THE RIVALS
and
POLLY HONEYCOMBE

broadview editions
series editor: L.W. Conolly

THE RIVALS
Richard Brinsley Sheridan

and

POLLY HONEYCOMBE
George Colman the Elder

edited by David A. Brewer

broadview editions

Library and Archives Canada Cataloguing in Publication

Sheridan, Richard Brinsley, 1751-1816
   The rivals / Richard Brinsley Sheridan. Polly Honeycombe
/ George Colman ; edited by David A. Brewer.

(Broadview editions)
Includes bibliographical references.
ISBN 978-1-55481-006-2

   I. Colman, George, 1732-1794 II. Brewer, David A. (David
Allen), 1969- III. Colman, George, 1732-1794. Polly Honeycombe.
IV. Title. V. Title: Polly Honeycombe. VI. Series: Broadview editions

PR3682.R4 2012   822'.6   C2012-903306-5

Broadview Editions
The Broadview Editions series represents the ever-changing canon of literature in English by bringing together texts long regarded as classics with valuable lesser-known works.

Advisory editor for this volume: Michel Pharand

Broadview Press is an independent, international publishing house, incorporated in 1985.

We welcome comments and suggestions regarding any aspect of our publications—please feel free to contact us at the addresses below or at broadview@broadviewpress.com.

North America
Post Office Box 1243, Peterborough, Ontario, Canada K9J 7H5
2215 Kenmore Avenue, Buffalo, NY, USA 14207
Tel: (705) 743-8990; Fax: (705) 743-8353
email: customerservice@broadviewpress.com

UK, Europe, Central Asia, Middle East, Africa, India, and Southeast Asia
Eurospan Group, 3 Henrietta St., London WC2E 8LU, United Kingdom
Tel: 44 (0) 1767 604972; Fax: 44 (0) 1767 601640
email: eurospan@turpin-distribution.com

Australia and New Zealand
NewSouth Books
c/o TL Distribution, 15-23 Helles Ave., Moorebank, NSW, Australia 2170
Tel: (02) 8778 9999; Fax: (02) 8778 9944
email: orders@tldistribution.com.au

www.broadviewpress.com

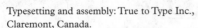

This book is printed on paper containing 100% post-consumer fibre.

Typesetting and assembly: True to Type Inc.,
Claremont, Canada.

PRINTED IN CANADA

Contents

List of Illustrations • 7

Acknowledgements • 9

Introduction • 11

George Colman the Elder and Richard Brinsley Sheridan:
A Brief Chronology • 43

A Note on the Texts • 47

Polly Honeycombe, A Dramatick Novel of One Act,
George Colman the Elder • 57

The Rivals, A Comedy, Richard Brinsley Sheridan • 111

Appendix A: The Original Casts of the Plays • 255

Appendix B: Novel-Reading and Its Discontents • 261
1. From [Samuel Johnson], *The Rambler* (31 March 1750) • 261
2. From [Francis Coventry], *The History of Pompey the Little:
or, The Life and Adventures of a Lap-Dog* (1752) • 264
3. [William Whitehead], *The World* (10 May 1753) • 267
4. From [William Dodd], *The Sisters; or, The History of Lucy
and Caroline Sanson, Entrusted to a false Friend* (1754) • 271
5. From [Owen Ruffhead], *The Monthly Review* (1761) • 273
6. From *The Critical Review* (1765) • 274
7. From [James Fordyce], *Sermons to Young Women* (1766) • 275
8. From [Hester Chapone], *Letters on the Improvement of
the Mind, Addressed to a Young Lady* (1773) • 277
9. From *The Monthly Review* (1773) • 278
10. From [William Enfield], *The Monthly Review* (1775) • 278
11. From *The Critical Review* (1775) • 279

Appendix C: "Such Paragraphs in the News-Papers!" • 281
1. Report of Sheridan's Elopement with Elizabeth Linley,
The Daily Advertiser (26 March 1772) • 281
2. Thomas Mathews's Denunciation of Sheridan, *The Bath
Chronicle* (9 April 1772) • 281
3. Report of the First Duel, *The London Evening-Post* (2-5 May
1772) • 283
4. Contradiction of *The London Evening-Post* Report, *The Bath
Chronicle* (7 May 1772) • 283
5. Mathews's Apology to Sheridan, *The Bath Chronicle* (7 May
1772) • 285
6. Draft of an unsent (?) letter from Sheridan (c. late June
1772) • 285
7. Report of Sheridan's Second Duel with Mathews, *The Bath
Chronicle* (2 July 1772) • 287

8. Report of Sheridan's Wounding in the Second Duel, *The London Chronicle* (2-4 July 1772) • 287

9. Another Report of the Second Duel, *The London Evening-Post* (2-4 July 1772) • 287

10. Report on Sheridan's Wounds, *The Public Advertiser* (8 July 1772) • 288

11. Another Report on Sheridan's Wounds, *The Bath Chronicle* (9 July 1772) • 288

12. From "Anecdotes *of the* Maid of Bath (*With an* Elegant Engraving)," *The London Magazine* (September 1772) • 289

13. Yet Another Report on Sheridan's Wounds, *The St. James's Chronicle* (10-12 November 1772) • 294

14. "Miss Linley, the syren of Bath," *The Westminster Magazine* (March 1773) • 294

15. Report of a Sheridan-Linley Marriage, *The Bath Chronicle* (1 April 1773) • 294

16. Letter probably written by Sheridan, *The Bath Chronicle* (15 April 1773) • 294

17. Report on *The Rivals, The Gazetteer and New Daily Advertiser* (17 January 1775) • 296

18. Another Report on *The Rivals, The Town and Country Magazine* (January 1775) • 296

Appendix D: The Narrative Possibilities of Bath • 297

1. From [Christopher Anstey], *The New Bath Guide: or, Memoirs of the B—r—d Family. In a Series of Poetical Epistles* (1766) • 297

2. From [Tobias Smollett], *The Expedition of Humphry Clinker* (1771) • 306

3. Report of an Elopement, *The Bath Chronicle* (9 September 1773) • 318

Select Bibliography • 321

List of Illustrations

Figure 1: The playbill for the opening night of *Polly Honeycombe* • 14

Figure 2: The playbill for the disastrous first night of *The Rivals* • 16

Figure 3: The playbill for the initial performance of the revised version of *The Rivals* • 17

Figure 4: A diagram of the Theatre-Royal, Drury Lane • 22

Figure 5: A diagram of the Theatre-Royal, Covent Garden • 23

Figure 6: A painting of a performance of *Macbeth* at Covent Garden • 25

Figure 7: An engraving of a 1763 riot at Covent Garden • 28

Figure 8: The title page for the first edition of *Polly Honeycombe* • 57

Figure 9: A map of London, showing the locations mentioned in *Polly Honeycombe*, the theaters, the principal circulating libraries, and the sites involved in Sheridan's first duel • 58

Figure 10: The title page for the first edition of *The Rivals* • 111

Figure 11: The spine and front of a "half-bound volume, with marbled covers" (the typical binding for books from a circulating library) • 262

Figure 12: Thomas Gainsborough's portrait of *Elizabeth and Thomas Linley* (c. 1768), which was exhibited in his studio in Bath • 282

Figure 13: Thomas Gainsborough's portrait of *The Linley Sisters*, which was exhibited at the Royal Academy in London in 1772 • 284

Figure 14: The "Elegant Engraving" of Elizabeth Linley in *The London Magazine* • 290

Figure 15: A map of Bath in 1775 • 298

Figure 16: An etching and stipple engraving of the North Parade in Bath (1785) • 319

Acknowledgements

This edition has been a long time in the making, and could never have come together as well as (I hope) it has without the assistance of many friends, colleagues, and students. Eileen Cottis, Elizabeth Frengel, Bruce Heiden, Drew Jones, Steven Moore, Larry Neal, John Sullivan, Linda Troost, and the members of c18-l helped answer a host of increasingly arcane queries, while Andrew Bricker, Dorothy Chalk, Lisa Cody, Frank Donoghue, Emily Friedman, Benedict Leca, Nush Powell, Sandra Macpherson, and Roxann Wheeler provided smart questions and encouragement at just the right moments. The students in my Winter 2010 section of English H590.03, especially John Hoffman and Jacky Werman, helped me determine what and how much to annotate, as did my experience, more than a dozen years ago, working with Cathy Gallagher on her edition of *Oroonoko*. Matt Kinservik and Danny O'Quinn cast the eyes of expert theater historians over my introduction, while Helen Burke, Alison Hurley, Stuart Sherman, and Mark Vareschi kindly shared their forthcoming work. Figures 9 and 11 would not exist without the generosity of Amy Spears, who taught me Photoshop, and Eric Johnson, who allowed me to browse the closed stacks of our Rare Books and Manuscripts Library looking for half-bindings with marbled boards. And there would be far fewer illustrations of any sort without the support of the Department of English and the Division of Arts and Humanities at The Ohio State University. I owe particular debts to Rob Hume, whose discontent with most of the existing editions of plays has shaped the alternative I've tried to provide here; to Marjorie Mather, for her astonishing patience and indulgence of my maximalist tendencies; and to Tera Pettella, who endured hours of proofreading, and yet could still conjure up her former self as a proxy for the needs and knowledge of our likely audience. However, my deepest love and gratitude go, as always, to Rebecca Morton, who understands the appeal of Mrs. Malaprop.

Introduction

The fundamental goal of any classroom edition should be to give its users the tools they need in order to understand how the texts it includes worked in the world, back when they were new, and what connections can be drawn between those past workings and the pleasures and puzzles of our own reading experience. Toward that end, I have organized this Introduction as a series of overviews of the most important contexts for imagining how *Polly Honeycombe* and *The Rivals* might have struck their initial audiences in the 1760s and 1770s, when they were clever competitors in a marketplace of theatrical pleasure, rather than canonical literature to be read for credit. We begin with an account of the experience of playgoing itself, and then move on to considerations of the often dubious reputation of novel-reading, the dynamics of celebrity, and the preexisting narrative possibilities of Bath (the resort city in which *The Rivals* takes place). Each of these sections has a corresponding appendix of documents illustrating, respectively, the associations surrounding the initial casts of these plays, the often hysterical ways in which novels and circulating libraries were denounced in the eighteenth century, the press coverage of Sheridan's elopement with Elizabeth Linley (which made him famous before he ever wrote a play), and the kinds of stories that a setting in Bath would have conjured up for most early audiences. The Introduction closes with a few observations about how these plays fit into their authors' careers and the generic conventions of the theater for which they were writing. Further information on all of these issues, and the broader social and cultural history in which they're embedded, may be found in the Note on the Texts, the Chronology, the annotations to the texts themselves, and the additional reading listed in the Bibliography. I have deliberately chosen not to provide any "readings" of these plays (I think this sort of edition should open up, rather than foreclose interpretive possibilities). But it is my fervent hope that with the material here presented, we can collectively rediscover the sheer range of pleasures and provocations offered by these two dazzling and deeply knowing plays about novel-reading girls gone wild.

Now by most of our usual accounts, print and performance—say, novels and plays—are polar opposites: letter versus spirit, disembodiment versus corporeality, permanence versus ephemerality. And most of the stories we tell about print and performance in the eighteenth century end up being stories of supercession, in which, say, the drama is where the action is up to about 1740, and then the novel or the newspaper just takes over and we don't have to worry about the playhouse anymore.[1] The reality is, as always, a bit more complicated. Print and performance were, in the third quarter of the eighteenth century, as they were long before and as they remain today, completely intertwined with one another. Print prompted performance, performance fed into print, so any attempt to disentangle the two will, at best, get things only momentarily or partially right. In many ways, this is something that the eighteenth century understood better about itself, than we, as students of the period, do, despite all the advantages of hindsight. But one of the best places in which we can begin to catch up are plays like *Polly Honeycombe* and *The Rivals*, which stage—in every sense—just how delightfully complex, and complexly delightful, the relations between print and performance could be. Both plays are, of course, chock-full of characters imitating or pretending to be kinds of people whom they'd read about, and often doing so, it seems, in the hope that their actions could become further reading material. So, for example, both Polly Honeycombe and Lydia Languish model their behavior on that of the heroines of the novels they read, but they do so not as mindless automata, but rather because it could make for what Polly calls "an excellent chapter in a new Novel" (86). They are quixotic, but knowingly, deliberately so. But it's not only our heroines who are imitating what they've read about. Pretty much everyone in the worlds of these plays is doing something along these lines: whether it be Polly's parents pretending to be genteel, Scribble pretending to be a footman, Captain Absolute pretending to be an impoverished ensign and "Mr. Saunderson," Mrs. Malaprop pretending to be "Delia," Bob Acres pretending first to be a fop and then a bloodthirsty duelist, Faulkland pretending to be a murderer. And, lest we forget, all of these different performances within each play are doubled and redoubled by the world outside the play: actors play these parts on stage to an audience that has probably already read about both the plays and the performances, and may well not only read more after leaving the playhouse, but also fashion their own subsequent performances in everyday life based upon what

---

1 For some welcome recent exceptions to this tendency, see Moody, O'Quinn, Sherman, and Stern (*Documents of Performance*).

they've read and seen and heard. In short, *Polly Honeycombe* and *The Rivals* are not just delicious (and still highly actable) comedies; they're also a splendidly illuminating way into understanding the full complexity of the relations between print and performance in the age which gave birth to so many aspects of our own time.

Print and Performance around the Playhouse

Perhaps the best way to grasp what it would be like to be part of the world into which *Polly Honeycombe* and *The Rivals* first appeared is to walk through the day of a hypothetical eighteenth-century playgoer.[1] Not all days would involve all the elements here described, and the particular weight and significance of each would vary, depending on the play, the playgoer, his or her location (London versus the provinces or colonies), etc. But they all might well figure in a given playgoer's day, and even if they didn't, the possibility that they could have would often color the situation.

Unless our hypothetical audience member had been at the theater the previous night (when the proposed next day's offering would be announced; see below), his or her playgoing day would probably begin by learning which plays were to be performed that evening. For most of the eighteenth century (i.e., after the Licensing Act of 1737), there were only two theaters in London that were legally permitted to perform plays during the regular theatrical season of mid-September through late May or early June. Each morning, except Sunday (when the playhouses were closed), the theaters advertised their offerings of the day in the newspapers and with playbills. The latter were pasted or nailed up around the city, and passed out as handbills, especially in places where prospective audience members were likely to congregate, such as coffeehouses, booksellers, law schools (the so-called Inns of Court), and the theaters themselves. Sometimes the newspaper ads gave slightly different details than the playbills, but they both provided the same basic information. Consider, for example, the playbill for the opening night of *Polly Honeycombe* on 5 December 1760 (Figure 1):

---

1 For more on the topics dealt with in this section, see Bevis (*The Laughing Tradition*), Hughes, Hume (*The London Theatre World*), Nicoll, Price (*Theatre in the Age of Garrick*), both titles by Stern, and Stone.

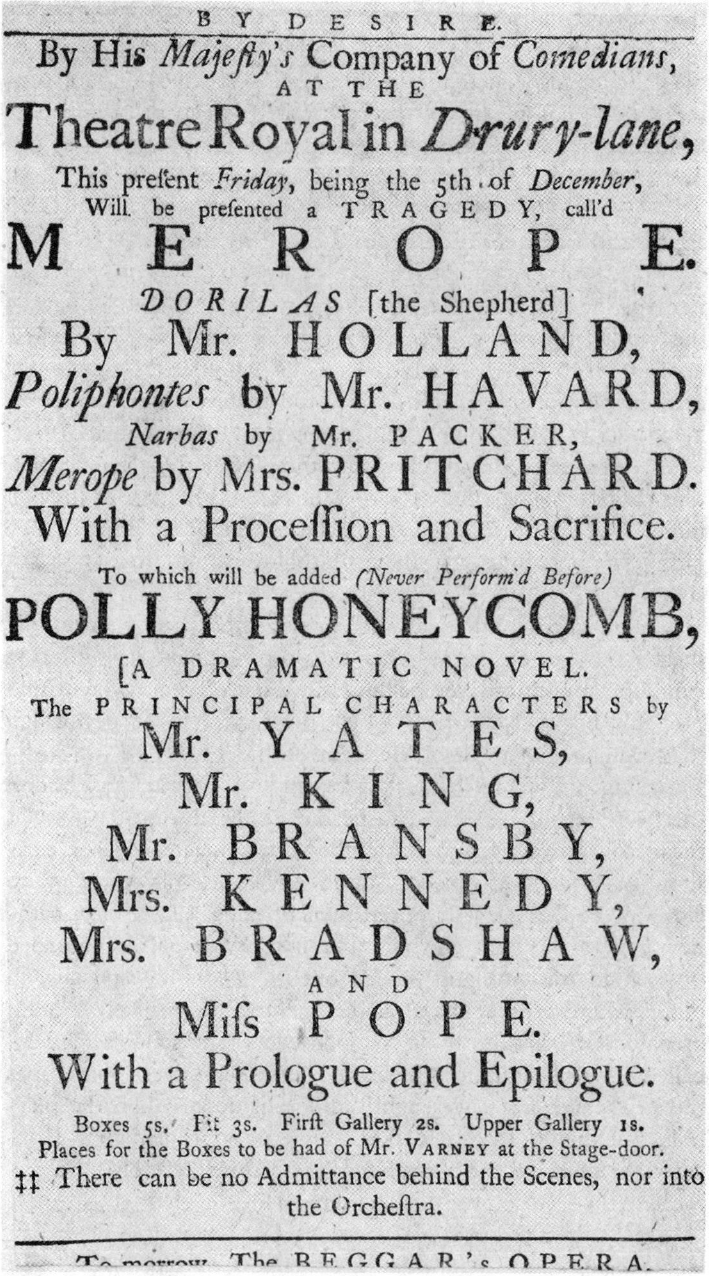

BY DESIRE.

By His *Majesty's* Company of *Comedians*,
AT THE

Theatre Royal in *Drury-lane*,

This present *Friday*, being the 5th of *December*,
Will be presented a TRAGEDY, call'd

MEROPE.

DORILAS [the Shepherd]

By Mr. HOLLAND,

Poliphontes by Mr. HAVARD,

Narbas by Mr. PACKER,

Merope by Mrs. PRITCHARD.

With a Procession and Sacrifice.

To which will be added *(Never Perform'd Before)*

POLLY HONEYCOMB,

[A DRAMATIC NOVEL.

The PRINCIPAL CHARACTERS by

Mr. YATES,
Mr. KING,
Mr. BRANSBY,
Mrs. KENNEDY,
Mrs. BRADSHAW,
AND
Miss POPE.

With a Prologue and Epilogue.

Boxes 5s. Fit 3s. First Gallery 2s. Upper Gallery 1s.
Places for the Boxes to be had of Mr. VARNEY at the Stage-door.
‡‡ There can be no Admittance behind the Scenes, nor into
the Orchestra.

To-morrow The BEGGAR's OPERA.

Figure 1: The playbill for the opening night of *Polly Honeycombe*. This item is reproduced by permission of The Huntington Library, San Marino, California.

It tells potential audience members that the Theatre-Royal in Drury Lane was performing a tragedy entitled *Merope*, "to which will be added (*Never Perform'd Before*) Polly Honeycombe, A Dramatic Novel ... with a Prologue and Epilogue." The playbill also lists who will be performing the principal roles in both plays, mentions that *Merope* will include "a Procession and Sacrifice," suggests that the program is "By Desire" (presumably of someone rich and powerful), and gives information on prices and theater rules.

Compare this to the playbill for the opening night of *The Rivals* at the Theatre-Royal, Covent Garden (Figure 2). Here again we learn about the novelty of the offering (its having been "Never Perform'd"), the cast, the presence of a prologue and epilogue, and what else was on the bill for that evening: "the Musical Entertainment of The Chaplet." But we also get an additional pitch regarding the "New Scenes and Dresses" prepared for this production, and a suggestion as to how "Ladies and Gentlemen" could best reserve their seats. And the playbill for the return of *The Rivals* "with Alterations" also includes mention of "a Dance call'd The Frolick" (Figure 3).[1]

This is a lot of information; more than we often get in modern theatrical advertising. But it's hardly exhaustive, and we can get some sense of the eighteenth-century theater's priorities by considering what doesn't generally appear on the playbills and in the advertisements in the newspapers: illustrations, excerpts from favorable reviews, authorial names.[2]

---

1 For the story of the play's disastrous first night, and Sheridan's quick revision of the script, see "A Note on the Texts."

2 Illustrations rarely appeared in any capacity in eighteenth-century newspapers, but they were a standard part of other sorts of printing in the period (such as broadside ballads), and so could have been included in playbills, if it had been thought profitable to do so. There were no previews for critics in the eighteenth-century theater, so it is unreasonable to expect quotations from reviews in the advertisements for the opening night of a new play; however, at least from the 1750s on, there was enough reviewing in the newspapers and magazines that the managers could have included such in their notices of the subsequent nights of a run, or for revivals of a play after it had passed into the repertory. Playwrights' names were rarely provided in any form by the theaters, although they were pretty routinely included on the title pages of printed plays. The would-be wits and tastemakers in the audience seem to have so enjoyed guessing at the authorship of new plays that the managers intentionally withheld that information, so as to carve out a space for public speculation (although, as the Prologue to *Polly Honeycombe* reminds us, such conjectures were not always accurate).   (*continued*)

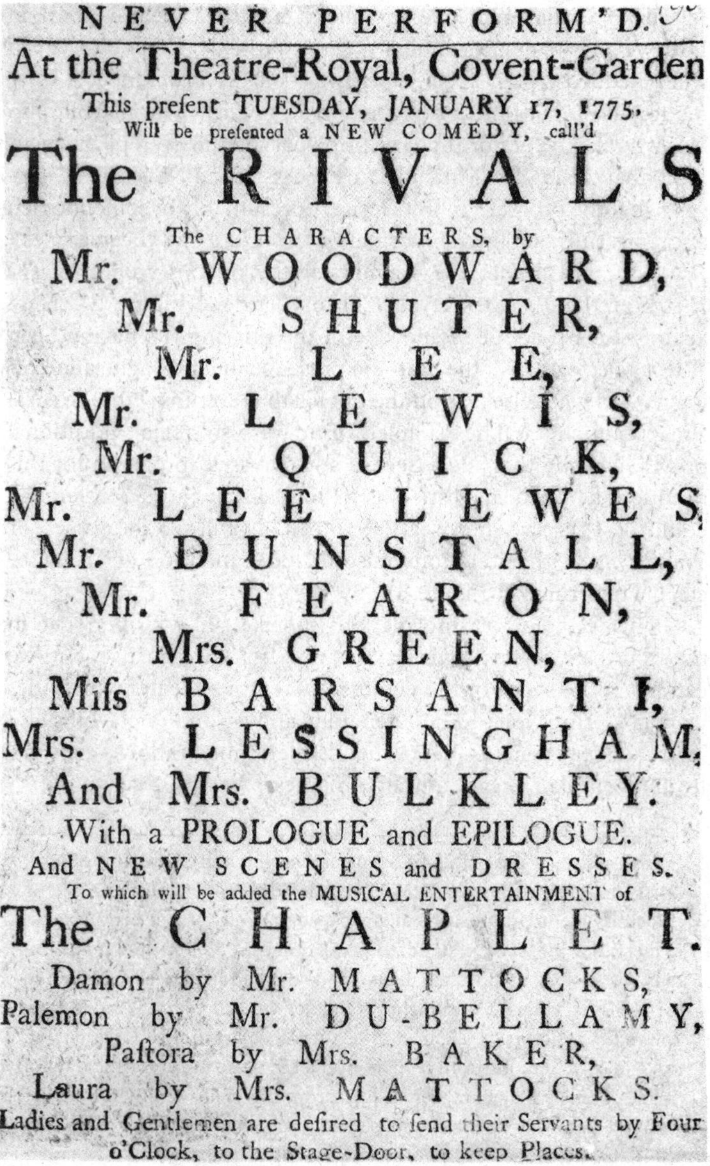

NEVER PERFORM'D.

At the Theatre-Royal, Covent-Garden

This prefent TUESDAY, JANUARY 17, 1775,
Will be prefented a NEW COMEDY, call'd

The RIVALS

The CHARACTERS, by

Mr. WOODWARD,

Mr. SHUTER,

Mr. LEE,

Mr. LEWIS,

Mr. QUICK,

Mr. LEE LEWES,

Mr. DUNSTALL,

Mr. FEARON,

Mrs. GREEN,

Mifs BARSANTI,

Mrs. LESSINGHAM,

And Mrs. BULKLEY.

With a PROLOGUE and EPILOGUE.

And NEW SCENES and DRESSES.

To which will be added the MUSICAL ENTERTAINMENT of

The CHAPLET.

Damon by Mr. MATTOCKS,

Palemon by Mr. DU-BELLAMY,

Paftora by Mrs. BAKER,

Laura by Mrs. MATTOCKS.

Ladies and Gentlemen are defired to fend their Servants by Four
o'Clock, to the Stage-Door, to keep Places.

Figure 2: The playbill for the disastrous first night of *The Rivals*. This
item is reproduced by permission of The Huntington Library, San
Marino, California.

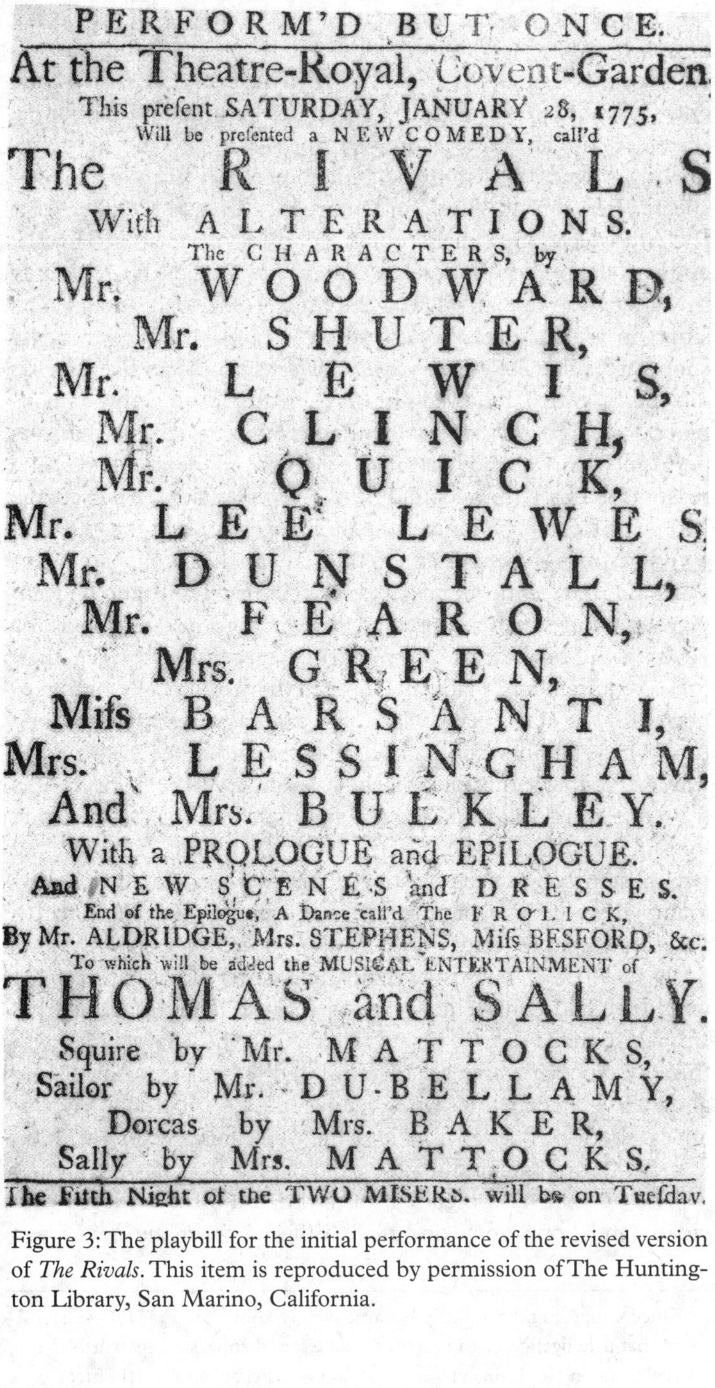

PERFORM'D BUT ONCE.
At the Theatre-Royal, Covent-Garden,
This present SATURDAY, JANUARY 28, 1775,
Will be presented a NEW COMEDY, call'd

The R I V A L S

With ALTERATIONS.
The CHARACTERS, by

Mr. WOODWARD,
Mr. SHUTER,
Mr. LEWIS,
Mr. CLINCH,
Mr. QUICK,
Mr. LEE LEWES,
Mr. DUNSTALL,
Mr. FEARON,
Mrs. GREEN,
Miss BARSANTI,
Mrs. LESSINGHAM,
And Mrs. BULKLEY.

With a PROLOGUE and EPILOGUE.
And NEW SCENES and DRESSES.
End of the Epilogue, A Dance call'd The FROLICK,
By Mr. ALDRIDGE, Mrs. STEPHENS, Miss BESFORD, &c.
To which will be added the MUSICAL ENTERTAINMENT of

THOMAS and SALLY.

Squire by Mr. MATTOCKS,
Sailor by Mr. DU-BELLAMY,
Dorcas by Mrs. BAKER,
Sally by Mrs. MATTOCKS.

The Fifth Night of the TWO MISERS. will be on Tuesday.

Figure 3: The playbill for the initial performance of the revised version of *The Rivals*. This item is reproduced by permission of The Huntington Library, San Marino, California.

These three playbills are unusual in that they're all presenting new or fairly new work (the comparatively oldest offering was *The Chaplet*, which first appeared in 1749). Most of what Drury Lane and Covent Garden produced was older than that, often quite a bit older. In the years leading up to *The Rivals*, the most frequently staged full-length comedies included plays by Shakespeare, Ben Jonson, Sir John Vanbrugh, Susanna Centlivre, Sir Richard Steele, George Farquhar, John Gay, Benjamin Hoadly, and a collaboration between Colman and David Garrick. Only the latter two were still alive at the time of Sheridan's debut. The situation wasn't quite as stark when it came to afterpieces, the short farces like *Polly Honeycombe*, or musical pieces like *Thomas and Sally*, which followed the five-act tragic or comic "mainpieces" (such as *The Rivals*). But there too, much of what was performed was already familiar to much of the audience. The reason for this is fairly simple. In 1737, Parliament passed the Licensing Act, which limited the number of London theaters that could perform spoken drama to those that held a royal patent (for much of the century, this was just Drury Lane and Covent Garden), and which required all new plays to be submitted to a government official for pre-performance censorship. Together, these requirements made it far safer, both politically and economically, to stage plays whose appeal was already established (and whose authors would not have to be paid, since the standard way of compensating playwrights was to give them the profits from the third, sixth, and ninth nights, should a run last that long). Indeed, out of the seventy-five or eighty different plays the two theaters staged each season, they each averaged only two new mainpieces and two or three new afterpieces, not all of which passed into the repertory for revival in future seasons. This obviously meant that few playwrights, and fewer still aspiring playwrights, could confidently hope to make a living at their craft. But it also made for a very savvy audience, whose familiarity with this (by modern standards, astonishingly large) repertory could allow them, when they wished, to compare different performances—both of a given role and by a particular actor—with an eye that few of us could match today.

The playbills also highlight how varied a bill each night provided (and how much one night differed from the next, even

---

Once a playwright's identity became widely known, though, possession of that intelligence lost most of its cachet, and so was rarely worth the real estate it would occupy in a playbill or newspaper advertisement.

during the initial run of a successful play). This too was a form of ensuring the theater's economic security, an attempt to guarantee that there were enough different kinds of pleasure on offer that no segment of the potential audience was likely to stay away for too long.[1] Indeed, for many playgoers the very incongruity of the juxtapositions may have been part of their appeal. So, for example, in addition to *Merope* (Aaron Hill's adaptation of Voltaire's tragedy of the same name), *Polly Honeycombe* was paired in its first season with, among other things, *The Beggar's Opera*, *Hamlet*, Centlivre's fast-paced comedy, *The Wonder*, two of Nicholas Rowe's "she-tragedies," and Samuel Foote's cruel satire on Methodism, *The Minor*. Beyond the specifically dramatic offerings, there was also the music of the orchestra, the spectacle afforded by one's fellow audience-members and the playhouse itself, and not infrequently some singing and comic dancing (including "the Cow Keepers" and "the Italian Gardener").[2] Since afterpieces were generally comic, the juxtapositions involving *The Rivals* are perhaps not quite as striking, but there too we get pairings with a musical farce, Kane O'Hara's *The Two Misers*, and two musical adaptations of seventeenth-century masques: *The Druids* and Milton's *Comus*. Presumably not every aspect of every bill appealed to every playgoer, but enough did so that, with competent management, the owners of the playhouses could do very well for themselves, and an even halfway "game" member of the audience never had to fear boredom.

So let's presume that our hypothetical playgoer has learned what both houses were offering for the evening, and come to a

---

1 Unlike many of their counterparts in Continental Europe, Drury Lane and Covent Garden received no state support, and so were wholly dependent upon ticket sales for their financial viability (although with this freedom to fail came a comparatively high level of freedom from government interference, even after the Licensing Act).

2 It is worth emphasizing just how much music was available at the theater (both vocal and instrumental). Handel's *Messiah* was first performed in London at Covent Garden, while "Rule Britannia" (the unofficial national anthem) and "God Save the King"—the official anthem—gained their respective statuses by virtue of their frequent performance at Drury Lane. Songs from plays were often published, even when their accompanying scripts were not, and most actors were more than able to carry a tune. A similar point could be made about dance: for many years, Covent Garden spent upwards of a quarter of its entire salary budget on dancers, which suggests their felt importance to the overall experience.

decision as to which performance to attend (although the two theaters were close enough together that one could switch from one to the other mid-performance if one wished). This decision might well have been shaped by various kinds of print beyond the playbills and advertisements, including critiques or "puffs" of various actors and plays in the newspapers and monthly reviews (such as those mentioned in the Preface to *Polly Honeycombe*), accounts of audience behavior (especially when it got unruly), pamphlets on the merits of various performers and styles of performance, scenes in novels depicting visits to the theater, and/or one or more of the plays themselves.[1]

Getting to the theater could itself be an adventure, depending on the distance and mode of transportation—foot, boat, sedan chair, hired or private carriage—but even when it wasn't, obtaining a seat often was. The show would begin at 6 p.m., but the doors would typically open one to three hours earlier, and there would often be a mad rush to purchase tickets and claim seats, such that anyone unable to show up well ahead of time would either have to risk being turned away, squeeze in wherever he or she could, or switch with a servant whom one had sent ahead to hold a place (see Figure 2 again). And to talk of "seats" is a bit of a misnomer: there were only unreserved benches. Officially, the managers of the theaters allotted 21 inches per patron (an economy airline seat today is 17.2 inches wide), but for popular shows, that guideline was often disregarded—and, of course, that space had to accommodate dresses far wider than our own fashions, not to mention gentlemen's swords. While waiting (in a theater that was warmed only by body heat), the audience—or their placeholder servants—could get quite loud, and not infrequently threw things on stage or elsewhere in the playhouse: generally orange peels, apple cores, or nut shells, but occasionally more dangerous objects, such as a half-pound of cheese or even lit fireworks.

These flying objects could damage one's clothing, and so add to what was already likely to be a fairly expensive outing for most playgoers. The playbill for *Polly Honeycombe* (Figure 1) gives the standard ticket prices: five shillings for a seat in the boxes, three shillings for one in the pit, two shillings for admission to the First

---

1 The opening act of Sheridan's *The Critic* (first staged 1779; first published 1781) delightfully, and deeply self-consciously, mocks how much the theaters relied upon the publicity and controversy provided by the newspapers.

Gallery, and one shilling for entrance to the Upper Gallery (see below for what these different areas of the theater were). Often, though not always, one could be admitted for half-price after Act Three of the mainpiece. Once the curtain went up, there were no refunds. Now it is foolish even to attempt to convert these prices to a modern equivalent (the relative costs of things like food and lodging and labor have just changed too much), but we can give them some context.[1] A cheap meal would run three pence (with twelve pence to a shilling) or six to eight pence if it included meat, a quart of beer would cost four pence, a dozen oranges—for eating and throwing—would go for close to a shilling, as would a decent but unglamorous steak dinner. A nice dinner would run more like two-and-a-half shillings, while a bottle of (highly taxed) French wine could cost somewhere between five and eight shillings. Coming at this from the other end, it is worth remembering that an unskilled manual laborer might only make nine shillings a week, and even a skilled tradesman rarely got more than twenty shillings a week, unless he owned his own business. Servants would often get far less, though they at least had room and board included in their compensation. For example, footmen, like the one Scribble pretends to be, often only received £8 (160 shillings) a year, plus whatever tips they could get from their employer's guests. Gentlemen and the upper end of the "middling sort" would, on the other hand, live on anywhere from three or four hundred pounds a year on up to many thousands. Given these sums, it is not hard to see that becoming a regular at the theaters was beyond the means of most of the population. And yet going to the theater, at least occasionally, was hardly restricted to an elite coterie. In 1747, Foote estimated that at least 12,000 Londoners (out of a total urban population of a scant 700,000) could be "called Play-followers,"[2] a figure that is equal to probably upwards of a third of the city's inhabitants who had enough disposable income to regularly indulge in some kind of commercial entertainment. This is not to say that a generous third of those who could afford to go periodically to the theater did so—at this distance, it's very hard to tell such things, and, of course, much poorer people could occasionally splurge, or be

---

1   The following figures are all drawn from Picard. For more on prices, and the difficulties of comparing purchasing power across time, see Hume ("The Economics of Culture").

2   [Foote], *A Treatise on the Passions, so far as they regard the Stage* (London, 1747), 3.

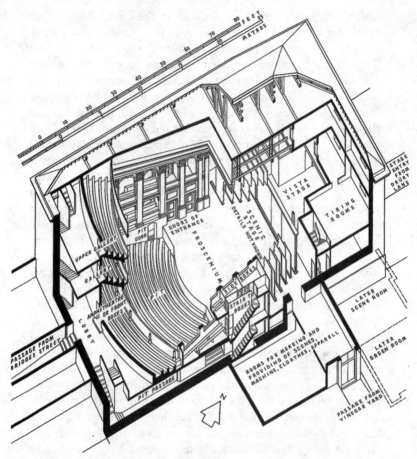

Figure 4: A diagram of the Theatre-Royal, Drury Lane [not including the renovations of the early 1760s]. This reconstruction first appeared in Richard Leacroft, *The Development of the English Playhouse* (London: Eyre Methuen, 1973).

taken as guests. But it does suggest the felt centrality of the theater to the middling and upper ranks of life in London (including both its full-time residents, and those who "came up" to the metropolis for business or pleasure).

The experience of our hypothetical playgoer would depend in part on where he or she sat. The interior of the auditorium was divided into three principal areas, not counting the stage, each of which attracted a fairly distinct group (see the diagrams in Figures 4 and 5). The most expensive area, the boxes, formed a

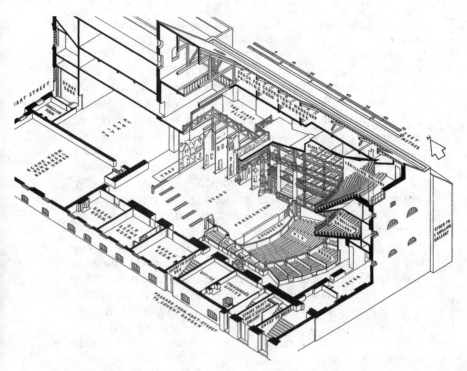

Figure 5: A diagram of the Theatre-Royal, Covent Garden. This reconstruction first appeared in Richard Leacroft, *The Development of the English Playhouse* (London: Eyre Methuen, 1973).

horseshoe around the perimeter of the theater at the level of the stage, with additional boxes also on the higher levels of the side walls. Directly in front of and below the stage was the next most expensive area, the pit. Above the boxes in the rear of the theater was the First (or Two-Shilling) Gallery, and above that was the Upper (or One-Shilling or Footman's) Gallery. The boxes tended to attract wealthy playgoers who didn't mind being on display (anyone who sat in the first row or two of a box would be visible to the entire house), but who weren't interested in being part of the often more boisterous activity of the pit or the galleries. Typically this meant that the boxes held ladies and older gentlemen. The pit, on the other hand, was the haunt of younger men, gentle or otherwise, who were interested in showing off (their wit, their clothing, their ability to interrupt the show). The First Gallery usually drew respectable people of "the middling sort," who wanted to see without being much seen. And the Upper Gallery was the home of servants and sailors and other quite exuberant playgoers who were unafraid to halt a performance until they got what they wanted. Every area was potentially visible to every other, since the house lights (wax candles) were never dimmed, but audience members hoping for anonymity could often find a place to hide at the back of one of the galleries. None of these seating areas was exclusive: people of all ranks could be found in all areas of the theater, as could prostitutes cruising for clients. And it was necessary to appeal to most or all of them in order for a play to succeed. But the respective characters of these different parts of the playhouse were well-established: prologues and epilogues often attempted to play one area off against the others, and the experience of going to the theater included learning where one "belonged" (both supposedly and actually), and discerning how the physical geography of the theater intersected with the social geography of its patrons. After all, the theaters were probably the largest (and certainly the best lit) secular meeting places in all of eighteenth-century Britain, though they're dwarfed by modern theaters and concert venues: after some renovations in the early 1760s (not shown in the diagram of Figure 4), Drury Lane increased its capacity to about 1,800, while Covent Garden probably held 1,400, though it was fairly rare for either one to be more than two-thirds full.[1]

As soon as it was 6:00, the orchestra began to play. After three pieces (generally totaling about twenty minutes), the house servants would come out and light the chandeliers and sconces that illuminated the stage. Prior to the mid-1760s, two grenadiers would also come out and flank the stage as a visible reminder that the theaters were operating under a royal patent, and so audiences should behave accordingly (one of them is visible on the right side of the stage in the crude painting of Figure 6).

Once the stage was lit, one of the leading actors would come out to speak the prologue (if a new mainpiece was being performed, or it was some sort of a special occasion), and then the curtain would rise.[2] Prologues and epilogues are perhaps

---

1 For photos of the only surviving theaters built along these lines (both of which are significantly smaller than the London patent houses), go to <http://www.theatrestrust.org.uk/resources/theatres/show/736-theatre-royal-bristol> and <http://www.georgiantheatreroyal.co.uk/history/1788_to_present.html>.

2 The prologue for a new afterpiece would be spoken right before the latter began.

Figure 6: A painting of a performance of *Macbeth* at Covent Garden in the early 1760s. © Victoria and Albert Museum, London.

best thought of as an attempt to quiet down the audience, draw their attention to the stage, and then cajole or otherwise rouse them to support a new play. Typically, they were comic or patriotic in tone, regardless of what sort of play they were framing, and they were valued largely independently of their plays. Indeed, a good prologue or epilogue could help a mediocre play limp along until its author had received the profits from its third, sixth, and ninth nights. Generally, they were dropped after the ninth night of a run (if a play got that far), but on occasion, as with the extremely popular epilogue to *The Rivals*, they could be continued or revived indefinitely. The newspapers often printed them immediately (whether or not their accompanying play was published), and certain actors, including Thomas King (the original Scribble), became famous for their performances of the genre. Prologues were usually delivered by men (often as comic taunts to one segment of the audience, or as attempts to bond with the audience at the expense of "our poet"), while epilogues were typically the purview of attractive young women, who could add their erotic allure to the pitch being made for the play.

So let's presume that the curtain is up and the mainpiece begun. What would our hypothetical playgoer have seen? First and foremost, he or she would have seen a set of very familiar actors, playing roles of a sort that he or she had encountered many times before (presuming that this wasn't his or her first time at the playhouse). As suggested above, the eighteenth-century theater was a repertory theater in which favorite plays would be produced again and again, often with roughly the same casts, over many years. But the repertory was large and shifting enough that the principal actors in each company would often have to know fifty, seventy, even upwards of ninety different parts, and be ready to perform them on a day's notice, depending on what plays the managers (informed by the audience) decided to do next. The practical solution was to specialize. Accordingly, most actors had their own "lines": kinds of characters that they typically performed (blustering villains, comic Irishmen, resourceful servants, fluttering ingénues). Once a part had been assigned to an actor, he or she in effect owned it until given a better part, or leaving the company. The result was often what to us would seem a mismatch between the bodies of the actors and the roles they were playing. For example, Jane Pope began playing Polly Honeycombe while she was still a teenager, like Polly. But she held onto the role until she was in her mid-thirties (close to middle age, by eighteenth-century standards). Similarly, Henry Woodward had long played roles like Captain Absolute, and so had a presumptive right to that part, even though he was in ill health and fourteen years older than the actor playing his father.[1] However, whatever disadvantages this lack of verisimilitude may have had, it at least provided a convenient shorthand for the audience. One might not know what a particular play was about, but if it was a comedy starring John Quick or Edward Shuter one could reasonably expect a lot of buffoonery—just as one can make a pretty good guess as to what sort of film one is likely to see, if one knows that it features Julia Roberts or Cameron Diaz or Russell Crowe. A similar sort of shorthand was often provided by the costumes: if one saw an actor enter wearing the latest ridiculous fashion, or a red coat, or a livery, one could be close to certain that a fop or an army

---

1 For descriptions of these performers, and the other members of the original casts, see Appendix A.

officer or a footman (or someone pretending to be a footman) was at hand.

As Figures 6 and 7 should suggest, the actors did most of their performing on the relatively bare platform at the front of the stage: what the diagrams of Figures 4 and 5 call the "proscenium." Most entrances and exits would be done through the doors adjacent to the side-boxes. Behind the performers was all the scenery (what Figure 4 terms the "scenic stage" and Figure 5 just the "stage"). The scenery here functioned more as a backdrop to the action than a typical part of it—though it could be used to "discover" (i.e., open and reveal) a scene *in medias res.* This bipartite division of the stage allowed for a real intimacy with the audience (just look how close the actors are to the pit and side-boxes, and how much they're not hidden away behind a "fourth wall"), without sacrificing the pleasures of spectacle. The latter was largely furnished by, in addition to the costumes and the generally attractive cast, painted canvas "wings" and "shutters" which slid in and out of position from the sides of the stage along grooves in the floor (occasionally a painted "drop" would also be rolled down from above the stage). Scene changes were generally done in full view of the audience (though anything particularly elaborate, or involving items that had to be carried in, could be prepared behind a closed set of shutters or a drop), and the rapidity and variety of the transformations wrought seem to have been part of the fun, especially after the mid-1760s when the lighting and sight-lines improved with the replacement of overhead chandeliers by better sidelights and footlights. Most of the scenery was fairly generic (a tomb, a prison, a bedchamber, a street), but productions that were expected to make a lot of money often had "new scenes" of specific places painted for them, such as the views of the North and South Parades of Bath that appear in *The Rivals,* and are advertised on its playbills (Figures 2 and 3).

With the exception of some of these "new scenes," the visual pleasures afforded by the eighteenth-century theater do not seem very bound up with mimesis. The point was to offer splendor, variety, familiarity, and exoticism (remember the "procession and sacrifice" of the *Polly Honeycombe* playbill; Figure 1), rather than a world in which one could get lost. The same could be said of the entire evening: there were seven-minute breaks between each act of the mainpiece, in which the advertised singing and dancing frequently took place, or else the orchestra played; there was the often tonally different afterpiece; sometimes there was tightrope walking or other sorts of circus acts; not to mention the various

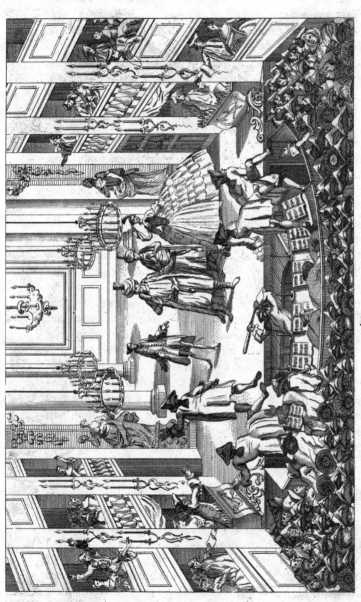

Riot at Covent Garden Theatre in 1763; in consequence of the Managers refusing to admit half-price in the Opera of Artaxerxes.

Figure 7: An engraving of a 1763 riot at Covent Garden. © Trustees of the British Museum.

distractions and delights of one's fellow audience members (many of whom were as visible as the actors on stage). Going to the theater was an event in which one was necessarily a participant; it wasn't an illusion from which one could keep a safe or aesthetic distance. As such, it's worth remembering that there was at least as much performance off-stage as there was on-stage. Actual riots, of the sort depicted in Figure 7, were comparatively rare (though significantly more frequent than in the modern theater), but there was far less respectful silence than we are accustomed to. The theater was a gathering place and full of all sorts of social interaction, not all of which had anything to do with the official performance at hand. Audiences would laugh, cry, applaud, hiss, throw things, demand encores, and otherwise make their pleasures and preferences known. But they would also sometimes engage in purposeful distraction: laughing or humming or dropping things into the pit during particularly tragic moments, calling across the theater to their friends, loudly coughing or blowing their noses, demanding a favorite song. James Boswell once imitated the lowing of a cow to great applause from the galleries, while Thaddeus Fitzpatrick stood up and whinnied in the midst of *King Lear*. Sometimes this behavior was spontaneous; other times it was premeditated and organized through printed handbills or advertisements in the newspapers (or simply incited by press reports of the previous night's activities).[1] And even when the audience was not interrupting, claims were still being made on their attention by the splendor of the inhabitants of the boxes or the glamour of the celebrities in attendance (often including members of the royal family) or the sensual appeal of the prostitutes and orange sellers doing their

---

1 For example, the riot depicted in Figure 7 was solicited earlier that day by a handbill "delivered at all the public places and coffee-houses in London," which called upon "frequenters of the theatres" to "convince the directors of *Covent-garden playhouse*" to abandon their attempt to do away with admission at half-price after Act Three of the mainpiece (*An Historical and Succinct Account of the Late Riots at the Theatres of Drury-Lane and Covent-Garden* [London, 1763], 5 and 21). The result was that "all the benches of the boxes and pit [were] entirely tore up, the glasses [i.e., mirrors] and chandeliers broken, and the linings of the boxes cut to pieces. The rashness of the rioters was so great, that they cut away the wooden pillars between the boxes, so that if the inside of them had not been iron, they would have brought down the galleries upon their heads. The damages done amount to at least [£]2000" (*The Gentleman's Magazine* 33 [1763], 97).

rounds. In short, the bustle and noise and number of potential things on which to focus was probably more akin to a Lolla-palooza-like festival or a sporting event than a modern theatrical performance in the dark. Audiences were there to see and be seen, and while most of them were genuinely interested in the performance, they weren't nearly as automatically deferential as we've been trained to be. The theaters may not always have liked this, but, at least in the period we're primarily concerned with, they couldn't do much about it. As Samuel Johnson put it, "Ah! let not Censure term our Fate our Choice, / The Stage but echoes back the publick Voice. / The Drama's Laws the Drama's Patrons give, / For we that live to please, must please to live."[1]

By the time the company had gotten through the mainpiece, the afterpiece, the music, and any additional entertainment, it was often close to 11 p.m. But before the remaining audience members would depart, they had one last, fiercely cherished per-formance to make. The prompter of the theater, or a leading actor serving as his deputy, would come on stage and "give out"—i.e., announce—what the house proposed to perform the next day (occasionally this had already been printed at the bottom of the day's playbill, as it is in Figure 1). If the audience mostly cheered, that would be the next night's offering (presum-ing that no one indispensable got sick). If the audience mostly groaned or hissed, or worse, the manager would quickly come up with an alternative, and the process would begin again. In this way, the audience ultimately determined not only the fate of par-ticular plays (including whether or not they would get to the third, sixth, or ninth nights out of whose profits the playwright would be paid), but also the repertory. No doubt this was often a cruel system, and one which could be gamed (enemies or cham-pions of a play could determine its fate by packing the house on a particular night), but it seems to have given the audience what it wanted most of the time: a task that cultural producers of any age have an extraordinarily difficult time bringing about.

Once home, our hypothetical playgoer could continue his or her engagement with both the play and the theater, if it seemed desirable to do so. In addition to reading the reviews and puffs and accounts of audience misbehavior already mentioned, and

---

1 Johnson, "Prologue Spoken by Mr. Garrick, at the Opening of the Theatre in *Drury-Lane* 1747," in *The Poems of Samuel Johnson*, ed. David Nichol Smith and Edward L. McAdam, 2nd ed. (Oxford: Clarendon P, 1974), 109.

possibly the plays themselves (which were generally published within a few days of their theatrical debut for one or one-and-a-half shillings), there were all sorts of possibilities: for impassioned or witty discussion in the coffeehouses, for writing pseudonymously to the newspapers to quarrel with or praise their reviews, for day-dreaming, for imitation of the fashions of the actors or the behavior of the characters, for bonding with or against one's friends and family regarding the worth of a particular play, or even the theater in general. In short, just because a performance on stage had drawn to a close, that didn't mean that the play, both as a text and as an event, didn't continue to resonate in ways that fostered still new feedback loops of print and performance, all of which could affect our hypothetical playgoer very deeply. Or, not at all: for some, perhaps many, audience members, the theater was simply a passing entertainment, no more consequential than a random night of television or web-browsing might be today. Either way, though, we need to remember that any attempt to regard plays like *Polly Honeycombe* or *The Rivals* as either purely theatrical or purely textual is going to very quickly tie itself into knots. The two were inescapably (and for most audience members, delightfully) intertwined in the eighteenth-century theater, both inside the playhouse and beyond.

Print and Performance around the Circulating Library

As my last paragraph should suggest, playgoing varied tremendously in terms of its place in the hearts and minds of the public. Many people, including the real-life counterparts to several of the dramatis personae in *Polly Honeycombe* and *The Rivals*, preferred to get their entertainment from reading. Mr. Honeycombe and Ledger are great readers of the newspapers, as is, in her own way, Lydia Languish (who hopes for "such paragraphs ...!" about her elopement). More importantly for dramatic purposes, however, Polly and Lydia—and implicitly Scribble and Captain Absolute and Faulkland—are devotees of the novel.

There isn't space here to rehearse the long-running debate over the "rise" or "elevation" or "making" or other supposed transformation of the novel in eighteenth-century Britain. A range of stories can be told, all of which depend on how one defines one's terms.[1] What matters for the present, however, isn't

---

1   For the most influential accounts, see Downie, Gallagher, Hunter (*Before Novels*), McKeon, Warner, and Watt.

so much which scholarly account one finds most compelling, as the simple fact that the eighteenth century itself regarded the novel as "novel." Prose fiction, as a broad category of story-telling, was generally agreed to date back centuries or even mil-lenia, but the specific forms that contemporaries of Colman and Sheridan thought of when they heard the word "novel" were widely regarded as innovations, and potentially dangerous ones at that. As the excerpts in Appendix B make clear, novels were thought of as less chaste and more realistic—and so more likely to encourage imitation of their characters—than previous kinds of fiction, such as the long heroic romances to which the Pro-logue to *Polly Honeycombe* refers. Not infrequently, this fear of readerly imitation led to a real hysteria on the part of traditional authorities: there isn't that much of a gap between the rantings of Mr. Honeycombe or Sir Anthony Absolute and those of figures like James Fordyce, who claimed that "she who can bear to peruse" such books "must in her soul be a prostitute, let her rep-utation in life be what it will,"[1] or the reviewer for *The London Magazine* who insisted that two recent publications were "written solely for the use of the circulating library, and very proper to debauch all young women who are still undebauched."[2] Indeed, in addition to being accessories to the seduction of young women, novels were routinely charged with making them unfit for their domestic duties and proper station in life, with making them reject suitable partners because they didn't behave like nov-elistic heroes, with undermining respect for parental authority (especially when it came to marriage), and with otherwise cor-rupting the bodies and souls of the rising generation.[3] As these phrasings should indicate, the widespread presumption was that novels were mostly read by what Johnson termed "the Young, the Ignorant, and the Idle,"[4] and so had a particularly impressionable audience. For opponents of the form, this meant that novels were especially treacherous, and the mere perusal of one—or at least the wrong one—could be regarded as itself a sign of moral depravity. Supporters of the novel, on the other hand, often made readers' supposed impressionability into a virtue, and hailed how

---

1 See Appendix B, p. 276.

2 Review of *The Way to Lose Him; or, The History of Miss Wyndham*, in *The London Magazine* 41 (1772), 543.

3 For further examples of all these concerns (beyond what is provided in Appendix B), see John Tinnon Taylor and Williams.

4 See Appendix B, p. 263.

the form permitted its audience to engage in a sort of emotional training regimen—what Johnson calls "mock Encounters" (p. 264)—which could help better prepare them for the actual world of love and deceit and moral dilemmas. Implicit in both positions, however, is a sense of the significant power of this new form, and the ways in which the print on its pages could become a script for new kinds of social performance in the world.

Much of this power (whether it was feared or lauded) stems from the ways in which the impact of individual novels was allegedly multiplied by a new institution for reading: the circulating library.[1] Most novels in the eighteenth century were published in small editions (500-750 copies) and sold for high prices: at the time of *Polly Honeycombe* and *The Rivals*, each volume would typically go for two-and-a-half or three shillings, and most novels ran to at least two or three, and sometimes up to six or seven volumes. Not surprisingly, given how fast one can tear through a novel, many readers were reluctant to spend so much on what might be only a day or two's entertainment. Obviously, there were other ways of getting one's hands on a novel: browsing, borrowing from friends, buying second-hand, shoplifting. But those didn't satisfy the pent-up demand, and so renting entered the scene (governmentally supported free libraries are largely an invention of the nineteenth century). Booksellers had been periodically loaning out their stock for a fee since the 1660s, and there were stand-alone circulating libraries in the provinces from the 1720s on. But it was really only in the 1740s that the institution took off, especially in London. In return for 10½ or 12 shillings a year—the price went up in the mid-1760s—or three or four shillings a quarter, one could join a circulating library and read as much as one liked of its collection. There were also possibilities for renting an individual volume for a few pence a week.[2] Depending on the library, collections ranged from a few hundred to several thousand titles, and included a variety of books: novels, to be sure, but also plays, poetry, history, medical texts, sheet music, etc. Customers chose what they wanted from a preprinted catalog, like the one supplied in *Polly Honeycombe*, though, as Act One, Scene Two, of *The Rivals* suggests, not everything was likely to be available at any given moment. Additionally, many libraries only allowed their patrons to have one volume out at a time, so it

---

1 For more on the issues raised in this paragraph and the next, see Allan, Donoghue (*The Fame Machine*), and the titles by Raven.

2 In Bath, it was fashionable for "the quality" to pay double these rates.

was not unusual for, say, only Volume Two of a given text to be on the shelves at the time of request, which could make for a rather different relation to plot than what we are generally accustomed to.

Part of the apparent appeal of circulating libraries—beyond their provision of an entire year's reading for the cost of two or three novels—was the way in which they gave readers, including young women under the protection of a parent or guardian, a sense of control over their own amusement. Elsewhere in their lives, pleasure came mostly preselected and preapproved (by fathers, husbands, teachers, clergy, employers, theater managers, et al.). But with a circulating library, one could choose—at least from the available selections.[1] For most of the usual authorities, however, such choice was at best a mixed, and probably a bad thing. Sentiments like these spurred on the development of a counter-institution for reading: monthly magazines devoted exclusively to book reviews. In 1749, *The Monthly Review* was launched as a sort of filter between the supposedly unscrupulous book trade and the reading public. In 1756, it gained a competitor, *The Critical Review*. Together, the reviews purported to protect the public from imperiling its morals and wasting its money by guiding its choices only toward what was both innocent and of lasting value. It's unclear how much influence they had upon actual novel-readers, since their reviews, especially of prose fiction, often lagged months behind, but—as the selections in Appendix B illustrate—they certainly played up the form's dubious reputation, and probably helped further inflame opposition to it. At the very least, the reviews (like many of their modern successors) provided many opportunities to feel snarkily superior to more abject segments of the reading public—such as teenage girls.

The felt threat of novel-reading, as it was amplified by the circulating libraries and (intermittently) thwarted or regulated by the reviews, ultimately hinges upon what might seem a paradox: novels were a problem *either* because they so absorbed readers as to take them out of the world, *or* because they so convincingly portrayed the world that readers became quixotic, and mistook fiction for reality. The two don't seem like they should both be able to be true, and perhaps they can't be so simultaneously. But

---

1 "Sukey Saunter" indignantly underscores this point in a letter to *The Morning Post* (3 February 1775): "I should be glad to know what are most of the modern comedies but *dialogue novels*? Are the two playhouses better than circulating libraries? Only that at Mr. *Noble*'s we may chuse our entertainment, and there the managers chuse it for us."

both fears (not to mention the growing popularity of the form itself, and the number of readers who may have changed their practices in order to avoid becoming the targets of anti-novelistic hysteria) testify to the felt power of the novel, its ability to shape and determine lives, and so transform print into performance, and performance—such as the "intrigues and contrivances" that Polly is planning—into still more kinds of print. After all, Miss Honeycombe was hardly alone in her conviction that "a Novel is the only thing" (72).

Print, Performance, and Celebrity

Play-acting, playgoing, and various forms of quixotism are hardly the only ways in which print and performance fed into one another in the eighteenth century. Another point at which the two converged was the cluster of reading and viewing practices surrounding celebrity. Celebrity, at least in its modern sense as something distinct from fame or reputation, is largely an eighteenth-century invention. Through gossipy accounts in the newspapers (sometimes involving the paid insertion—or suppression—of rapturous or defamatory "paragraphs," such as we see in the opening scene of Sheridan's *The School for Scandal*), publicly exhibited images, and recognizable mimicry in the theaters, readers, viewers, and playgoers were solicited to join in the creation and destruction of an ever-changing set of idols.[1] Then, as now, the public persona of a celebrity was an odd sort of being: a widely available—and highly mediated—collective image that most people would acknowledge probably didn't bear that much of a resemblance to its supposed referent, but that nonetheless prompted a craving for an unobtainable intimacy with the person in question. That is, at some level we know that the "Brad Pitt" and "Angelina Jolie" of the tabloids are unlike the actual Mr. Pitt and Ms. Jolie in any number of ways, but yet we think we know them, perhaps better than we know people in our own lives, and we find ourselves drawn to learn ever more details about their marriage, children, changing bodies, etc. Much the same dynamic was at work in the eighteenth century, with much the same results: attractive young people with a compelling story could find themselves objects of public fascination almost overnight.

---

1   For more on the matters touched upon in this paragraph, see Bourque, Braudy, Moody, Roach, and Werkmeister.

The most important eighteenth-century celebrities for our purposes are Sheridan and Elizabeth Linley, whose high-profile elopement together, and the subsequent duels Sheridan fought on her behalf, captured the public imagination in the early 1770s. Appendix C offers a sampling of images and press coverage of the two, but since the story those snippets tell is (necessarily) fragmentary—events were reported as they happened, often on the basis of incomplete or incorrect information—it is worth rehearsing the entire affair, so as to allow for a fuller grasp of how it reappears in complex and delightfully refracted ways in *The Rivals*.

In 1754, Elizabeth Linley was born into a celebrated musical family in Bath. Her father directed the concerts at the Assembly Rooms (for more on these, see the next section), her brother would become, in his short lifetime, a significant composer and a friend of Mozart's, and her sister would become an accomplished singer. But it was Elizabeth who was to be the most famous Linley of all. By the time she was nine, she was singing in public, and by her mid-teens she was regularly performing to wild acclaim—and being hailed as an extraordinary beauty—in both Bath and London. In 1770, when she was sixteen, her parents forced her into an engagement with Walter Long, a wealthy man traditionally said to have been fifty-nine—though it has been recently claimed he was only in his mid-forties. Shortly before the wedding, the engagement was broken off, and the already active rumor mill began to turn at top speed. It is unclear whether Long charitably released Linley from a marriage that she clearly didn't want, or if he was alarmed by the attention being paid to her by other men, including Thomas Mathews (a married friend of her father's), or if it was something else entirely. Foote quickly dramatized the tale as *The Maid of Bath*, suggesting that the real reason for the break-up was that Linley refused to engage in premarital sex. It must have been mortifying for Linley to have her story, especially with this spin on it, put upon the London stage. But audiences loved it, and it was performed forty-one times between the summer of 1771 and the debut of *The Rivals*.

After her parting with Long, Linley continued to perform, but found herself regularly tormented by Mathews, who supposedly threatened to ruin her reputation and/or commit suicide, if she didn't succumb to his advances. Despairing, she turned to some friends for help. Those friends were Sheridan's sisters, Lissy and Betsy, and it didn't take much for Sheridan (who was already in love with Linley, as were his brother and his best friend) to agree to escort her to a convent in France, where she could take refuge until she came of age and could decide her own fate. So the two left Bath in secret in the middle of the night, and made their way to France (along the way, Sheridan told a friend who was helping them that she was an heiress named "Miss Harlow," as if the whole affair were a spin-off from Samuel Richardson's novel *Clarissa*).[1] Once in France, Sheridan convinced Linley that they should marry in order to preserve her reputation, although any such ceremony would have been invalid under English law, since it would have been a Catholic service, and the two were underage. Soon thereafter, Linley's father tracked the couple down, and convinced them to come home. In the meantime, though, Mathews, apparently feeling cheated, had been abusing Sheridan's family in Bath, and had put a notice in *The Bath Chronicle* insulting Sheridan, and effectively challenging him to a duel. Sheridan found Mathews in London, and, after some evasions on Mathews's part, they fought. Sheridan won, and broke Mathews's sword (a form of ritual humiliation), but promised to keep the latter secret if Mathews apologized through another paragraph in the newspaper and didn't contradict the public account of the duel. These conditions rankled Mathews, and he was soon spreading rumors that things had gone very differently than Sheridan would have everyone believe. Since this amounted to a new insult, the two again dueled, this time near Bath. Both men's swords quickly broke, but Mathews retained enough of a shard to stab the probably drunken Sheridan repeatedly in a very unsporting way (duels were supposed to be about demonstrating one's courage, and thereby one's right to be called a gentleman, rather than anything more bloodthirsty). Mathews then fled the scene, and Sheridan was left to die. Indeed, some newspapers reported that he was on the verge of death, which the audiences listening to Linley perform found particularly alluring and poignant (there may be echoes of these rumors in the proliferating reports of Sir Peter Teazle's non-existent duel in the penultimate scene of *The School for Scandal*). The second duel only further infuriated Sheridan's and Linley's fathers, who both determined to keep the lovers apart (Thomas Sheridan thought it beneath his family's dignity for his son to marry the daughter of a musician; Thomas Linley scorned the poverty and Irishness of the Sheridans, and—rightly—feared that Sheridan's extravagance would quickly exhaust all of the couple's money). Sheridan was sent to live in the country and prepare himself to study law;

1   See O'Toole, 57.

Linley continued to perform and earn huge sums for her father (a newspaper estimated that she had brought him £10,000). Her triumph as both a singer and a "public beauty" may have come in the winter of 1773 when the young Frances Burney recorded that "the whole Town seem[s] distracted about her. Every other Diversion is forsaken—Miss Linley Alone engrosses all Eyes, Ears, Hearts."[1] According to Horace Walpole, even George III "ogle[d] her as much as he dare[d] to do in so holy a place as an oratorio."[2] During their forced separation, Sheridan and Linley nonetheless contrived to see one another—often with stratagems that would have pleased Lydia Languish—and by the next spring they somehow obtained Thomas Linley's permission for them to marry (since Elizabeth was still underage). Sheridan immediately decided that it would be an affront to his status as a gentleman for his wife to perform any more for money, and so began to cast about for a way to make ends meet. The result was *The Rivals*, a play that takes all of the elements of their courtship—elopement, duels, multiple suitors, deceived parents, the prospect of losing a dowry—and transmutes them into something that, while hardly a simple transcription, nonetheless tantalizingly conjures up the romantic adventures (and in Linley's case, spectacular desirability) of a couple already deeply familiar to the celebrity-gazing public.

The Narrative Possibilities of Bath

Part of why the Sheridan-Linley romance seemed so compelling to readers and viewers in the early 1770s was the way in which it drew upon the pre-existing narrative possibilities of Bath. Now all story-telling relies upon geography to some extent—indeed Franco Moretti has argued that "*without a certain kind of space, a certain kind of story is simply impossible*" (100, Moretti's emphasis) but some spaces and places are far more highly conventionalized in their narrative uses than others. For example, a whole range of tales were set in London in the eighteenth century, and still new possibilities could be created by combining those already in circulation (witness only the ways in which *Polly Honeycombe* places

---

1   *The Early Journals and Letters of Fanny Burney*, ed. Lars E. Troide (Kingston: McGill-Queen's UP, 1988), 1:248-49.
2   Walpole to Lady Ossory, 16 March 1773, in *Horace Walpole's Correspondence with the Countess of Upper Ossory*, ed. W.S. Lewis and A. Dayle Wallace (New Haven: Yale UP, 1965), 106.

a tale of quixotism—traditionally associated with the West End social elite—squarely in the wealthy, but unfashionable commercial district of the City: see Figure 9 [p. 58]). Bath, on the other hand, was far more circumscribed in its associations. This is not necessarily a bad thing—just think of how many recent films and television shows have been able to successfully exploit the fairly one-dimensional reputations of Las Vegas or Miami—but it does create a more binding set of expectations on the part of the public.

So what would early audiences of *The Rivals* have conjured up when they thought of Bath? Eighteenth-century Bath was renowned for two seemingly contradictory things: it was a place for the sick to get better, and a place for the healthy to indulge themselves.[1] The medical side of the city hardly figures in *The Rivals*, and so need not much concern us here (the short version is that bathing in or drinking from the local hot springs were thought to be good for all sorts of ailments, including the gout of which Sir Anthony complains). The leisure side of the city, on the other hand, looms large in the play, and is further illuminated by the excerpts in Appendix D. "The busiest idle place in the world,"[2] as Mary Delany called Bath, offered ample opportunities for young people to meet one another, dance, gossip, gamble, find potential mates, polish or reinvent themselves, gain or lose a fortune, and otherwise engage in a more sustained quest for pleasure than was generally available at home. As this last phrase should suggest, most of the inhabitants of Bath—and the entire dramatis personae of *The Rivals*—were not full-time residents of the city, but rather visitors there (usually for the "season" in Autumn, Spring, or, more rarely, Winter). The temporariness of their stay, along with the suspension of social distinctions that was enforced by the Master of Ceremonies at the Assembly Rooms (the center of social life for most visitors), meant that there was something of a camp- or resort-like atmosphere. People who would never meet in their lives elsewhere (because of geography, rank, or religion) could stroll or dance or listen to music together, strike up conversations, and try out new versions of their selves—often in the hope of making a match: Bath was one

---

1   For more on the subjects explored in this paragraph, see Borsay, Briggs, Eglin, and the titles by Fawcett.
2   Delany to Anne Dewes, 28 October 1760, in *Autobiography and Correspondence of Mary Granville, Mrs. Delany*, ed. Lady Llanover (London, 1861), 3:606.

of the central marriage markets in the nation. Not surprisingly, this suspension of distinction, along with the fact that most of the visitors were previously unknown to one another, encouraged not a little dressing-up and misrepresentation. Sometimes this was innocent enough (say, Bob Acres refashioning himself as a fop); other times it was in the service of fortune hunting: impoverished Irish gentlemen, like Sir Lucius O'Trigger, or Sheridan himself, were supposedly particularly prone to the latter. But either way, the possibility that one could step outside one's regular life—into pleasure, maybe into a bit of danger—seems to have been a big part of Bath's allure, at least for the middling, gentry, and titled visitors who came there to play (this was not a resort for the lower orders, except for the servants who accompanied their employers). One result was that the usual sites and kinds of amusement in Bath became known, both through print and prior theatrical performance, to people well beyond those who had actually spent any time there: readers and playgoers would have had no difficulty understanding references to—or scenery showing—the Parades, the Orange Grove, the Circus, or Queen Square as fashionable places in which to stroll, or the Assembly Rooms as where one went to dance, or the many opportunities for eating, shopping, gambling, and people-watching. Nor would they have had any trouble believing that, of all the places in the world, Bath was the most probable and fitting setting for a tale, like *The Rivals*, which was full of flirtation, gossip, romantic entanglements, contemplated elopements, duels, and people pretending to be someone else.

These Plays and Our Playwrights

For most users of this edition, of course, the issues we've been exploring are going to be of interest in direct proportion to the degree to which they can serve as useful contexts for understanding *Polly Honeycombe* and *The Rivals*. Accordingly, it makes sense to close with a brief consideration of these plays and our playwrights.

Both plays mark the advent, on the theatrical scene, of ambitious young men. Each saved its author from an unwanted career in the law, and launched him upon a more satisfying vocation as a playwright and theater manager (and in Sheridan's case, a politician as well). Each play is, in effect, a job application, an attempt to show the managers and the public that a new and significant talent had arrived, and should be rewarded accordingly.

And in each case, the application worked. Unlike most new plays, both *Polly Honeycombe* and *The Rivals* were successful, and lastingly so. *Polly Honeycombe* was the most popular afterpiece of the 1760s, and stayed in the repertory, both in London and elsewhere, for decades. *The Rivals* has never left the repertory, and remains one of the few eighteenth-century plays to be performed with any regularity by modern actors.[1]

Much of this success stems from how well Colman and Sheridan knew the resources and conventions of their theaters. They each seem to have written with particular actors (and their "lines") in mind. And they each very knowingly echo the plots and characters and pleasures of many of the most successful comedies of the repertory. This is not to say that they're engaged in the plagiarism that Sheridan so anxiously denies in his Preface, only that both plays are really good at hitting their generic marks. Their innovation comes largely from how well, and how audaciously, they deploy long familiar conventions (young lovers deceiving their elders, servants and hapless suitors unable to speak except in the jargon of their professions, etc.), rather than from any great defiance of the past: though the ending of *Polly Honeycombe* is the significant departure that the author's mother complains of in the Preface, and *The Rivals* is more concerned with the details of everyday life—such as servants ceasing to wear wigs—than most of its predecessors and competitors.[2] Such loving adherence to convention may be at odds with how we like to think of the texts we call "literature," but it describes quite well how most of those texts have actually worked in the world (and how most of the current film and television we enjoy functions as well). Convention, like other markers of genre, solicits desire, and solicitations that come off as startling or unprecedented are likely to fall flat. It's in the realm of the mostly familiar, the clever take on the already largely known, that bids for literary and theatrical success have their best chance, and where print and performance can most intriguingly intertwine to create lasting, and yet ever new forms of pleasure. Polly and Lydia already know this; it's time for us to follow their lead.

---

1   For an intriguing production from 2004, see Kavanaugh.
2   In an apparent puff for *Polly Honeycombe*, "a young lady" praised "the conclusion" as "so droll and diverting, and so different from every thing else!" (*The Public Ledger* 8 December 1760). For the ways in which Sheridan echoes other plays, see Auburn, Bevis (*The Laughing Tradition*), Freeman, and Loftis.

George Colman the Elder and Richard Brinsley Sheridan: A Brief Chronology

1732   Colman born in Florence to Francis and Mary Colman (c. 15 April).

1733   Francis Colman dies; William Pulteney, Colman's extraordinarily rich uncle, becomes his guardian.

1737   The Licensing Act restricts the number of theaters in London that can perform spoken drama, and requires submission of all new and revised scripts for pre-performance censorship.

1741   Colman sent to Westminster School, where he develops many of his closest literary friendships (with Charles Churchill, William Cowper, Robert Lloyd, and Bonnell Thornton). Several of these men later form the Non-sense Club (a weekly social group devoted to clever mockery of contemporary art and literature) with Colman.

1751   Colman goes to Christ Church, Oxford; Sheridan born in Dublin to Thomas and Frances Sheridan (September or October).

1754   Colman and Bonnell Thornton start *The Connoisseur* (which runs through 1756); Elizabeth Linley born in Bath (early September).

1755   Colman begins his legal training at Lincoln's Inn in London (he was called to the bar in 1757 and worked intermittently as a lawyer between 1758 and 1761).

1757   Colman writes *A Letter of Abuse to D—d G——k, Esq.* (actually an ingenious bit of praise), which leads to his becoming friends with David Garrick, the most cele-brated actor of his day and the manager of the Theatre-Royal, Drury Lane.

1760   Premiere of *Polly Honeycombe* (5 December) at Drury Lane.

1761   Premiere of Colman's first mainpiece, *The Jealous Wife* (12 February); Colman, Thornton, and Garrick start the *St. James Chronicle*, which regularly "puffed" Drury Lane.

1762   Sheridan sent to Harrow School near London, where he stays until 1767 or 1768. His family was in France (where it was cheaper to live) for most of his time in boarding school and so, because of their finances, he rarely saw them.

1763   Colman takes charge of theatrical matters at Drury Lane for two seasons, while Garrick is recovering from exhaustion in France; premiere of Colman's *The Deuce is in Him* (4 November), a possible influence on the Julia-Faulkland plot in *The Rivals*.

1764   Pulteney, by then Earl of Bath, dies and leaves his fortune to his brother, thus ending Colman's hope of becoming independently wealthy.

1766   Premiere of Colman and Garrick's *The Clandestine Marriage* (20 February); Frances Sheridan dies.

1767   Mary Colman dies; Colman becomes partner and manager at the Theatre-Royal, Covent Garden.

1768   Colman marries Sarah Ford, his longtime mistress and the mother of his son, George (who would himself become a major playwright).

1770   Thomas Sheridan moves his family to Bath (September), where they get to know the Linleys; Elizabeth Linley is forced by her parents into an engagement with Walter Long (December).

1771   Sheridan revises a burlesque written by a friend, Nathaniel Halhed, changes its title from *Ixion* to *Jupiter*, and offers it to Samuel Foote, Colman, and Garrick, but no one is interested; Sarah Colman accidentally poisons herself and dies; Long breaks off the engagement with Linley; Foote transmutes the whole affair into *The Maid of Bath* (premiered 26 June at the Haymarket—a theater that had a royal patent to present spoken drama in the summer).

1772   Sheridan elopes to France with Elizabeth Linley (18 March); Thomas Mathews publishes a challenge to Sheridan in *The Bath Chronicle* (9 April); Sheridan returns to England (28 April); Sheridan and Mathews's first duel (4 May); Sheridan and Mathews's second duel (1 July).

1773   Premiere of Oliver Goldsmith's *She Stoops to Conquer* at Covent Garden (15 March); Sheridan and Linley marry (13 April), and move to London.

1774   Colman steps down as manager at Covent Garden.

1775   Premiere of *The Rivals* at Covent Garden (17 January); the play is immediately withdrawn for revision; *The*

Rivals "with alterations" performed to acclaim at Covent
Garden (28 January); premiere of Sheridan's *The
Duenna*, with music by several of the Linleys, at Covent
Garden (21 November).

1776 Garrick retires as partner and manager of Drury Lane;
Foote retires as manager of the Haymarket, and sells the
theater to Colman; Sheridan becomes partner and
manager at Drury Lane, borrowing heavily to do so, and
opens the season with a prologue by Colman: *New
Brooms! An Occasional Prelude.*

1777 Sheridan invited to join the Club, a weekly dining
society (other members include James Boswell, Edmund
Burke, Colman, Garrick, Samuel Johnson, Sir Joshua
Reynolds, and Adam Smith); Sheridan becomes friends
with many aristocrats, and begins to live far beyond his
(still considerable) means, and to have affairs; premiere
of Sheridan's *The School for Scandal* at Drury Lane (8
May), with an epilogue by Colman; premiere of
Colman's adaptation of Pierre Augustin Caron de Beau-
marchais's *The Barber of Seville* at the Haymarket (30
August).

1778 Sheridan and Thomas Harris, the manager of Covent
Garden, purchase the King's Theatre, an opera house
(further plunging Sheridan into debt).

1779 Garrick dies and is eulogized at Drury Lane by Sheridan's *Verses to the Memory of Garrick*; premiere of Sheridan's *The Critic* at Drury Lane (30 October).

1780 Sheridan elected to Parliament, financing his campaign
(and later ones as well) by borrowing against his share of
Drury Lane; management of the latter is largely left to
others.

1781 Sheridan sells his interest in the King's Theatre.

1785 Colman has a stroke, which leaves him partially para-
lyzed, making it difficult for him to speak, though he
continues to manage the Haymarket.

1787 Sheridan attacks Warren Hastings, Governor General of
Bengal, in the first of four roughly five-hour speeches in
Parliament (the others were in 1788), as part of the
impeachment of Hastings for corruption and the tyran-
nical oppression of India. Hastings is ultimately acquit-
ted, but Sheridan's speeches are widely hailed as almost
miraculous feats of oratory, and tickets to the trial were
sold for over £50 each.

1788   Thomas Sheridan dies; George III goes mad from por-
        phyria, and Sheridan becomes the Prince of Wales's
        closest advisor as Parliament contemplates the possibility
        of a Regency.

1790   The Sheridans' marriage is so strained by Richard's
        affairs that Elizabeth expects they will separate. Instead
        she has an affair of her own; Colman goes mad and has
        to be institutionalized; his son runs the Haymarket in his
        absence.

1791   Drury Lane closed for renovation, which puts Sheridan
        into still more debt.

1792   Elizabeth Sheridan dies, reconciled with Richard, two
        months after giving birth to her lover's child.

1794   Colman dies (14 August); Drury Lane reopens with a
        much larger capacity, but Sheridan often fails to pay its
        bills.

1795   Sheridan marries Hester Jane Ogle.

1799   Premiere of Sheridan's adaptation of August von Kotze-
        bue's *Pizarro* (24 May).

1809   Drury Lane burns down.

1812   Drury Lane reopens, but without Sheridan (he was
        excluded from its management as a condition of raising
        the necessary funds for rebuilding); Sheridan loses his
        bid for reelection and leaves Parliament virtually bank-
        rupt.

1813   The Prince of Wales, officially Regent since 1811, breaks
        off his friendship with Sheridan.

1814   Sheridan, no longer possessing his parliamentary immu-
        nity, is arrested for debt (as he would be again in 1815).

1816   Sheridan dies with almost no available cash, surrounded
        by bailiffs trying to recover the thousands of pounds
        owed to their clients (7 July), and is buried in Poet's
        Corner in Westminster Abbey.

A Note on the Texts

Playtexts are, as anyone with acting experience can attest, considerably more fluid than their non-theatrical counterparts. Words, lines, and even entire scenes are routinely cut, revised, or inserted (sometimes on an almost daily basis), depending on the available cast, rehearsal or running time, production resources, and audience reactions. The result, actors and managers hope, is a text that works well in the ever-shifting world of the playhouse. But the exact contours of the script, as it was performed on a given night—what was and was not said, much less what was gestured or otherwise conveyed non-verbally—are typically beyond recovery, especially for productions that predate recording technology. All we have are whatever written playtexts have survived, which offer us imperfect snapshots of particular moments in the production process, along with the equally imperfect evidence of advertisements and promptbooks, and perhaps some theatrical anecdotes (often recorded long after the fact, and sometimes of dubious reliability). Obviously, this means that any claims we might want to make about the life of a playtext in, say, the eighteenth-century theater are going to be, at least in principle, a bit of a reach, an informed guess based upon texts that were preserved for reasons other than giving posterity an accurate transcription of the words and movements of a given performance. But what else can we do, if we want to understand these plays, and their place in an institution central to eighteenth-century society? Moreover, similar problems haunt every sort of historical inquiry: archives are always imperfect, always assembled with intentions other than those driving later students and researchers. However, imperfection need not stand in the way of our understanding the past "well enough." We just need to remember that there will always (at least theoretically) be a gap between what we know and "how things actually were," and so we should be properly self-conscious about the ultimately speculative nature of our work.

In the case of the plays here reproduced, we have five broad kinds of evidence regarding their texts: manuscripts submitted by the theaters for pre-production censorship, the first published editions of the plays, advertising done by the theaters, later published editions, and various promptbooks and production anecdotes. Each has its own strengths and limitations, but collectively they give us a decent picture of how these playtexts both endured and changed over their first few decades. A brief consideration of each type of evidence, working in rough chronological order, should help contextualize the specific versions of *Polly Honeycombe* and *The Rivals* being presented here, and in so doing, further underscore all the ways in which these are, after all, plays written for and produced in a commercial theater. That is, we always need to remember that what we're reading are ultimately scripts intended for performance on a particular kind of stage, and with a particular sort of actors, rather than, say, novels that just happen to be broken into acts and scenes, instead of chapters.

In 1737, after close to a decade of increasingly outrageous political satire (and upwards of a century of opposition from business owners, who thought their employees were being led astray by the theater), the London playhouses began to be required to submit all new or revised plays, which they hoped to produce, to a government Licenser for pre-production censorship. The manuscripts of these submissions have largely survived (bureaucracies produce good archives), and offer an often fascinating glimpse into how the theaters were planning to produce a given play. In some cases, especially with farces or other fairly low-status forms, the manuscript text (hereafter called the Larpent text, after John Larpent, a longtime Licenser of Plays) is the only version we have.[1] In other cases, the Larpent text opens a window onto how the text read prior to its premiere. Accordingly, the Larpent manuscripts can often get us as close as we're ever going to get to the text performed on the first night (although, as the Preface to *Polly Honeycombe* reminds us, such performances were often "nothing more than a Publick Rehearsal," after which bits that didn't work would be revised or cut, and so the Larpent text doesn't necessarily represent the state of the script for anything beyond that first night).

If a play was successful in its first few performances (and sometimes if it wasn't), it would generally be printed as a stand-alone playbook—that is, a thick pamphlet that contained the playtext, and often a dedication or preface describing the playwright's supposed intentions and/or the play's initial fate on the stage. In general, such playbooks at least claimed to present the

---

1   Despite being public property, the Licenser's collection was sold by
    Larpent's widow in the 1830s and has mostly ended up in the hands of
    the Huntington Library in San Marino, California.

text "as it is acted" at whatever theater had staged it, but a comparison of their texts to those of the Larpent manuscripts often reveals some significant differences, and so we're forced to decide on a case-by-case basis whether those changes are the trace of revisions to the playtext as it was staged after the first night, or if they're an instance of a playwright's attempting to alter the playtext in order to make it a better, perhaps more "literary," reading experience.

One of the ways in which we can try to make these decisions is by looking at the theaters' advertising over time. Since the theaters relied upon both familiarity and novelty to draw in their audiences, their advertising often highlighted major changes to the playtexts: new prologues or epilogues, new scenes, the restoration of scenes previously cut, etc. If these changes line up with the text of the printed playbooks, we can be reasonably confident that the playbooks are offering a fairly good representation of what was then being staged. If they don't line up, chances are that the playbooks are taking their texts in a direction other than that of the theater. Such departures are not necessarily underhanded or bad: plays were popular reading material, and a playwright could often fetch a higher price for the sale of his or her copyright if the play in question made for good reading, as well as good viewing. But scholars and students interested in the plays as theatrical events should be wary of how far to trust the text of printed playbooks without some sort of external verification.

Plays that were successful, either in the theater or as reading material, were often republished to further supply their apparent market. These later editions not only share all of the uncertainties of their predecessors, but sometimes introduce still new questions. If the play was still an active part of the repertory, these later editions can often provide a useful glimpse into how a playtext changed after its initial run (see, for example, my description below of how the third scene of *Polly Honeycombe* was reworked). But even more than with the first edition, these subsequent editions often widen the gap between stage and page with additional authorial revision (often to "clean up" a text for inclusion in an author's collected works).

Finally, we have a number of promptbooks—copies of a play marked up by the prompter of a theater to indicate cuts, necessary props, entrances, and exits—and various theatrical anecdotes, all of which can shed light upon particular productions (a few of the most significant anecdotes are mentioned in my notes to *The Rivals*). It's difficult to know how representative this sort of evidence is: the fact that a scene was cut in a provincial production in the 1790s may or may not tell us anything useful about what audiences saw at other times and in other places. But, if nothing else, this sort of material offers yet another reminder that we need to be cautious about hanging *theatrical* significance on something, simply because it appears in the printed playtext. Print and performance were, as the Introduction suggests, deeply intertwined with one another. They were not, however, synonymous or interchangeable.

In the interest of not overcomplicating matters for an initial reading, I have chosen to present each play in the version offered by its first published edition, while giving below a chronological overview of how that particular version figures in the unfolding history of the playtext. This strategy, while admittedly imperfect for all the reasons outlined above, has, I believe, the advantage of capturing these plays in something close to the versions in which they achieved their initial success, with their initial casts. Those moments are not, of course, the only ones of interest, but, I suspect, they're likely to be of first and greatest interest to most students and scholars using this edition. Readers interested in learning more about the differences between the various extant versions of these plays than I've provided here, or in the notes to the plays themselves, should consult the textual notes to the editions of Thomas Price, Richard Little Purdy, and Cecil Price listed in the bibliography.

The version of *Polly Honeycombe* reproduced here is what appeared as the first edition of the play, published on 9 December 1760 (four days after its premiere) and probably represents what audiences saw and heard for the overwhelming majority of the forty-four performances of its first two seasons, excluding, of course, the Preface, the Extract, and Colman's note on the Prologue—which were all, obviously, not intended for the stage—and the Prologue and the Epilogue, which were dropped after the tenth performance, one more than was customary. There are three other principal versions of the play: the Larpent manuscript, which probably gets us as close as we can to the version staged at the "Publick Rehearsal" of the first night; the "Third Edition with Alterations" of 1762, which includes some quite significant authorial revisions, and probably corresponds to what was staged from May 1762 on; and the text that appears in the 1777 *Dramatick Works of George Colman* and includes a few additional revisions, none of which seem to have carried over to the theater. Additionally, there were several unauthorized editions of the play published in 1761 in Cork, Dublin, Edinburgh, and London, and a number of later eighteenth- and early nineteenth-century reprints, none of which are important enough to describe here.

The biggest differences between the text of the Larpent manuscript and that of the first edition reproduced here are in the Prologue, the Larpent text of which offers several additional lines and alternate phrasings (though they're all in the same vein), and in the final scene—where there's a bit less blustering by Mr. Honeycombe toward Polly and the Nurse, a little less impertinence from Polly and Scribble, one more financially-minded speech by Ledger, and a significantly shorter, and so less ostentatiously self-pitying, final speech by Mr. Honeycombe. It's likely, though impossible to prove, that the cuts and additions of the first edition represent the results of the "Publick Rehearsal" of the first night (i.e., the Prologue was thought to work just as well with a little truncation, and the farcical interactions of Mr. Honeycombe, Polly, and Scribble were thought to need a little further pumping up, as were Mr. Honeycombe's closing pleas to the audience—which collectively drove home all the ways in which the play's ending broke with comic convention).

The most significant departures from the first edition text made by the "Third Edition with Alterations" are the omission of the entire paragraph regarding the Lutestrings in the Preface, presumably because its references to the death of George II had become dated (this had the perhaps inadvertent side-effect of making the author's mother no longer responsible for the Extract), an almost wholesale reworking of the third scene, and some further amplifying of the farcical aspects of the fourth scene: Mr. Honeycombe's indignation, Polly's and Scribble's impudence, the Nurse's penchant for clichés, Mrs. Honeycombe's drunken incomprehension, etc. In the new version of the third scene, which the theater was advertising in May 1762, Mr. Honeycombe discovers Scribble and throws him out of the house, under the impression that he is only a footman sent to deliver a love letter. Mr. Honeycombe then threatens Polly with "the Whole Duty of Man, or the Practice of Piety to read,—or a chair, a screen, or a carpet to work with your needle.—We'll find you employment.—Some other books than Novels, and some better company than Mr. Scribble's footman.——Have done with your nonsense—and learn to make a pudding, you impudent, idle young baggage!" (28-29). The scene ends with the

Nurse slipping Polly out of the house. A number of lines from the first edition text were retained in this new scene, including Polly's comparison of herself to Sophy Western, her considering taking the screws off the door, and Scribble's proposal to conduct her through the streets as if he were her footman. But Polly also invents some new plans, including setting fire to the house, so that she can be carried away like stolen goods in the confusion.

The only significant further change made in the 1777 *Dramatick Works* was the rather inexplicable alteration, in the Preface, of "my Mother" as the source of the indirect praise of the play's ending to "a maiden aunt." Perhaps Colman had come to think that the passage was disrespectful to his actual mother (who had died in the interim)?

The textual history of *The Rivals* is a bit more complicated. With the exception of the Prologue "Spoken on the Tenth Night," what is reproduced here is what appeared as the first edition of the play, which was published on 11 February 1775, two weeks after the debut of Sheridan's revised version of the play. It probably represents something close to what audiences saw and heard for the sixteen performances of that version in its first two seasons at Covent Garden, excluding, of course, the Preface, and, for some of those performances, one or both of the prologues and/or the epilogue. It appeared in an unusually large edition of 3,000 copies, which suggests that its publisher expected it to be a big hit. There are two other principal versions of the play: the Larpent manuscript, which probably gets us as close as we can get to the disastrous first performance of the play (about which more below), and the "Third Edition Corrected" of May 1776, which was the first to include the Prologue "Spoken on the Tenth Night." There were a number of other editions of the play published in Sheridan's lifetime, none of them important enough to describe here.

As Sheridan's Preface to the play suggests, the opening night of *The Rivals* did not go well. Apparently over-confident in the "buzz" of anticipation surrounding the play, Sheridan put forward—and Covent Garden performed—a script that was, as "*A Friend to Comedy*" complained a few days later, "a *full hour* longer in the representation than any piece on the stage" (another account suggests that it ran four hours).[1] Moreover, several of the main characters were thought to be offensive, most of the actors

---

1 *The Morning Chronicle*, 20 January 1775.

didn't know their lines (especially Edward Shuter, who was playing Sir Anthony Absolute), and there was a general sense that the new playwright was far too delighted by his own puns and double entendres. When, at the close of the opening night, the play was "given out" to be performed again the next evening, the audience was not pleased, but the theater decided to press on anyway, going so far as to print up playbills for the next day's performance. However, Sheridan then withdrew the play and quickly revised it, largely in response to the criticism he received from the newspapers. In addition to the length, punning, and indecency, the reviewers objected to the portrayal of Sir Lucius O'Trigger, both as a role, and as it was performed by John Lee, and to some aspects of the other characters, especially Sir Anthony. The result of Sheridan's revision was, a mere eleven days later, a significantly new play, with a new actor, Lawrence Clinch, in the part of Sir Lucius (see Appendix A for all of these performers). This new version was much applauded, and quickly passed into the repertory, out of which it has never fallen.

A full account of the differences between the original version of the play, as represented by the Larpent manuscript, and the revised version—as represented by the first edition—is beyond our scope here (for a side-by-side comparison and various cautions, see Purdy). But it's worth rehearsing some of the principal changes made, since they shed some intriguing light upon what playgoers of 1775 were and were not willing to accept. The chief source of offense in the original version was Sir Lucius, who came off as a bloodthirsty fortune hunter eager to instruct Acres in how to "Put [Beverley] to Death,"[1] and even willing to duel with himself, when it seemed as if he had inadvertently sent himself a challenge. *The Morning Chronicle* (18 January 1775) thought his character "so far from giving the manners of our brave and worthy neighbours, that it scarce equals the picture of a *respectable* Hotentot; gabbling in an uncouth dialect; neither Welch, English, nor Irish." The latter complaint, echoed two days later by the same paper's reference to Sir Lucius's "horrid medley of discordant brogues," may be an indication that part of the problem was Lee's attempt at an Irish accent. But the part, as originally written, can't have helped, especially at a time when English audiences were generally prone to congratulate themselves on their affectionate tolerance of alleged (and allegedly harmless) Irish eccentricities. Being amusingly prickly in

---

1 Purdy, 64.

response to "a jest ... at the expense of my country" (Sir Lucius's supposed provocation for the duel with Captain Absolute in the revised version), and inordinately concerned with the decorum of challenges, was one thing; being out to slaughter Englishmen for the sheer joy of it, and then marry their women, and take their money, was quite another. There were also some significant changes to Sir Anthony, who, in the original version, was far more lascivious, frequently hinting to Jack and Mrs. Malaprop what he'd like to do to Lydia, and otherwise going well beyond the bounds of propriety, even for a cranky old man. For example, his condemnation of circulating libraries extended to include "Oh, our London Nunneries are more obliged to them than to all the Recruiting Officers in the Kingdom,—The vicious Trash they send forth, not only disturbs the Imaginations of our Girls, but sets their Passions afloat—And then, rely on it, Mrs Malaprop, if they cannot find an Oroondates, they will take up with Thomas" (17). Given the widespread habit, in the eighteenth century, of referring to brothels as "nunneries," and the long-standing use of "Thomas" as not only a stock name for servants, but also a slang term for the penis, this is a rather inflammatory charge, tantamount to suggesting that Mrs. Malaprop's ward is well on her way toward becoming a prostitute or nymphomaniac. The other characters were also toned down: for example, Lucy no longer proclaimed, regarding her stack of books from the circulating library, that "the top one is Roderick Random, and Emily Montagu, under" (10),[1] while Captain Absolute stopped crying out "O shame! shame! that in a civiliz'd Country, like this, Women should be suffer'd to have a will of their own" (90). Even the song that Acres heard Julia sing in Devonshire was changed from "Variety is Charming" (the first line of which is "I'm in love with twenty"), presumably so as to remove any suggestion of promiscuity. And malapropisms, which had previously been part of several of the servants' ways of talking, as well as that of Mrs. Malaprop, were made her exclusive purview.

Beyond these many cuts and reworkings, the first edition also departed from the Larpent text by adding quite a few lines in the Julia and Faulkland plot. Here too Sheridan seems to have been responding to the reviews of the disastrous first night, which generally praised that part of the story. There are also a number of

---

1 Emily Montague is the sensitive and virtuous heroine of Frances
   Brooke's *The History of Emily Montague* (1769), and so not whom we
   would expect to find "under" the often unscrupulous hero of Tobias
   Smollett's *The Adventures of Roderick Random* (1748).

moments inserted in the first edition text that don't really advance the plot (such as Captain Absolute's flattery of Sir Anthony in Act Three, Scene One). It's unclear whether all of these additional lines were staged or not. If they were, then the play doesn't seem like it could have been shortened as dramatically as it needed to be, and there aren't any further complaints about its length. However, there is no direct evidence of their being cut for performance, other than the fact that many of them drop out of the subsequent versions of the printed playtext.

The third edition of 1776, which was advertised as "corrected by the Author," cuts the Preface, adds the Prologue "Spoken on the Tenth Night," and generally trims the play, removing overly topical allusions (such as the contest between "High-roomians and Low-roomians" in Bath), seemingly redundant dialogue, and some further oaths and double-entendres—such as Mrs. Malaprop's mention of "salivation going on in the fields" in Act Five, Scene One (salivation was a rather nasty side-effect of treatment for syphilis). The overall effect was to make the play a bit more streamlined and correct, which may have been more theatrically satisfying, but it diminished some of the wit and sheer exuberance that have long been among the play's principal attractions. The trade-off between these two may be part of why Sheridan was never able to come up with a final version that satisfied him (although his general difficulty focusing and his perennial writer's block presumably had something to do with that as well).

Both the plays and the various texts in the appendices appear in their original spelling and with their original punctuation, including a wide variety of dashes (which may indicate the duration of pauses, or the speed with which oaths were spoken). However, I have regularized the speech prefixes, italicized book titles, silently corrected a few obvious mistakes that the playwrights themselves corrected in later editions, and added quotation marks where they would help clarify that the words in question came from somewhere other than the speaker's own mind (say, from a letter being read aloud, or a customary phrase being echoed). The level of annotation is a bit more extensive than is typical in editions of this sort, but it's aimed at giving students and scholars the kind of knowledge that the original audience would have had at its fingertips. For playgoers and readers of the 1760s and 1770s, the allusions here would have been as readily apparent as the cultural references in any given episode of *The Simpsons* are today.

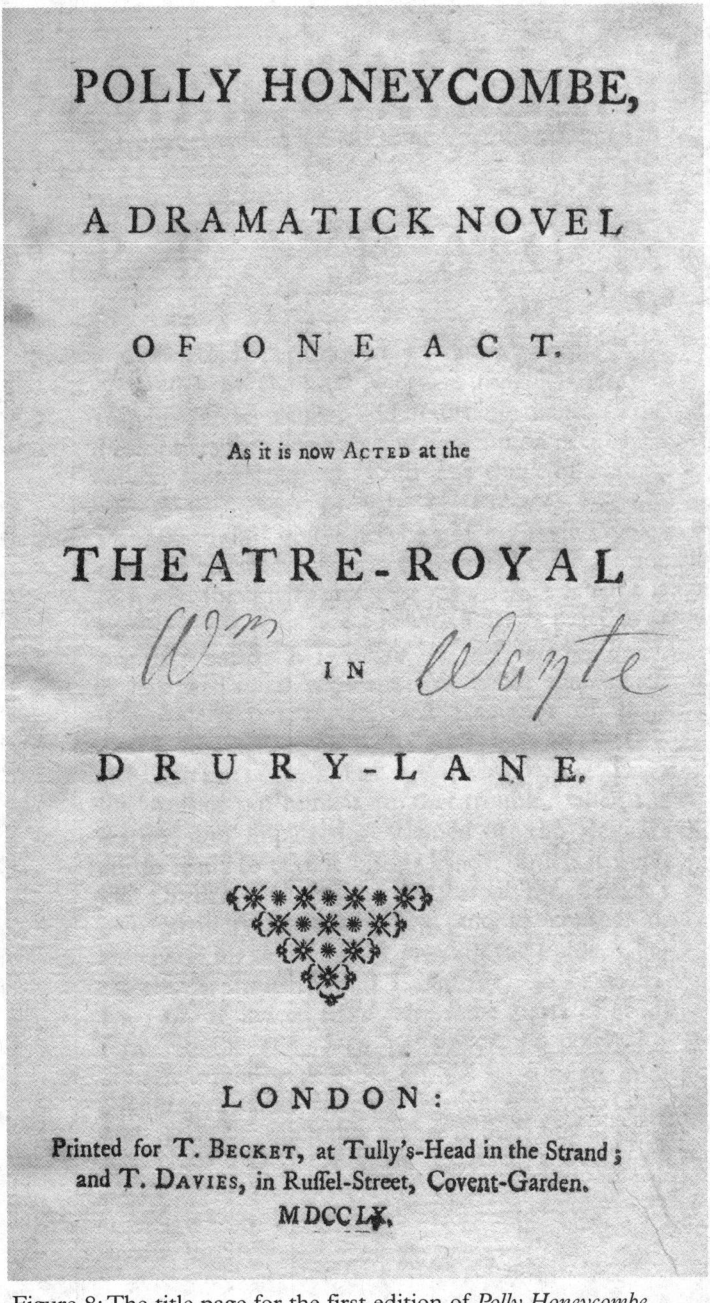
POLLY HONEYCOMBE,

A DRAMATICK NOVEL

OF ONE ACT.

As it is now ACTED at the

THEATRE-ROYAL

IN

DRURY-LANE.

LONDON:

Printed for T. BECKET, at Tully's-Head in the Strand; and T. DAVIES, in Ruffel-Street, Covent-Garden.

MDCCLX.

Figure 8: The title page for the first edition of *Polly Honeycombe*. Courtesy of The Ohio State University Rare Books and Manuscripts Library.

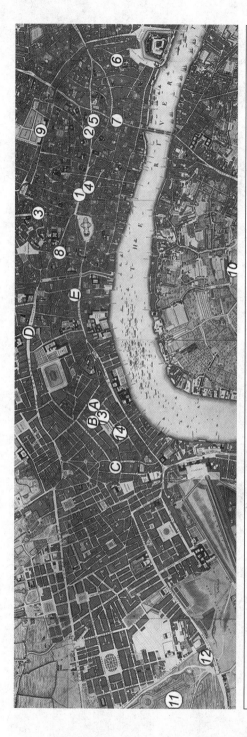

Places in London mentioned in Polly Honeycombe.: 1: Cheapside; 2: The Royal Exchange; 3: Aldersgate Street; 4: Bow Church; 5: Cornhill; 6: Crutched Friars; 7: Gracechurch Street; 8: Newgate Prison; 9: Bethlem Hospital ("Bedlam"); 10: St. George's in the Fields

Theatres and Circulating Libraries in London: A: Theatre-Royal, Drury Lane; B: Theatre-Royal, Covent Garden; C: John Noble's Circulating Library; D: Francis Noble's Circulating Library; E: Thomas Lownds's Circulating Library

Places in London which figure in Sheridan's first duel: 6: Crutched Friars; 11: Hyde Park; 12: the Hercules Pillars Inn; 13: the Bedford Coffee-house; 14: the Castle Tavern

Figure 9: A map of London, showing the locations mentioned in *Polly Honeycombe*, the theaters, the principal circulating libraries, and the sites involved in Sheridan's first duel. These locations are all plotted onto John Rocque's *A Plan of the Cities of London and Westminster and the Borough of Southwark* (1747). The latter is courtesy of Motco Enterprises.

PREFACE

After expressing my Gratitude to the Publick for the kind reception they have given to Miss Honeycombe, and returning thanks to the Performers for their care and uncommon excellence in the Representation, I did not think of adding any thing further by way of Preface: but my Publisher insists on the necessity of my saying something in behalf of the Piece, which, I think, ought to speak for itself, and that my friend's scheme is much of the same colour with Bayes's[1] practice of printing papers *to insinuate the plot into the Boxes.* It has been usual with the Writers of the French Theatre, it is true, to tack Examens of their Plays, like a sting or *melius non tangere*[2] to the Criticks, to the tail of them. But why need an English Author put himself to that trouble, when the learned and impartial gentlemen of the Reviews are so ready to take it off his hands, unless it were, like Dryden,[3] to turn the thunder of the Critick's own artillery against himself, and to confute or anticipate his censures, by proving the Fable, Characters, Sentiments, and Language, to be excellent, or, if indeed there were some parts of it inferior to the rest, such parts were purposely *underwritten*, in order to set off the superior to more advantage? This, indeed, Dryden has often done, and done so inimitably; that I shall not attempt it after him. To the Gentlemen, therefore, above mentioned, the self-impannelled Jury of the English Court of Criticism, without Challenge, I put myself

---

1 Bayes is a bombastic playwright from George Villiers, Duke of Buckingham's *The Rehearsal* (first staged 1671; first printed 1672), a perennially popular farce. At one point, when some gentlemen question whether the audience will be able to follow his ridiculously complicated tragedy, Bayes informs them that "I have printed above a hundred sheets of papyr, to insinuate the Plot into the Boxes" (8), so there's no need to worry about the theatrical intelligibility of his work. As the Prologue will suggest, the name Bayes soon became a comic shorthand for any ambitious playwright or poet.

2 Latin for "better not touch."

3 John Dryden (1631-1700), poet laureate for most of the late seventeenth century, wrote lengthy prefaces to many of his plays in which he attempted to articulate their underlying aesthetics (and sometimes preemptively counter any objections). There is a long-standing, if not wholly accurate, tradition that Bayes, in *The Rehearsal*, was a portrait of Dryden.

on my Trial for the High Crime of writing for the Stage, trusting that their candour[1] will send me a good deliverance.

I could, indeed, in compliance with the request of my Publisher, have obliged the Publick, by printing, entire, an original Manuscript, now in my possession, containing several strictures on the following scenes; being no other than a Letter from my Mother, occasioned by the first night's representation, which, like most other first nights, was nothing more than a Publick Rehearsal, with ten thousand fears and apprehensions, that never attend a private one.[2] The Good Gentlewoman, hurt at the confusion, and in pain for my success, tells me with much warmth, and as dogmatically as any Male Critick could possibly do, that She is astonished at my attempting to violate the received laws of the Drama——That the *Catastrophe* (that was really her word) is directly contrary to all known rules—That the several Characters, instead of being dismissed, one by one, should have been industriously kept together, to make a bow to the audience at the dropping of the curtain——That, not withstanding any confusion, created by the Girl's whimsical passion for Novels, in the course of the Piece, all parties should be perfectly reconciled to each other at last. Polly, having manifested her affection for him, should, to be sure, have been married to Scribble; and the Parents should have been thoroughly, though suddenly, appeased by the declared reformation of both. Ledger might, with much propriety and great probability, have been disposed of to the Nurse: and the whole Piece, instead of concluding bluntly with a sentence in Prose, should have been tagged with a Couplet or

---

1 In the eighteenth century, in addition to its modern meaning of speaking freely and frankly, "candor" (and related terms like "candid") often meant being kindly disposed and free from malice. The "candour" of the Reviews ("the self-impannelled Jury of ... Criticism") is thus their supposed predisposition to overlook a play's shortcomings, if possible. For more on the Reviews, see Introduction (pp. 31-35).

2 There is no evidence that the real Mary Colman had anything to do with her son's play. William Hopkins, the prompter for Drury Lane, noted that on the first night "the Farce" was "indifferently received, partly oweing to the Fright and Confusion of the Performers, who omitted some speeches on which the plot depended" (quoted in Stone, 2:828). For more on first nights as "publick rehearsals," see the Preface to *The Rivals* (pp. 113-16), "A Note on the Texts," and Stern, *Rehearsal*.

Two; and then every thing would have gone off smoothly and roundly, á lá mode du Théatre.[1]

Having thus presented the Publick with a small specimen of my good Mother's talents for Criticism, I shall not, by attempting to answer them, heap Remarks upon Remarks; rather chusing to leave Her and all other Criticks, Male and Female, to meditate on the following extract from Ben Jonson; but must, at the same time, desire not to be understood to take to myself that confidence, with which He presumes to speak of his own abilities.

"Though my Catastrophe may, in the strict rigour of Comick Law, meet with censure; I desire the learned and charitable Critick, to have so much faith in me, to think it was done of industry: for, with what ease I could have varied it nearer his scale (but that I fear to boast my own faculty) I could here insert."[2] To this quotation I shall add a short story, and then conclude my Preface with the remainder of my good Mother's Letter. The Story is as follows:

A Nobleman of Madrid, being present at the Spanish Comedy, fell asleep during the first act, and never woke again till the end of the play. Then rubbing his eyes, and observing his friends laughing at the hearty nap he had taken, he cried out, *How now? Gentlemen! What! Is it* OVER *then? Are the Actors all* MARRIED?

The remainder of the Letter is in these words:——"And then I was the more alarmed at this unseasonable attempt at Novelty, lest it should put it out of my power to preserve my credit with my worthy friend, Mr. Lutestring, the silk-mercer, in Cheapside.[3]

---

1 *À la mode du Théâtre* is French for "in the (current) fashion of the theater." The author's mother's suggestions, if followed, would make *Polly Honeycombe* into a far more conventional comedy. A letter from a supposed audience member to *The Public Ledger* (8 December 1760) praised "the conclusion, so droll and diverting, and so different from every thing else!" Colman may well have had a hand in this "puff."

2 This is from the Epistle to "The Two Famous Universities" at the opening of Jonson's *Volpone* (1607). Like Dryden, Jonson (1572-1637) frequently wrote prefaces to attempt to guide the reception of his plays by readers.

3 "Lutestring" is glossy silk or a dress made out of that material. A "mercer" is someone who sells fine fabrics. "Cheapside," a major shopping street in the City of London (the area within the old city walls which constituted the commercial heart of the metropolis), attracted a respectable but not particularly fashionable clientele. For more on the geography of the play, see the map in Figure 9 (p. 58).

You know, Child, that just after you had informed me of Polly Honeycombe's being in rehearsal, a late melancholy event put the whole nation into deep Mourning.[1] The things, which I made up three years ago, on account of the death of the Princess of Orange, having since been used on several other occasions, could by no means be rendered capable of going through the present Mourning: a six months mourning! quite a thing impossible. This gave me some little uneasiness, especially as I had just got my Blue-Tabby cleaned for the winter's wear. However, I did not doubt but that, on the strength of your Farce, my good friend Lutestring would give me credit for two and twenty yards of Bombazine, to make me up a sack and petticoat; and accordingly I went immediately up to his house.[2] When I got there, Mr. Lutestring was not at home; but the Young Man very civily desired me to walk into the little parlour behind the shop, till his master's return, and there I found Mrs. Lutestring, who received me with her usual good-nature. The Good Woman was sitting alone (the Two Girls being gone, it seems, to see the scaffolding in Westminster Abbey) industriously employed in making up her own Mourning; but her Daughters' Gowns, just come from the Mantua-Maker's, lay in the window; and black caps, black fans, black gloves, &c. from the milliner's, were scattered carelessly about the table, together with three or four books, half-bound, and a bulky pamphlet.[3] These I had the curiosity to examine, and found them to be, (though much thumbed, and in a greasy con-

---

1 George II died on 25 October 1760. Two days later, an order was issued that "expected" all British subjects to "put themselves into the deepest mourning" (somber black clothing) for the next six months (*The London Gazette*, 26-28 October 1760).

2 A "tabby" is silk taffeta, often striped or watered, or a dress made out of that material. "Bombazine" is a silk or wool or cotton twill, often used for mourning. A "sack" is a gown, open in the front (to show off the petticoat, which was not then a form of underwear) and pleated in the back.

3 It's presumably telling that the mercer's daughters, whom we learn are avid novel readers, aren't making their own mourning (as their mother is doing), but rather have purchased it, and that their parents have apparently gone along with this. Books from circulating libraries were typically half-bound with marbled covers (i.e., they had leather spines and marbled paper boards). Given the libraries' reputation for stocking little or nothing but fiction, such a binding would visually mark a book as being most likely a novel. For a photograph of such a binding, see Figure 11 (p. 262).

dition, indeed, for the perusal of such fine ladies) the first volume of the Adventures of Mr. Loveil, the third volume of Betsy Thoughtless, the New Atalantis for the year 1760, and the Catalogue of the Circulating Library. The books I was too well acquainted with to be tempted to any further perusal of them; but (on Mrs. Lutestring's being called into the shop to speak to a particular customer) I made the inclosed Extract from the Catalogue, which, as it falls exactly in with your design, I now send for your consideration. Heaven bless you, My Dear Child! and send that your Farce may do some good on the Giddy Girls of this Age!"

EXTRACT[1]

Accomplished Rake, or the modern fine Gentleman.
Adventures of Miss Polly B— ch—rd and Samuel Tyrrel, esq.
Adventures of Jerry Buck.
Adventures of Dick Hazard.
Adventures of Jack Smart.
Adventures of Lindamira, a Lady of Quality.
Adventures of David Simple.
Adventures of a Turk.
Adventures of Daphnis and Chloe.
Adventures of Prince Clermont and Mad. de Ravezan.
Adventures of Mr. Loveil.
Adventures of Joseph Andrews.
Adventures of Hamilton Murray.
Adventures of a Rake.

Adventures of a Cat.
Adventures of a Black Coat.
Adventures of Frank Hammond.
Adventures of Mr. George Edwards, a Creole.
Adventures of a Valet.
Adventures of Capt. Greenland.
Adventures of Roderick Random.
Adventures of Peregrine Pickle.
Adventures of Ferdinand Count Fathom.
Agenor and Ismeaa, or the War of the tender Passions.
Amelia, by Mr. Fielding.
Amelia, or the Distressed Wife.
Amours of Philander and Sylvia, or Love-Letters between a Nobleman and his Sister.
Amorous Friars, or the Intrigues of a Convent.

---

1 Like the titles just mentioned, the titles listed here are all real, and about three quarters of them had come out in the previous decade (and so were likely to ring some bells). For details, see Scott. It is unclear, though, whether Colman worked from an actual circulating library catalog (not many have survived from the period), or simply devised his own list for satiric or comic effect. Certainly the selective use of italics and the pointed inclusion of certain subtitles (and not others) suggest that the list is more than a simple transcription.

Anti-Gallican, or the History and Adventures of Harry Cobham.

Anti-Pamela, or feigned Innocence detected.

Apparition, or Female Cavalier, a Story founded on Facts.

Auction.

Beauty put to its Shifts, or the Young Virgin's Rambles, being several Years Adventures of Miss * * * * in England and Portugal.

Bracelet, or the Fortunate Discovery; being the History of Miss Polly * * *.

Brothers.

Bubbled Knights, or successful Contrivances; plainly evincing, in two familiar Instances lately transacted in this Metropolis, *the Folly and Unreasonableness of Parents laying a Restraint upon their Childrens Inclinations in the Affairs of Love and Marriage.*

Card.

Chiron, or the mental Optician.

Chit-chat, or a Series of interesting Adventures.

Chrysal, or the Adventures of a Guinea, with curious Anecdotes.

Clarissa, or the History of a young Lady; comprehending the most important Concerns of private Life, and particularly shewing the Distresses that may attend the Misconduct both of Parents and Children in relation to Marriage.

Cleora, or the Fair Inconstant: an authentick History of the Life and Adventures of a Lady, lately very eminent in high Life.

Clidanor and Cecilia, a Novel, designed as a Specimen of a Collection, *adapted to form the Mind to a just Way of thinking, and a proper Manner of behaving in Life.*

Clio, or a secret History of the Amours of Mrs. S—n—m.

Cry, A Dramatick Fable.

Dalinda, or the Double Marriage.

Devil upon Crutches in England, or Night Scenes in London.

Emily, or the History of a Natural Daughter.

Fair Adultress.

Fair Moralist.

Fair Citizen, or the Adventures of Charlotte Bellmour.

Fanny, or the Amours of a West-country young Lady.

Female Foundling; shewing the happy Success of constant Love, in the Life of Mademoiselle D—— R——.

Female Rambler, or Adventures of Madam Janeton De * * *.

Female Banishment, or the Woman Hater.

Female Falshood.

Fortunate Villager, or Memoirs of Sir Andrew Thompson.

Fortune-Teller, or the Footman Innobled.

Friends, a *sentimental* History.

Gentleman and Lady of Pleasure's Amusement, in Eighty-eight Questions, with their Answers, on Love and Gallantry. To which are added, the Adventures of Sophia, with the History of Frederick and Caroline.

Henrietta.

History of Charlotte Villars.

History of Miss Kitty N——, containing her Amours and

Adventures in Scotland, Ireland, Jamaica, and England.

History of Barbarossa and Pollyane.

History of Two Persons of Quality.

History of Lavinia Rawlins.

History of two Orphans, by W. Toldervy.

History of Henry Dumont, Esq; and Miss Charlotte Evelyn; with some critical Remarks on comic Actors, by Mrs. Charke.

History of Benjamin St. Martin, a Fortunate Foundling.

History of the Life and Adventures of Mr. Anderson.

History of Honoria, or the Adventures of a young Lady; interspersed with the History of Emilia, Julia, and others.

History of Betty Barnes.

History of Jemmy and Jeney Jessamy.

History of Dicky Gotham and Doll Clod.

History of Fanny Seymour.

History of Sophia Shakespear.

History of Sir Charles Grandison.

History of a young Lady of Distinction.

History and Adventures of Frank Hammond.

History of Jasper Banks.

History of J. Trueman, Esq; and Miss Peggy Williams.

History of Sir Harry Herald and Sir Edw. Haunch.

History of Will Ramble, a Libertine.

History of Miss Polly Willis.

History of my own Life.

History of Lucy Wellers.

History of a Fair Greek, who was taken out of a Seraglio at Constantinople.

History of Hai Ebor Yokdhan, an Indian Prince.

History of the human Heart, or Adventures of a young Gentleman.

History of Charlotte Summers.

History of Cornelia.

History of Tom Jones, a Foundling.

History of Tom Jones in his married State.

History of two modern Adventurers.

History of Sir Roger, and his Son Joe.

History of Miss Sally Sable.

History of Mira, Daughter of Marcio.

History of Amanda, by a young Lady.

History of a Woman of Quality, or the Adventures of Lady Frail.

History of Pompey the Little, or the Adventures of a Lap Dog.

History of Wilhelmina Susannah Dormer.

History of Porcia.

History of the Countess of Dellwyn.

History of Ophelia.

History of the Marchioness de Pompadour, Mistress to the French King, and first Lady of Honour to the Queen.

History of Tom Fool.

History of the *Intrigues* and *Gallantries* of Christiana Queen of Sweden.

History of Jack Connor.

History of Miss Betsy Thoughtless.

Histories of some of the Penitents in the Magdalen-House.

Jilts, or Female Fortune-hunters.

Impetuous Lover, or the Guilt-
less Parracide; shewing *to
what Lengths Love may run,*
and the extreme Folly of
forming Schemes for Futu-
rity.
Intriguing Coxcomb.
Journey through every Stage of
Life.
Juvenile Adventures of David
Ranger, Esq.
Juvenile Adventures of Miss
Kitty Fisher.
Lady's Advocate, or Wit and
Beauty a Match for Treachery
and Inconstancy; containing
a Series of Gallantries,
Intrigues, and Amours, fortu-
nate and sinister; Quarrels
and Reconciliations between
Lovers; conjugal Plagues and
Comforts, Vexations and
Endearments; with many
remarkable Incidents and
Adventures, the Effects of
Love and Jealousy, Fidelity
and Inconstancy.
Ladies Tales.
Life and Adventures of Miranda.
Life's Progress, or the Adven-
tures of Natura.
Life and Adventures of Joe
Thompson.
Life of Harriot Stuart.
Life of Patty Saunders.
Life and History of a Pilgrim.
Life and Adventures of Sobrina.
Life of Corporal Bates, a
broken-hearted Soldier.
Life and Adventures of Coll-
Jack.
Life and Adventures of James
Ramble, Esq.
Life of Charles Osborn, Esq.
Life of Mr. John Van.
Life and Opinions of Miss
Sukey Shandy, of Bow-Street,

Gentlewoman.
Love and Friendship, or the
Fugitive.
Lydia.
Marriage Act.
Memoirs of the Countess of
Berci.
Memoirs of Fanny Hill.
Memoirs of a Man of Quality.
Memoirs of the Life of John
Medley, Esq.
Memoirs of a Coxcomb.
Memoirs of the Shakespear's-
Head Tavern.
Memoirs of the celebrated Miss
Fanny M——
Memoirs of B—— Tracey.
Memoirs of Fidelio and Harriot.
Memoirs of Sir Thomas Hough-
son and Mr. Joseph Williams.
Memoirs of an Oxford Scholar.
Memoirs of a young Lady of
Quality.
Memoirs of the noted Buck-
horse.
Memoirs of a certain Island.
Memoirs of a Man of Pleasure.
Memoirs of a young Lady of
Family.
Memoirs of sir Charles
Goodville.
Modern Characters illustrated
by Histories.
Modern Lovers.
Modern Story-Teller.
Mother.
Mother-in-Law.
New Atalantis for the Year One
thousand seven hundred and
fifty-eight.
New Atalantis for the Year One
thousand seven hundred and
fifty-nine.
New Atalantis for the Year One
thousand seven hundred and
sixty.
Nominal Husband.

Pamela.

Polydore and Julia.

Prostitutes of Quality, or Adultery a la Mode; being *authentic* and *genuine* Memoirs of several Persons of the *highest Quality.*

Reformed Coquet.

Revolutions of Modesty.

Rival Mother.

Rosalinda.

Roxana.

School of Woman, or Memoirs of Constantia.

Sedan, in which many new and entertaining Characters are introduced.

Sisters.

Skimmer.

Sopha.

Spy on Mother Midnight, or F——'s Adventures.

Stage-Coach.

Temple-Beau, or the Town-Rakes.

Theatre of Love, a Collection of Novels.

True Anti-Pamela.

Widow of the Wood.

Zadig, or the Book of Fate.

Zara and the Zarazians.

Zulima, or Pure Love.

&c. &c. &c. &c. &c.

&c. &c. &c. &c. &c.

&c. &c. &c. &c. &c.

&c. &c. &c. &c. &c.

PROLOGUE.

Spoken by Mr. KING.[1]

HITHER, in days of yore, from Spain *or* France
Came a dread Sorceress; her name, ROMANCE.
O'er Britain*'s Isle her wayward spells She cast.*
And Common Sense in magick chain bound fast.
In mad Sublime did each fond Lover wooe,
And in Heroicks ran each Billet-Doux*:*[2]
High deeds of Chivalry their sole Delight,
Each Fair a Maid Distrest, each Swain a Knight.[3]

---

1 Thomas King, who played Scribble (see Appendix A). The Prologue was dropped after the tenth performance (one more than was customary), but retained in most printed versions of the play.

2 "Heroicks" are here elevated, extravagant language. *Billet-doux* is the French term for a love-letter.

3 A "swain" is a poetic name for a rural laborer, especially a shepherd. In pastoral and romance, shepherds hardly ever need to work, and so can pass their days as lovers. The heroes of romance often spent some time either disguised as shepherds or being raised by them incognito.

Then might Statira Orondates *see,*
At Tilts and Tournaments, arm'd Cap-a-pè.[1]
She too, on Milk-white Palfrey, Lance in hand,
A Dwarf to guard her, pranc'd about the land.[2]
     This Fiend to quell, his sword Cervantes *drew.*
A trusty Spanish Blade, Toledo *true:*
Her Talismans and Magick Wand He broke——
Knights, Genii, Castles——vanish'd into smoke.[3]
     But now, the dear delight of later years,
The younger Sister of ROMANCE *appears:*
Less solemn is her air, her drift the same,
And NOVEL *her enchanting, charming, Name.*
ROMANCE *might strike our grave Forefathers' pomp,*
But NOVEL *for our Buck and lively Romp!*[4]
Cassandra's *Folios now no longer read,*
See, Two Neat Pocket Volumes in their stead![5]
And then so sentimental *is the Stile,*
So chaste, yet so bewitching all the while!
Plot, and elopement, passion, rape, and rapture,
The total sum of ev'ry dear—dear—Chapter.

---

1 Statira and Oroondates are the impossibly heroic stars of Gaultier de
   Coste, Seigneur de La Calprenède's *Cassandre* (1642-45), a ten-volume,
   close to 5,500-page romance ostensibly about the martial exploits and
   love affairs surrounding Alexander the Great (but the ancient Greeks,
   Scythians, and Persians come off as seventeenth-century French aristocrats pretending to be medieval knights and ladies). To be "armed cap-
   à-pie" is to be covered head to foot in armor.
2 A "palfrey" is a small horse for everyday riding, especially by women.
   Heroines in romance were sometimes accompanied by dwarves.
3 Miguel de Cervantes Saavedra's *Don Quijote* (1605-15) was widely cred-
   ited with dispelling the attractions of chivalric romance, which had long
   been the most popular form of fiction in Europe. A "blade, Toledo true"
   is a sword made in Toledo, Spain, which was renowned for its production of such.
4 A "buck" is here a high-spirited young man. A "romp" is here a playful
   young woman.
5 Like most seventeenth-century French romances, *Cassandre* was first
   published in English as a folio (a large and often thick book: in this
   case, almost a foot high and close to nine hundred pages long). Novels
   were generally far smaller (and multi-volume) objects and so could be
   more readily concealed in one's "pocket," which, for women, actually
   meant a bag tied around the waist beneath one's dress, with access
   through slits in the seams.

'*Tis not alone the Small-Talk and the Smart,*
'*Tis* NOVEL *most beguiles the Female Heart.*
Miss reads—she melts—she sighs—Love steals upon her—
And then—Alas, poor Girl!—good night, poor Honour!

*Thus of our Polly having lightly spoke,
Now for our Author!—but without a joke.
Though Wits and Journals, who ne'er fibb'd before,*
Have laid this Bantling[1] at a certain door,
Where, lying store of faults, they'd fain heap more,
*I now declare it, as a serious truth,
'Tis the first folly of a simple Youth,
Caught and deluded by our harlot plays:——
Then crush not in the shell this infant* Bayes!
*Exert your favour to a young Beginner,
Nor use the Stripling like a Batter'd Sinner!* [2]

PERSONS. [3]

HONEYCOMBE,	Mr. YATES.
LEDGER,	Mr. BRANSBY.
SCRIBBLE,	Mr. KING.
Mrs. HONEYCOMBE,	Mrs. KENNEDY.
POLLY,	Miss POPE.
NURSE,	Mrs. BRADSHAW.

---

* These Lines were added by Mr. GARRICK, on its being reported, that
  he was the Author of this Piece: and, however humourous and poetical,
  contain as strict matter of fact as the dullest Prose [Colman's note].

---

1 A small child, especially an illegitimate one.
2 A "stripling" is an adolescent boy (who presumably hasn't yet had that
   many opportunities to sin).
3 For more on the particular talents and reputations of these performers,
   see Appendix A.

POLLY HONEYCOMBE, A Dramatick NOVEL of One ACT.

SCENE I.

An Apartment in HONEYCOMBE'*s House.*

POLLY, *with a Book in her Hand.*[1]

Well said, Sir George!—O the dear man!—But so——"With these words the enraptured baronet [*reading*] concluded his declaration of love."—So!—"But what heart can imagine, [*reading*] what tongue describe, or what pen delineate, the amiable confusion of Emilia?"—Well! now for it!——"Reader, if thou art a courtly reader, thou hast seen at polite tables, iced cream crimsoned with rasberries; or, if thou art an uncourtly reader, thou hast seen the rosy-fingered morning, dawning in the golden east";—Dawning in the golden east!—Very pretty!——"Thou hast seen, perhaps, [*reading*] the artificial vermilion on the cheeks of Cleora, or the vermilion of nature on those of Sylvia; thou hast seen—in a word, the lovely face of Emilia was overspread with blushes."——This is a most beautiful passage, I protest! Well, a Novel for my money! Lord, lord, my stupid Papa has no taste. He has no notion of humour, and character, and the sensibility of delicate feeling. [*affectedly*] And then Mama,—but where was I?— Oh here—"Overspread with blushes. [*reading*] Sir George, touched at her confusion, gently seized her hand, and softly pressing it to his bosom, [*acting it as she reads*] where the pulses of his heart beat quick, throbbing with tumultuous passion, in a plaintive tone of voice breathed out, Will you not answer me, Emilia?"——Tender creature!——"She, half raising [*reading and acting*] her downcast eyes, and half inclining her averted head, said in faltering accents—Yes, Sir!"—Well, now!—"Then gradually recovering with ineffable sweetness she prepared to address him; when Mrs. Jenkinson bounced into the room, threw down a set of china in her hurry, and strewed the floor with porcelain fragments: then turning Emilia round and round, whirled her out of the apartment in an instant, and struck Sir George dumb with astonishment at her appearance. She raved; but the baronet resuming his accustomed effrontery——"

---

1 Unlike most of the other novels Polly mentions, *The History of Sir George Trueman and Emilia* seems to be Colman's invention (though it certainly includes many of the stock conventions of the actual novels of the 1740s and 1750s).

Enter NURSE.

Oh, Nurse, I am glad to see you,—Well, and how——

NURSE.
Well, Chicken!

POLLY.
Tell me, tell me all this instant. Did you see him? Did you give him my letter? Did he write? Will he come? Shall I see him? Have you got the answer in your pocket? Have you——

NURSE.
Blessings on her, how her tongue runs!

POLLY.
Nay, but come, dear Nursee, tell me, what did he say?

NURSE.
Say? why he took the letter——

POLLY.
Well!

NURSE.
And kiss'd it a thousand times, and read it a thousand times, and——

POLLY.
Oh charming!

NURSE.
And ran about the room, and blest himself, and, heaven preserve us, curst himself, and——

POLLY.
Very fine! very fine!

NURSE.
And vowed he was the most miserable creature upon earth, and the happiest man in the world, and——

POLLY.
Prodigiously fine! excellent! my dear dear Nursee! [*Kissing her.*]
Come, give me the letter.

NURSE.
Letter, Chicken! what letter?

POLLY.
The answer to mine. Come then! [*Impatiently.*]

NURSE.
I have no letter. He had such a *peramble* to write, by my troth I
could not stay for it.

POLLY.
Pshah!

NURSE.
How soon you're affronted now! he said he'd send it some time
to-day.

POLLY.
Send it some time to-day!—I wonder now, [*as if musing.*] how
he will convey it. Will he squeeze it, as he did the last, into the
chicken-house in the garden? Or will he write it in lemon-juice,
and send it in a book, like blank paper? Or will he throw it into
the house, inclosed in an orange? Or will he——

NURSE.
Heavens bless her, what a sharp wit she has!

POLLY.
I have not read so many books for nothing. Novels, Nursee,
Novels! A Novel is the only thing to teach a girl life, and the
way of the world, and elegant fancies, and love to the end of the
chapter.

NURSE.
Yes, yes, you are always reading your simple story-books. The
Ventures of Jack this, and the history of Betsy t'other, and sir
Humphrys, and women with hard christian names. You had
better read your prayer-book, Chicken.

POLLY.
Why so I do; but I'm reading this now—[*Looking into the book.*]
"She raved, but the baronet"—I really think I love Mr. Scribble
as well as Emilia did sir George.—Do you think, Nursee, I
should have had such a good notion of love so early, if I had not
read Novels?—Did not I make a conquest of Mr. Scribble in a
single night at a dancing? But my cross Papa will hardly ever let
me go out.—And then, I know life as well as if I had been in
the Beau Monde all my days. I can tell the nature of a masquerade as well as if I had been at twenty. I long for a mobbing
scheme with Mr. Scribble to the two-shilling gallery, or a snug
party a little way out of town, in a post-chaise[1]——and then, I
have such a head full of intrigues and contrivances! Oh, Nursee,
a Novel is the only thing.

NURSE.
Contrivances! ay, marry, you have need of contrivances. Here
are your Papa and Mama fully resolved to marry you to young
Mr. Ledger, Mr. Simeon the rich Jew's wife's nephew, and all
the while your head runs upon nothing but Mr. Scribble.

POLLY.
A fiddle-stick's end for Mr. Ledger! I tell you what, Nursee. I'll
marry Mr. Scribble, and not marry Mr. Ledger, whether Papa
and Mama chuse it or no.—And how do you think I'll contrive
it?

NURSE.
How? Chicken!

POLLY.
Why, don't you know?

NURSE.
No, indeed.

---

1   *Beau monde* is French for "the fashionable world." A "mobbing scheme"
    is a plan to form a crowd and make a commotion, especially in the
    cheaper seats at the theater. A "post-chaise" is a small fast carriage
    usually seating only two people.

POLLY.
And can't you guess?

NURSE.
No, by my troth, not I.

POLLY.
O lord, it's the commonest thing in the world.—I intend to elope.

NURSE.
Elope! Chicken, what's that?

POLLY.
Why, in the vulgar phrase, run away,——that's all.

NURSE.
Mercy on us!——Run away!

POLLY.
Yes, run away, to be sure. Why there's nothing in that, you know. Every girl elopes, when her parents are obstinate and ill natur'd about marrying her. It was just so with Betsy Thompson, and Sally Wilkins, and Clarinda, and Leonora in the history of Dick Careless, and Julia in the Adventures of Tom Ramble, and fifty others—Did not they all elope? and so will I too. I have as much right to elope, as they had, for I have as much love and as much spirit as the best of them.

NURSE.
Why, Mr. Scribble's a fine man to be sure, a gentleman every inch of him!

POLLY.
So he is, a dear charming man!—Will you elope too, Nursee?

NURSE.
Not for the varsal[1] world. Suppose now, Chicken, your Papa and Mama——

---

1 Universal or whole.

POLLY.

What care I for Papa and Mama? Have not they been married and happy long enough ago? and are not they still coaxing, and fondling, and kissing each other all the day long?—"Where's my dear Love, [*mimicking.*] My Beauty?" says Papa, hobbling along with his crutch-headed cane, and his old gouty legs: "Ah, my sweeting, my precious Mr. Honeycombe, d'ye love your nown dear wife?" says Mama; and then they squeeze their hard hands to each other, and their old eyes twinkle, and they're as loving as Darby and Joan—especially if Mama has had a cordial[1] or two——Eh! Nursee!

NURSE.

Oh fie, Chicken!

POLLY.

And then perhaps, in comes my utter aversion, Mr. Ledger, with his news from the Change, and his Change-alley wit,[2] and his thirty *per cent.* [*mimicking.*] and stocks have risen one and a half and three eighths.—I'll tell ye what, Nursee! they would make fine characters for a Novel, all three of them.[3]

NURSE.

Ah, you're a graceless bird!—But I must go down stairs, and watch if the coast's clear, in case of a letter.

POLLY.

Could not you go to Mr. Scribble's again after it?

NURSE.

Again! indeed, Mrs. Hot-upon't!

---

1 "Nown" means own. "Darby and Joan" are a proverbial happily married old couple. A "cordial" is a sweet, highly alcoholic medicine (often taken as a fashionable way to disguise the extent of one's drinking).

2 "The Change" is the Royal Exchange, the symbolic center of commercial activity in London. "Change-alley wit" is the (presumably feeble) humor characteristic of the stockbrokers of Exchange Alley, just south of the Royal Exchange. See the map in Figure 9 (p. 58).

3 Persons of the social standing of the Honeycombes and Mr. Ledger (well-to-do, respectable, but hardly fashionable members of "the middling sort") almost never appear in eighteenth-century novels, which tend to be populated by figures either higher or significantly lower in terms of their status.

POLLY.
Do now, my dear Nursee, pray do! and call at the Circulating Library, as you go along, for the rest of this Novel—The History of Sir George Truman and Emilia—and tell the bookseller to be sure to send me the British Amazon, and Tom Faddle, and the rest of the new Novels this winter, as soon as ever they come out.

NURSE.
Ah, pise[1] on your naughty novels! I say. [*Exit.*

POLLY.
Ay, go now, my dear Nursee, go, there's a good woman!——What an old fool it is! with her pise on it—and fie, Chicken—and no, by my troth—[*mimicking.*]——Lord! what a strange house I live in! not a soul in it, except myself, but what are all queer animals, quite droll creatures. There's Papa and Mama, and the old foolish Nurse.——[*Re-enter* Nurse *with a band-box.*] Oh, Nursee, what brings you back so soon? What have you got there?

NURSE.
Mrs. Commode's 'prentice is below, and has brought home your new cap and ruffles, Chicken![2]

POLLY.
Let me see—let me see—[*opening the box.*] Well, I swear this is a mighty pretty cap, a sweet pair of flying lappets![3] Aren't they, Nursee?——Ha! what's this? [*looking into the box.*]—Oh charming! a letter! did not I tell you so?——Let's see—let's see—— (*opening the letter hastily—it contains three or four sheets.*) "Joy of my soul—only hope,—eternal bliss—[*dipping into different places.*] The cruel blasts of coyness and disdain blow out the flame of love, but then the virgin breath of kindness and compassion blows it in again."—Prodigious pretty! is'nt it, Nursee? [*turning over the leaves.*]

---

1 An expression of mild disapproval (such as "pish").
2 Mrs. Commode's name is probably taken from the term for a tall, somewhat old-fashioned woman's head-dress made of wire covered with silk or lace. However, in eighteenth-century slang a "commode" could also be a procuress or bawd.
3 Pieces of fabric, often lace, hanging down from a cap.

NURSE.
Yes, that is pretty,—but what a deal there is on't! It's an old saying and a true one, the more there's said the less there's done. Ah, they wrote other guess sort of letters, when I was a girl! [*while she talks* Polly *reads.*]

POLLY.
Lord, Nursee, if it was not for Novels and Love-letters, a girl would have no use for her writing and reading.—But what's here? [*reading.*] Poetry!—"Well may I cry out with Alonzo in the Revenge—
'—*Where didst thou steal those eyes? From heaven?*
Thou didst, and 'tis religion to adore them!'"[1]
Excellent! oh! he's a dear man!

NURSE.
Ay, to be sure!——But you forget your letter-carrier below, she'll never bring you another, if you don't speak to her kindly.

POLLY.
Speak to her! why I'll give her sixpence, woman! Tell her I am coming.—I will but just read my letter over five or six times, and go to her.—Oh, he's a charming man! [*reading.*] Very fine! very pretty!—He writes as well as Bob Lovelace[2]—[*kissing the letter.*] Oh, dear, sweet Mr. Scribble! [*Exit.*

---

1 In Edward Young's *The Revenge* (1721), Alonzo is a victorious general who, after much hand-wringing, marries the woman formerly betrothed to his best friend, only to immediately discover—he thinks—that she has been unfaithful to him. Half-mad with jealousy he goes to stab her, but cannot bring himself to do it, in part because of her beauty: "But, O those Eyes! Those Murderers! O whence! / Whence didst thou steal their burning Orbs? from Heav'n? / Thou didst, and 'tis Religion to adore them." In isolation, these lines could be an extravagant compliment; in context ... (well, Polly doesn't seem to much care about context). *The Revenge* was performed at least twenty-eight times in the decade leading up to the debut of *Polly Honeycombe*, so these lines would have been fairly familiar to most members of the audience.

2 Robert Lovelace is the villain of Samuel Richardson's immensely influential *Clarissa* (1747-48). In order to escape a loathsome arranged marriage, Clarissa Harlowe runs away with the aristocratic Lovelace, only to discover that she is as much a prisoner with him as she was with her own family (he wants to marry her in order to revenge   (*continued*)

Scene changes to another Apartment.

HONEYCOMBE *and Mrs.* HONEYCOMBE *at breakfast—*
HONEYCOMBE *reading the News-paper.*

Mrs. HONEYCOMBE.
My dear! [*peevishly.*]

HONEYCOMBE.
What d'ye say, my Love? [*still reading.*]

Mrs. HONEYCOMBE.
You take no notice of me.—Lay by that silly paper—put it
down—come then—drink your tea.—You don't love me now.

HONEYCOMBE.
Ah! my beauty! [*looking very fondly.*]

Mrs. HONEYCOMBE.
Do you love your own dear wife? [*tenderly.*]

HONEYCOMBE.
Dearly.—She knows I do.—Don't you, my Beauty?

Mrs. HONEYCOMBE.
Ah, you're a dear, dear man! [*rising and kissing him.*] He does
love her—and he's her own husband—and she loves him most
dearly and tenderly—that she does. [*kissing him.*]

HONEYCOMBE.
My Beauty! I have a piece of news for you.

Mrs. HONEYCOMBE.
What is it: my Sweeting!

HONEYCOMBE.
The paper here says, that young Tom Seaton, of Aldersgate-

---

himself upon the Harlowes for their ill treatment of him). Eventually he
drugs and rapes her, after which she escapes and dies an exemplary
Christian death. The whole (very long) novel is epistolary and Lovelace's
letters are, indeed, quite eloquent and dramatic. But once again, it
would seem, Polly is overlooking a crucial bit of context.

Street, was married yesterday at Bow Church, to Miss Fairly of Cornhill.[1]

Mrs. HONEYCOMBE.
A flaunting, flaring hussy! she a husband!—

HONEYCOMBE.
But what does my Beauty think of her own daughter?

Mrs. HONEYCOMBE.
Of our Polly? Sweeting!

HONEYCOMBE.
Ay, Polly: What sort of a wife d'ye think she'll make? my Love!—I concluded every thing with Mr. Simeon yesterday, and expect Mr. Ledger every minute.

Mrs. HONEYCOMBE.
Think, my Sweetings!—why, I think, if she loves him half so well as I do my own dear man, that she'll never suffer him out of her sight—that she'll look at him with pleasure—[*they both ogle fondly.*]—and love him—and kiss him—and fondle him— oh, my dear, it's impossible to say how dearly I love you. [*kissing and fondling.*]

Enter LEDGER.

LEDGER.
Heyday! what now, good folks, what now? Are you so much in arrear? or are you paying off principal and interest both at once?

HONEYCOMBE.
My dear!——Consider——Mr. Ledger is——

---

1 "Aldersgate Street" was "a very broad street" in the City of London "more noted for the remains of its ancient grandeur, than for the modern taste of its buildings" (John Entick, *A New and Accurate History and Survey of London, Westminster, Southwark, and Places Adjacent* [London, 1766], 3:340). "Cornhill" was a similarly broad street, "covered with houses of the first class ... occupied by the most substantial dealers" (4:98). The implication seems to be that the Seatons and the Fairlys are wealthy and respectable, but not particularly fashionable. The church of St. Mary-le-Bow is midway between them. See the map in Figure 9 (p. 58).

Mrs. HONEYCOMBE.
What signifies Mr. Ledger?—He is one of the family, you know,
my Sweeting!

LEDGER.
Ay, so I am,—never mind me—never mind me.—Tho' by the
bye, I should be glad of somebody to make much of me too.
Where's Miss Polly?

HONEYCOMBE.
That's right—that's right.——Here, John!

Enter JOHN.

Where's Polly?

JOHN.
In her own room, Sir.

HONEYCOMBE.
Tell her to come here——and hark ye, John! while Mr. Ledger
stays, I am not at home to any body else. [*Exit* John.

LEDGER.
Not at home!—are those your ways?—If I was to give such a
message to my servant, I shou'd expect a commission of bank-
ruptcy out against me the next day.[1]

HONEYCOMBE.
Ay, you men of large dealings—it was so with me, when I was in
business.—But where's this girl? what can she be about?——My
Beauty, do step yourself, and send her here immediately.

---

1 People who moved in the fashionable world often instructed their servants to tell unwanted visitors that their employers were "not at home"
   (even if lights were blazing, conversation or music was audible, etc.).
   Such a strategy would, as Ledger notes, have been suicide in the commercial realm, where one's creditworthiness depended on one's visible
   industry and availability. For a merchant or banker to be "not at home"
   would be tantamount to suggesting that he couldn't cover his debts, and
   so his creditors should petition the Lord Chancellor to appoint a commission to seize his property and begin to liquidate it on their behalf.

Mrs. HONEYCOMBE.
I will, my Sweeting! [*offering to kiss him.*]

HONEYCOMBE.
Nay, my Love, not now——

Mrs. HONEYCOMBE.
Why not now?—I will. [*kissing him.*] Good bye, Love.—Mr.
Ledger, your servant!—B'ye, Dearest! [*Exit.*

HONEYCOMBE.
Ha! ha! you see, Mr. Ledger! you see what you are to come to—
but I beg pardon—I quite forgot—have you breakfasted?

LEDGER.
Breakfasted! ay, four hours ago, and *done* an hundred tickets
since, over a dish of coffee, at Garrayway's.[1]——Let me see,
[*pulling out his watch.*] bless my soul, it's eleven o'clock! I wish
Miss would come.—It's Transfer-Day—I must be at the Bank
before twelve, without fail.

HONEYCOMBE.
Oh, here she comes.—[*Enter* Polly].—Come, Child! where have
you been all this time?—Well, Sir, I'll leave you together.
——Polly, you'll——ha! ha! ha!——Your servant, Mr. Ledger,
your servant! [*Exit.*

---

1 The fashionable world operated on a much different schedule than the
world of business, often not rising until close to noon and then staying
up until two or three in the morning. Coffeehouses, like Garraway's (in
Exchange Alley), were prominent places in which to do financial business. Indeed, such locations were the norm in the eighteenth century:
e.g., the modern insurance giant, Lloyds of London—whose "list" of
shipping news is mentioned later in this scene—began as a group of
merchants and ship-owners meeting at Edward Lloyd's coffeehouse to
arrange the underwriting of their vessels. The "tickets" that Ledger has
been doing are transfer tickets, which record the sale of government-
backed stocks or bonds. Once a transaction was agreed to, a broker
would fill in the pre-printed blanks on such a ticket, and then take it to
a clerk at the Bank of England (just northwest of the Royal Exchange)
on "Transfer-Day," where it would be recorded in the official ledgers for
that stock.

[POLLY *and* LEDGER *remain,—they stand at a great distance from each other.*]

POLLY. [*Aside.*]
What a monster of a man!—What will the frightful creature say to me?—I am now, for all the world, just in the situation of poor Clarissa,—and the wretch is ten times uglier than Soames[1] himself.

LEDGER.
Well, Miss!

POLLY. [*Aside.*]
He speaks! what shall I say to him?—Suppose I have a little sport with him.—I will.—I'll indulge myself with a few airs of distant flirtation at first, and then treat him like a dog. I'll use him worse than Nancy Howe ever did Mr. Hickman.[2]—Pray, sir, [*to* Ledger.] Did you ever read the History of Emilia?

LEDGER.
Not I, Miss, not I.—I have no time to think of such things, not I.—I hardly ever read any thing, except the Daily Advertiser, or the list at Lloyd's—nor write neither, except its my name now and then.—I keep a dozen clerks for nothing in the world else but to write.

POLLY.
A dozen clerks!—Prodigious!

LEDGER.
Ay, a dozen clerks. Business must be done, Miss!—We have large returns, and the ballance must be kept on the right side, you know.—In regard to last year now—Our returns from the first of January to the last of December, fifty-nine, were to the amount of sixty thousand pounds, sterling. We clear upon an average, at the rate of twelve *per cent*. Cast up the twelves in

---

1 Roger Solmes is the wealthy, but physically and morally abhorrent man whom the Harlowes want Clarissa to marry.
2 Anna Howe is Clarissa's best friend and principal correspondent. Her parents urge her to marry Charles Hickman, a grave young man, but, for most of the novel, she mocks him as far too dull for her.

sixty thousand, and you may make a pretty good guess at our net profits.

POLLY.
Net Profits!

LEDGER.
Ay, miss, net profits.—Simeon and Ledger are names as well known, as any in the Alley, and good for as much at the bottom of a piece of paper.——But no matter for that——you must know that I have an account to settle with you, Miss.—You're on the debtor side in my books, I can tell you, Miss.

POLLY.
I in your debt, Mr. Ledger!

LEDGER.
Over head and ears in my debt, Miss!

POLLY.
I hate to be in debt of all things—pray let me discharge you at once—for I can't endure to be dunn'd.[1]

LEDGER.
Not so fast, Miss! not so fast. Right reckoning makes long friends.—Suppose now we should compound this matter, and strike a ballance in favour of both parties.

POLLY.
How d'ye mean? Mr. Ledger!

LEDGER.
Why then in plain English, Miss, I love you—I'll marry you— My uncle Simeon and Mr. Honeycombe have settled the matter between them—I am fond of the match—and hope you are the same—There's the Sum Total.

---

1 To be "dunned" is to be pestered by a debt collector. To "compound" a
   debt (as Ledger proposes to do in the next line) is to settle it by partial
   payment.

POLLY.
Lord, this is so strange!—Besides, is it possible that I can have any charms for Mr. Ledger?

LEDGER.
Charms! Miss; you are all over charms.—I like you—I like your person, your family, your fortune—I like you altogether—the Omniums—Eh, Miss!—I like the Omniums—and don't care how large a premium I give for them.[1]

POLLY.
Lord, sir!

LEDGER.
Come, Miss, let's both set our hands to it, and sign and seal the agreement, without loss of time, or hindrance of business.

POLLY.
Not so fast, sir, not so fast.—Right Reckoning makes long friends, you know——Mr. Ledger!

LEDGER.
Miss!

POLLY.
After so explicit and polite a declaration on your part, you will expect, no doubt, some suitable returns on mine.

LEDGER.
To be sure, Miss, to be sure—ay, ay, let's examine the *per contra*.[2]

POLLY.
What you have said, Mr. Ledger, has, I take it for granted been very sincere.

---

1 An "omnium" is the total public offering of a government stock or bond (which, because it gave its purchaser a monopoly over the subsequent market, might command a premium).
2 Italian for "the opposite" side of an account. In traditional bookkeeping, one side of a ledger records assets or income, while the other lists liabilities or expenditures.

LEDGER.
Very sincere, upon my credit, Miss!

POLLY.
For my part then, I must declare, however unwillingly——

LEDGER.
Out with it, Miss!

POLLY.
That the passion I entertain for you is equally strong——

LEDGER.
Oh brave!

POLLY.
And that I do with equal or more sincerity——

LEDGER.
Thank you, Miss; thank you!

POLLY.
Hate and detest——

LEDGER.
How! how!

POLLY.
Loath and abhor you——

LEDGER.
What! what!

POLLY.
Your sight is shocking to me, your conversation odious, and
your passion contemptible——

LEDGER.
Mighty well, Miss; mighty well!

POLLY.
You are a vile book of arithmetick, a table of pounds, shillings,

and pence—You are uglier than a figure of eight, and more tiresome than the multiplication-table.—There's the Sum Total.

LEDGER.
Flesh and blood——

POLLY.
Don't talk to me—Get along—Or if you don't leave the room, I will.

LEDGER.
Very fine, very fine, Miss!—Mr. Honeycombe shall know this. [*Exit.*

POLLY *alone.*

Ha! ha! ha!—There he goes!—Ha! ha! ha!—I have out-topped them all—Miss Howe, Narcissa, Clarinda, Polly Barnes, Sophy Willis, and all of them. None of them ever treated an odious fellow with half so much spirit.—This would make an excellent chapter in a new Novel.——But here comes Papa—In a violent passion, no doubt.—No matter—It will only furnish materials for the next chapter.

Enter HONEYCOMBE.

HONEYCOMBE.
What is the meaning, mistress Polly, of this extraordinary behaviour? How dare you treat Mr. Ledger so ill, and behave so undutifully to your Papa and Mama?——You are a spoilt child—Your Mama and I have been too fond of you——But have a care, young madam! mend your conduct, or you may be sure, we'll make you repent on't.

POLLY.
Lord, Papa, how can you be so angry with me?——I am as dutiful as any girl in the world.——But there's always an uproar in the family about marrying the daughter, and now poor I must suffer in my turn.

HONEYCOMBE.
Hark ye, Miss!——Why did not you receive Mr. Ledger as your lover?

POLLY.

Lover!—Oh, dear Papa!—He has no more of a lover about
him!——He never so much as cast one languishing look
towards me, never once prest my hand, or struck his breast, or
threw himself at my feet, or——Lord, I read such a delightful
declaration of love in the new Novel this morning! first, Papa,
sir George Trueman——

HONEYCOMBE.

Devil take sir George Trueman!——these cursed Novels have
turned the girl's head——Hark ye, hussy! I could almost find in
my heart to—I say, hussy, isn't Mr. Ledger a husband of your
Papa and Mama's providing? and ar'n't they the properest
persons to dispose of you?

POLLY.

Dispose of me!—See there now!—Why you have no notion of
these things, Papa!——Your head's so full of trade and com-
merce, that you would dispose of your daughter like a piece of
merchandise—But my heart is my own property, and at
nobody's disposal, but my own.——Sure you would not consign
me, like a bale of silk, to Ledger and Co.—Eh! Papa!

HONEYCOMBE.

Her impudence amazes me.—Hark ye, hussy, you're an undutiful slut——[1]

POLLY.

Not at all undutiful, Papa!——But I hate Mr. Ledger.——I
can't endure the sight of him——

HONEYCOMBE.

This is beyond all patience.——Hark ye, hussy, I'll——

POLLY.

Nay more; to tell you the whole truth, my heart is devoted to
another. I have an insuperable passion for him; and nothing
shall shake my affection for my dear Mr. Scribble.

---

1 In the eighteenth century, "hussy" and "slut" could simply mean "bold,
   impudent girl" (i.e., they didn't have to have the sexual connotations
   that they now possess).

HONEYCOMBE.
Mr. Scribble!—Who's Mr. Scribble?——Hark ye, hussy, I'll turn
you out of doors.—I'll have you confin'd to your chamber—Get
out of my sight——I'll have you lock'd up this instant.

POLLY.
Lock'd up! I thought so. Whenever a poor girl refuses to marry
any horrid creature, her parents provide for her, then she's to be
lock'd up immediately.——Poor Clarissa! poor Sophy Western! I
am now going to be treated just as you have been before me.[1]

HONEYCOMBE.
Those abominable books!——Hark ye, hussy! you shall have no
Novel to amuse you—Get along, I say—Nor no pen and ink to
scrawl letters—Why don't you go?——Nor no trusty companion.—Get along——I'll have you lock'd up this instant, and the
key of your chamber shall be in your Mama's custody.

POLLY.
Indeed, Papa, you need not give my Mama so much trouble.
——I have——

HONEYCOMBE.
Get along, I say.

POLLY.
I have read of such things as ladders of ropes—

HONEYCOMBE.
Out of my sight!

POLLY.
Or of escaping out of window, by tying the sheets together——

HONEYCOMBE.
Hark ye, hussy——

---

1 When Clarissa refuses to marry Solmes, she is locked in her room and
forbidden to write. Sophia Western, the heroine of Henry Fielding's *Tom
Jones* (1749), was similarly treated twice by her ill-mannered and impul-
sive father, who wants her to marry their (secretly villainous and deceitful) neighbor, William Blifil.

POLLY.
Or of throwing one's-self into the street upon a feather-bed——

HONEYCOMBE.
I'll turn you out of doors——

POLLY.
Or of being catch'd in a gentleman's arms——

HONEYCOMBE.
Zouns, I'll——

POLLY.
Or of——

HONEYCOMBE.
Will you be gone? [*Exeunt, both talking.*

Scene changes to POLLY*'s apartment.*[1]

Enter SCRIBBLE, *disguised in a livery.*[2]

So!—In this disguise mistress Nurse has brought me hither safe
and undiscovered.——Now for Miss Polly! here's her letter: a
true picture of her nonsensical self!——"To my dearest Mr.
Scribble." [*Reading the direction.*] And the seal Two Doves
Billing, with this motto:

"We two,
When we wooe,
Bill and cooe."

——Pretty!—And a plain proof I shan't have much trouble with
her.——I'll make short work on't——I'll carry her off to-day, if
possible.—Clap up a marriage at once, and then down upon
our marrow-bones,[3] and ask pardon and blessing of Papa and
Mama. [*Noise without.*] Here she comes.

---

1   This entire scene was significantly reworked in 1762. See "A Note on
    the Texts" for a description of the revision.
2   A fancy uniform for a servant, especially a footman.
3   In this context, shins and knees (what one would kneel upon when
    seeking forgiveness).

HONEYCOMBE, *without.*

Get along, I say,——Up to your own chamber, hussy!

POLLY, *without.*
Well, Papa, I am——

SCRIBBLE.
O the devil!——Her father coming up with her!——What shall
I do? [*Running about.*] Where shall I hide myself?——I shall certainly be discovered.——I'll get up the chimney.——Zouns!
they are just here——Ten to one the old cuff may not stay with
her——I'll pop into this closet. [*Exit.*

Enter HONEYCOMBE *and* POLLY.

HONEYCOMBE.
Here, mistress Malapert,[1] stay here, if you please, and chew the
cud of disobedience and mischief in private.

POLLY.
Very well, Papa!

HONEYCOMBE.
Very well!—What! you are sulky now! Hark ye, hussy, you are a
saucy minx, and it's not very well.——I have a good mind to
keep you upon bread and water this month. I'll—I'll—But I'll
say no more——I'll lock you up, and carry the key to your
Mama——She'll take care of you.——You will have Mr. Scribble.——Let's see how he can get to you now. [*Shewing the key.*]
[*Exit, locking the door.*

POLLY, *alone.*
And so I will have Mr. Scribble too, do what you can, Old
Squaretoes![2]——I am provided with pen, ink, and paper, in
spite of their teeth.——I remember that Clarissa had cunning
drawers made on purpose to secure those things, in case of an

---

1 "Mistress Malapert" is, presumably, the very personification of
   impudence.
2 Someone with overly strict ideas about how others should behave.

accident[1]——I am very glad I have had caution enough to
provide myself with the same implements of intrigue, tho' with
a little more ingenuity.——Indeed now they make standishes,
and tea-chests, and dressing boxes, in all sorts of shapes and
figures——But mine are of my own invention.——Here I've got
an excellent ink-horn in my pin-cushion—And a case of pens,
and some paper, in my fan. [*Produces them.*] I will write to Mr.
Scribble immediately. I shall certainly see him eaves-dropping
about our door the first opportunity, and then I'll toss it to him
out of the window. [*Sits down to write.*

SCRIBBLE *putting his head out of the door of the closet.*
A clear coast, I find——The old Codger's gone, and has lock'd
me up with his daughter——So much the better!——Pretty
Soul! what is she about? Writing?—A letter to me, I'll bet ten to
one—I'll go and answer it in *propriâ personâ.*[2]

[*Comes forward, and stands behind* Polly, *looking over her writing.*

POLLY, *writing.*
"Me—in—your—Arms."——Let me see——What have I
written? [*Reading.*] "My dearest dear, Mr. Scribble."

SCRIBBLE.
I thought so!

POLLY, *reading.*
"I am now writing in the most cruel confinement. Fly then, oh
fly to me on the wings of love, release me from this horrid
gaol,[3] and imprison me in your arms."

SCRIBBLE.
That I will with all my heart. [*Embracing her.*

POLLY.
Oh! [*Screaming.*]

---

1 When Clarissa suspects she is about to be locked up, she hides some of
   her writing supplies (so that she can continue to correspond even
   though her family has, they think, confiscated her pens, ink, and paper).
2 Latin for "in one's own person," usually used in reference to represent-
   ing oneself in court.
3 An alternate spelling for jail.

SCRIBBLE.
O the devil!—why do you scream so?—I shall be discovered in
spite of fortune. [*running about.*]

POLLY.
Bless me! is it you? Hush! [*running to the door.*] here's my father
coming up stairs, I protest.

SCRIBBLE.
What the duce shall I do?——I'll run into the closet again.

POLLY.
O no! he'll search the closet.——Lord, here's no time to—he's
here—get under the table——[Scribble *hides.*]—Lie still—What
shall I say? [*sits down by the table.*]

Enter HONEYCOMBE.

HONEYCOMBE.
How now? Hussy!——What's all this noise?

POLLY.
Sir! [*affecting surprise.*]

HONEYCOMBE.
What made you scream so violently?

POLLY.
Scream! Papa?

HONEYCOMBE.
Scream? Papa!—Ay, scream, hussy!—What made you scream? I
say.

POLLY.
Lord, Papa, I have never opened my lips, but have been in a
philosophical reverie ever since you left me.

HONEYCOMBE.
I am sure I thought I heard——But how now, hussy! what's
here?—pens—ink—and paper!——Hark ye, hussy!—How came
you by these?—So! so! fine contrivances!—[*examining them*]—
And a letter begun too——"cruel confinement——wings of love

——your arms." [*reading*] Ah, you forward slut!——But I am glad I have discovered this——I'll seize these moveables.[1]—— So! so! now write, if you can——Nobody shall come near you ——Send to him, if you can.——Now see how Mr. Scribble will get at you.——Now I have you safe, mistress!—and now—ha! ha!—now you may make love[2] to the table. [*Exit, locking the door.*

POLLY.
So I will.—We'll turn the tables upon you. Come, Mr. Scribble!

SCRIBBLE.
Here am I, my Love!——This is lucky, and droll too.—Under the table! ha! ha! ha! this is like making love in a pan-tomime[3]—But my Dear, you should not have screamed so.

POLLY.
Lord, who thought of you?—I was as much surprised as Sophy Western, when she saw Tom Jones in the looking-glass.[4]—But what brought you here?

SCRIBBLE.
Love.

POLLY.
What put you into that habit?

SCRIBBLE.
You and Love, my dear Polly, You.—I wear your livery.

---

1 Portable property (i.e., Polly's writing implements).
2 "Make love" here simply means "court," rather than anything more explicitly erotic.
3 Pantomimes were extremely popular in the mid-eighteenth-century theater (indeed, their profits underwrote many other sorts of produc-tions). Typically, their plots, such as they are, involve a pair of young lovers outwitting an elderly father or rival who is trying to block their union.
4 Sophia fled to London to avoid marrying Blifil. While staying at a rela-tive's house, she looked into a mirror and was startled to see the reflec-tion of Tom, her (temporarily disgraced) true love, whose whereabouts she hadn't known.

POLLY.
Lord! how well it becomes him!—But why a livery? Mr. Scribble.

SCRIBBLE.
Only to carry on our affair more securely—a little amour in masquerade.——Do you know me?[1] [*mimicking.*]

POLLY.
Comical creature!——But how did you get here?

SCRIBBLE.
Under this disguise, I pretended business to the Nurse, and she brought me hither.

POLLY.
Admirable!—this is a most charming Adventure.[2]

SCRIBBLE.
Isn't it?

POLLY.
And have you really a sincere passion for me?

SCRIBBLE.
A sincere passion!—true as the needle to the pole, or the dial to the sun.——

POLLY.
But Mr. Scribble!

SCRIBBLE.
My Dear!

---

1   At masquerade balls (which were widely regarded as licentious), conversations would often begin with one attendee asking another "do you know me?"

2   Respectable young ladies were not supposed to have "adventures" (e.g., in Charlotte Lennox's *The Female Quixote* [London, 1752], the worldly Miss Glanville is insulted when asked, by the romance-reading heroine, to recount her "adventures," a term which she takes to be synonymous with illicit sexual behavior, such as a woman's being "ready to run away with every Man" she "see[s]" [1:131]).

POLLY.
D'ye think I am as handsome as Clarissa, or Clementina, or
Pamela, or Sophy Western, or Amelia, or Narcissa, or——

SCRIBBLE.
Handsome!—you are a constellation of all their beauties
blended together.——Clarissa, and Sophy, and the rest of them,
were but mere types[1] of you.——But, my little Charmer, what
was the meaning of all that uproar I heard just now, and of your
being locked up in this manner?

POLLY.
You.

SCRIBBLE.
I?

POLLY.
Yes, you. You was the meaning of it. They brought me an odious
fellow for an husband; and so I told them that he was my utter
aversion; that I was enamoured with you, and you alone, and
that my attachment was inviolable to my dear Mr. Scribble.

SCRIBBLE.
The duce you did! You need not blush to own your passion for
me, to be sure—But things were not quite ripe for that yet.

POLLY.
Yes, but they were ripe, and ripe enough.—What d'ye think I
don't know how to manage for the best?

SCRIBBLE.
O to be sure! but then this being kept under lock and key, like
the old Curmudgeon's strong box, spoils the finest scheme.

POLLY.
What scheme?

---

1   "Types" are foreshadowings (the persons and events, or "types," of the
    Old Testament were thought to prefigure their more glorious counter-
    parts, or "antitypes," in the New Testament).

SCRIBBLE.
Why, a scheme to bring matters to issue at once. I was in hopes
of securing you for ever, this very day.——I intended to have
stolen slily down stairs with you, made a silent escape into the
street, have squeezed you into a chair in a twinkling, had you
conveyed to my lodging, and have strutted thither with a "By
your leave, gemmin!" before your chair, in this livery.[1]

POLLY.
A most excellent contrivance!—We must put it in execution—
How can we manage it?——Let's make our escape out of the
window!

SCRIBBLE.
I must beg to be excused.

POLLY.
Let us force the lock then——or take off the screws of it——or
suppose we should contrive to——[*noise at the door.*]

SCRIBBLE.
'Sdeath! here's somebody coming.

POLLY.
Hush!——Stay!——[*running to the door and peeping through the
key-hole.*]——O no! it's only Nurse.

After unlocking the door, Enter NURSE.

NURSE.
Well, Chicken!——Where's Mr. Scribble?

SCRIBBLE.
O, Mrs. Nurse, is it you?——I am heartily glad to see you.

POLLY.
Oh Nursee! you frighted us out of our little wits.——I thought
it had been Papa or Mama.

---

1   One of the duties of a footman was to clear the way for his employer's
    coach or sedan chair (and thereby call attention to the wealth or impor-
    tance of its occupant).

NURSE.
Ah, Chicken, I've taken care of your Mama—But I must not stay long——Mr. Honeycombe brought her the key in a parlous fury, with orders to let nobody go near you, except himself.—— But I——I can't chuse but laugh——I prevailed on Madam to take a glass extraordinary of her Cordial, and have left her fast asleep in her own chamber.

POLLY.
The luckiest thing in the world!——Now, Mr. Scribble, we may put your stratagem in practice this instant.

SCRIBBLE.
With all my heart.—I wish we were out of the house.

POLLY.
Away, away then!

NURSE.
Softly, Chicken, softly!—Let me go before, to see that there's nobody in the way. Come gently down stairs. I'll set open the door of your cage, and then you may take wing as fast as you please.—Ah, you're a sweet pair of turtles![1]—Come along.

SCRIBBLE.
Turtles indeed! Come, my Dear!——"We two, when we wooe, bill and cooe."

POLLY.
Very well!——You're to walk before my chair, remember!—— This is the finest Adventure I ever had in my life! [*Exeunt, following the* Nurse.

   Scene changes to Mrs. HONEYCOMBE's *Apartment.*

   Mrs. HONEYCOMBE *alone,—several phials on the table, with labels.*

I am not at all well to-day.—[*yawns, as if just waking.*]—Such a quantity of tea in a morning, makes one quite Nervous—and

---

1   "Turtles" are here turtle-doves (known for their affection and fidelity).

Mr. Honeycombe does not chuse it qualified.[1]——I have such a dizziness in my head, it absolutely turns round with me.—I don't think neither that the Hysterick Water is warm enough for my stomach.——I must speak to Mr. Julep[2] to order me something rather more comfortable.

Enter NURSE.

NURSE.
Did you call, Ma'am?

Mrs. HONEYCOMBE.
Oh Nurse, is it you?——No, I did not call—Where's Mr. Honeycombe?

NURSE.
Below stairs in the parlour, Madam.—I did not think she'd have wak'd so soon——If she should miss the key now, before I've an opportunity to lay it down again! [*Aside.*]

Mrs. HONEYCOMBE.
What d'ye say? Nurse!

NURSE.
Say? Ma'am!——Say!——I say, I hope you're a little better, Ma'am!

Mrs. HONEYCOMBE.
Oh Nurse, I am perfectly giddy with my Nerves, and so low-spirited.

NURSE.
Poor gentlewoman! suppose I give you a sup out of the case of Italian Cordials, Ma'am! that was sent as a present from Mr.

---

1   "Qualified" tea is tea mixed with something (Mrs. Honeycombe presumably prefers alcohol).
2   "Hysterick Water" is one of Mrs. Honeycombe's cordials (recipes vary, but they all involve herbs, roots, and other ingredients combined with a lot of alcohol). A "julep" is a sweet medicine (i.e., a cordial).

What-d'ye-call-him, in Crutched-Fryars[1]—The Italian merchant with the long name.

Mrs. HONEYCOMBE.
Filthy poison! don't mention it!—Faugh! I hate the very names of them.——You know, Nurse, I never touch any Cordials, but what come from the Apothecary's——What o'clock is it?—— Isn't it time to take my Draught?

NURSE.
By my troth, I believe it is—Let me see, I believe this is it—— [*Takes up a phial, and slips the key upon the table.*] "The Stomachick Draught to be taken an hour before dinner.[2] For Mrs. Honeycombe." [*reading the label.*]—Ay, this is it—By my troth, I am glad I've got rid of the key again. [*Aside.*]

Mrs. HONEYCOMBE.
Come then!—Pour it into a tea cup and give it me.—I'm afraid I can't take it. It goes sadly against me.

While she is drinking, HONEYCOMBE *without.*

Run, John, run!—After them immediately!—Harry, do you run too——Stick close to Mr. Ledger——Don't return without them for your life!

NURSE.
Good lack! good lack! they're discovered, as sure as the day. [*Aside.*]

Mrs. HONEYCOMBE.
Lord, Nurse, what's the matter?

---

1 "Crutched Friars" was an old, somewhat run-down street near the Tower of London (i.e., not the sort of place a fashionable woman would usually go shopping). See the map in Figure 9 (p. 58). Sheridan went to Crutched Friars to meet Thomas Mathews for their first duel, though they ended up fighting in Covent Garden—see Appendix C, items 3, 4, and 6.
2 "Dinner" was the midday meal (taken about three in the afternoon by people like the Honeycombes and as late as five to seven in the evening by members of the fashionable world).

NURSE.
I don't know, by my troth.

Enter HONEYCOMBE.

Mrs. HONEYCOMBE.
O, my Sweeting, I am glad you are come.—I was so frighted
about you. [*Rises, and seems disorder'd.*]

HONEYCOMBE.
Zouns, my Dear——

Mrs. HONEYCOMBE.
O don't swear, my Dearest!

HONEYCOMBE.
Zouns, it's enough to make a parson swear——You have let
Polly escape——She's run away with a fellow.

Mrs. HONEYCOMBE.
You perfectly astonish me, my dear!——I can't possibly conceive——My poor head aches too to such a degree—Where's
the key of her chamber? [*Seems disorder'd.*]

NURSE.
Here, Madam, here it is.

HONEYCOMBE.
Zouns, I tell you——

Mrs HONEYCOMBE.
Why here's the key, my Sweeting!——It's absolutely impossible—it has lain here ever since you brought it me—not a soul
has touched it—have they, Nurse? [*disordered.*]

NURSE.
Not a creature, I'll take my Bible oath on't.

HONEYCOMBE.
I tell you, she's gone.—I'm sure on't—Mr. Ledger saw a strange
footman put her into a chair, at the corner of the street—and
He and John, and a whole Posse, are gone in pursuit of them.

Mrs. HONEYCOMBE.
This is the most extraordinary circumstance—It's quite beyond my comprehension——But my Sweeting must not be angry with his own dear wife—it was not her fault. [*fondling.*]

HONEYCOMBE.
Nay, my Love, don't trifle now!——

Mrs. HONEYCOMBE.
I must——I will——

HONEYCOMBE.
Zouns, my Dear, be quiet!—I shall have my girl ruined for ever.

LEDGER, *without.*
This way—this way—bring them along!

HONEYCOMBE.
Hark! they're coming—Mr. Ledger has overtaken them—they're here.

LEDGER, *without.*
Here!—Mr. Honeycombe is in this room——Come along!

Enter LEDGER, POLLY, *and* SCRIBBLE, *with Servants.*

LEDGER.
Here they are, Mr. Honeycombe!——We've brought them back again.——Here they are, Madam.

HONEYCOMBE.
Hark ye, Hussy! I have a good mind to turn you out of doors again immediately.——You are a disgrace to your family.— You're a shame to——

Mrs. HONEYCOMBE.
Stay, my dear, don't you put yourself into such a passion!—— Polly, observe what I say to you—Let me know the whole circumstances of this affair——I don't at all understand——Tell me, I say——[*Disorder'd.*]

HONEYCOMBE.
Zouns! I have no patience.—Harke ye, hussy!——Where was

you going?——Who does this fellow belong to?——Where does
he live?——Who is he?

POLLY.
That gentleman, Papa, is Mr. Scribble.

HONEYCOMBE.
This! is this Mr. Scribble?

SCRIBBLE.
The very man, sir, at your service——An humble admirer of
Miss Honeycombe's.

POLLY.
Yes, Papa, that's Mr. Scribble.——The sovereign of my heart
——The sole object of my affections.

Mrs. HONEYCOMBE.
What can be the meaning of all this?

HONEYCOMBE.
Why you beggarly slut!——What, would you run away from
your family with a fellow in livery? a footman?

POLLY.
A footman! ha! ha! ha! very good; a footman!——

SCRIBBLE.
A footman, eh, my dear!——An errand boy!——A scoundrel
fellow in livery——A good joke, faith! [*Laughing with* Polly.]

POLLY.
Why, Papa, don't you know that every gentleman disguises
himself in the course of an amour?——Don't you remember
that Bob Lovelace disguised himself like an old man?[1] And Tom
Ramble like an old woman?——No Adventure can be carried
on without it.

---

1 After the rape, Lovelace tracked down the fleeing Clarissa and gained
   entrance to the house in which she had been hiding by being "slouched,
   and muffled up" as "an old clumsy fellow" (5:15). Once again, Polly
   seems to completely disregard narrative context.

HONEYCOMBE.
She's certainly mad—stark mad.——Hark ye, sir! Who are
you?——I'll have you sent to the Compter[1]—You shall give an
account of yourself before my Lord-Mayor.

SCRIBBLE.
What care I for my Lord-Mayor, or the whole court of Alder-
men?——Hark ye, old Greybeard, I am a gentleman——A gentleman as well known as any in the city.

Mrs. HONEYCOMBE.
Upon my word, I believe so.—He seems a very proper gentle-
man-like young person.

LEDGER.
As well known as any in the city!——I don't believe it—He's no
good man—I am sure he's not known upon Change.[2]

SCRIBBLE.
Damme, sir, what d'ye mean?

LEDGER.
Oho! Mr. Gentleman, is it you?——I thought I knew your
voice—Ay, and your face too.——Pray, sir, don't you live with
Mr. Traverse, the attorney, of Gracechurch-Street?[3]——Did not
you come to me last week about a policy of insurance?

SCRIBBLE.
O the Devil! [aside.] I come to you? sir!——I never saw your
face before. [to Ledger.]

NURSE.
Good lack! he'll certainly be discovered. [aside.

---

1 A prison for misdemeanors, attached to a City court. There were two
   within a short distance of the other locations mentioned in the play.
2 Creditworthiness depended upon personal reputation, so not being
   "known upon Change" suggested (in the commercial world) that one
   was not a "good man," at least in the financial sense of being able to
   fully cover one's debts.
3 In the law, a "traverse" is a formal denial of the facts alleged by the
   other side. "Gracechurch Street" is a major, but unremarkable (and certainly unfashionable) street in the City of London. See the map in
   Figure 9 (p. 58).

HONEYCOMBE.
An attorney's clerk![1]——Hark ye, friend——

SCRIBBLE.
'Egad, I'd best sneak off before it's worse. [*going.*

HONEYCOMBE.
Hark ye, woman! [*to* Nurse.]——I begin to suspect—Have not I heard you speak of a kinsman, clerk to Mr. Traverse?——Stop him!

SCRIBBLE.
Hands off, Gentlemen!——Well then—I do go through a little business for Mr. Traverse—What then? What have you to say to me now? sir!

POLLY.
Do pray, Mama, take Mr. Scribble's part, pray do!

NURSE.
Do, ma'am, speak a good word for him.

Apart, while they are searching Scribble.

Mrs. HONEYCOMBE.
I understand nothing at all of the matter.

HONEYCOMBE.
Hark ye, Woman!——He's your nephew——I'm sure on't—— I'll turn you out of doors immediately.——You shall be——

NURSE.
I beg upon my knees that your honour would forgive me——I meant no harm, Heaven above knows—— [Nurse *kneeling.*

---

1 An attorney's clerk was a scribe and errand-boy for a lawyer, and so occupied a significantly lower social position than Ledger, a partner in a highly profitable financial firm, or Mr. Honeycombe, who is retired from such a firm. All three fell within the broad "middling" ranks of society, but an attorney's clerk would have been close to the opposite end of those ranks from Ledger and Honeycombe, both in terms of status and financial resources. At least in literature, pretenders to wit or fashion often seem to turn out to be attorneys' clerks (presumably because they spend their days pen in hand, and have frequent contact with their social superiors).

HONEYCOMBE.
No harm! what to marry my daughter to——I'll have you sent
to Newgate[1]——And you, [*to* Polly.] you sorry baggage; d'ye
see what you was about?——You was running away with a
beggar—With your Nurse's nephew, hussy!

POLLY.
Lord, Papa, what signifies whose nephew he is? He may be
ne'er the worse for that.—Who knows but he may be a
Foundling, and a gentleman's son, as well as Tom Jones?[2]——
My mind is resolved,——And nothing shall ever alter it.

SCRIBBLE.
Bravo, Miss Polly!——A fine generous spirit, faith!

HONEYCOMBE.
You're an impudent slut—You're undone.——

Mrs. HONEYCOMBE.
Nay, but, look ye, Polly!——Mind me, child!——You know that
I——

POLLY.
As for my poor Mama here, you see, sir, she is a little in the
nervous way, this morning——When she comes to herself, and
Mr. Julep's draughts have taken a proper effect, she'll be convinced I am in the right.

HONEYCOMBE.
Hold your impertinence!—Hark ye, Polly——

POLLY.
You, my angelick Mr. Scribble— [*to* Scribble.]

---

1 One of the principal prisons for felons in London (which suggests that
   Mr. Honeycombe thinks the Nurse's offense greater than Scribble's,
   since the latter was only threatened with the Compter). See the map in
   Figure 9 (p. 58).
2 Tom Jones began his story as a foundling (a baby left at a stranger's
   house by parents who are unable or unwilling to care for him), but turns
   out at the end to be the illegitimate nephew of the gentleman who
   raised him.

SCRIBBLE.
Ma chere Adorable![1]

POLLY.
You may depend on my constancy and affection. I never read of
any lady's giving up her lover, to submit to the absurd election
of her parents——I'll have you let what will be the consequence.——I'll have you, though we go through as many distresses as Booth and Amelia.[2]

HONEYCOMBE.
Peace, hussy!

POLLY.
As for you, you odious Wretch, [*to* Ledger.] how could they ever
imagine that I should dream of such a creature? A great He-
monster! I would as soon be married to the Staffordshire
Giant——I hate you. You are as deceitful as Blifil, as rude as the
Harlowes, and as ugly as Doctor Slop.[3] [*Exit.*

LEDGER.
Mighty well, Miss, mighty well!

SCRIBBLE.
Prodigious humour! high fun, faith!

HONEYCOMBE.
She's downright raving—Mad as a March hare——I'll put her
into Bedlam[4]——I'll send her to her relations in the country
——I'll have her shut up in a nunnery——I'll——

---

1 *Ma chère Adorable* is French for "my dear adorable" one.
2 Amelia is the long-suffering wife of Captain William Booth in Henry
   Fielding's *Amelia* (London, 1751). Among their other distresses, Booth
   is imprisoned twice and has an affair, while Amelia has "her lovely Nose
   ... beat all to pieces" (1:95) when a carriage overturns.
3 Edward Bamford, "The Staffordshire Giant," stood seven foot four and
   frequently exhibited himself around London. After his death in 1768,
   the curious could visit a life-size waxwork of him at a local museum.
   "Dr. Slop" is the short, fat obstetrician who botches the delivery of the
   narrator in Laurence Sterne's *Tristram Shandy* (1759-67).
4 The popular nickname of Bethlem Hospital, London's insane asylum.
   See the map in Figure 9 (p. 58).

Mrs. HONEYCOMBE.
Come, my Sweeting, don't make your dear self so uneasy—
Don't——

HONEYCOMBE.
Hark you, woman, [*to the* Nurse.] I'll have you committed to
Newgate—I'll——

NURSE.
Pray, your dear honour!— [*Kneeling.*]

HONEYCOMBE.
As for you, sir! [*to* Scribble.]—Hark ye, Stripling——

SCRIBBLE.
Nay, nay, Old Gentleman, no bouncing![1]—You're mistaken in
your man, sir! I know what I'm about.

HONEYCOMBE.
Zouns, sir, and I know——

SCRIBBLE.
Yes, sir, and I know that I've done nothing contrary to the
twenty-sixth of the King[2]—Above a month ago, sir, I took lodgings in Miss Polly's name and mine, in the parish of St.
George's in the Fields[3]——The bans have been asked three
times, and I could have married Miss Polly today——So much
for that.——And so, sir, your servant.——If you offer to detain
me, I shall bring my action on the case for false imprisonment,
sue out a bill of Middlesex, and upon a *Non est inventus*, if you
abscond, a *Latitat*, then an *Alias*, a *Pluries*, a *Non omittas*, and so
on——Or perhaps I may indict you at the sessions, bring the

---

1 In this context, "blustering" or "scolding."
2 All of the steps Scribble proceeds to list were required, by a law passed
   in 1753 (the twenty-sixth year of the reign of George II), in order for a
   marriage to be legal. To ask "the bans" is to publicly announce, in a
   couple's parish church, their intention to wed, so that anyone opposed
   to the union can have the opportunity to object.
3 St George's in the Fields was a fairly poor, undeveloped area on the
   south edge of London (far enough away that the Honeycombes would
   not hear of the bans being asked for their daughter's marriage). See the
   map in Figure 9 (p. 58).

affair by *Certiorari* into *Bancum Regis, et cætera, et cætera, et cætera*[1]———And now———Stop me at your peril. [*Exit.*

[*While* Scribble *speaks* Nurse *sneaks off.*]

HONEYCOMBE.
I am stunn'd with his jargon, and confounded at his impudence.———I'll put an end to this matter at once———Mr. Ledger, you shall marry my daughter to-morrow morning.

LEDGER.
Not I indeed, my friend! I give up my interest in her.———She'd make a terrible wife for a sober citizen.———Who can answer for her behaviour?———I would not underwrite her for ninety *per cent.*[2] [*Exit.*

HONEYCOMBE.
See there! see there!———My girl is undone.—Her character is ruined with all the world———These damn'd Story Books!—What shall we do? Mrs. Honeycombe, what shall we do?

Mrs. HONEYCOMBE.
Look ye, my Dear! you've been wrong in every particular———

HONEYCOMBE.
Wrong!———I! Wrong!———

Mrs. HONEYCOMBE.
Quite wrong, my Dear!———I wou'd not expose you before company—My Tenderness, you know, is so great———But leave the whole affair to me———You are too violent———Go, my dear,

---

1   Scribble's flourishes of legal Latin all have to do with a court's gaining jurisdiction over a case regardless of where its defendant might be located (essentially Scribble is warning Mr. Honeycombe that his City connections will be no match for Scribble's ability to manipulate the legal system to his own advantage). Colman trained to be a lawyer, though he only practiced for a few sporadic years before devoting himself full-time to the theater.
2   That is, Ledger wouldn't insure Polly's good behavior, even if the premium were ninety percent of the value of the policy, because her conduct could ruin the reputation (and so creditworthiness) of even the most "sober citizen." Like a woman's honor, creditworthiness, once lost, was thought very difficult, if not impossible, to restore.

go and compose yourself, and I'll set all matters to rights——
[*Going turns back.*] Don't you do any thing of your own head
now—Trust it all to me, my Dear!—Be sure you do, my Love!
[*Exit.*

HONEYCOMBE, *alone.*
Zouns, I shall run mad with vexation—I shall—Was ever man
so heartily provoked?—You see now, Gentlemen, [*coming
forward to the audience.*] what a situation I am in!—Instead of
happiness and jollity,—My friends and family about me,—A
wedding and a dance,—And every thing as it should be,—Here
am I, left by myself,—Deserted by my intended son-in-law—
Bully'd by an attorney's clerk—My Daughter mad—My Wife in
the Vapours—And all's in confusion.——This comes of Cordials and Novels.——Zouns, your Stomachicks are the Devil—
And a man might as well turn his Daughter loose in Covent-
garden, as trust the cultivation of her mind to
A CIRCULATING LIBRARY.[1]

EPILOGUE.

Written by Mr. GARRICK.

Spoken by Miss POPE.[2]

Enter, as POLLY, *laughing—Ha! ha! ha!—*

My poor Papa's in woeful agitation—
While I, the Cause, feel here, [striking her bosom.] *no palpitation—*
We Girls of Reading, and superior notions,
Who from the fountain-head drink love's sweet potions,
Pity our parents, when such passion blinds 'em,
One hears the good folks rave—One never minds 'em.

---

1 In addition to being where the theaters were located, Covent Garden
   was notorious as a cruising ground for prostitutes. It was also, in a nice
   irony, close to John Noble's circulating library, one of the largest in
   London (see the map in Figure 9, p. 58).
2 Jane Pope, who played Polly (see Appendix A). The Epilogue was
   dropped after the tenth performance (one more than was customary),
   but retained in most printed versions of the play. More unusually, it was
   twice revived in later repertory performances.

Till these dear books infus'd their soft ingredients,
Asham'd and fearful, I was all Obedience.
Then my good Father did not storm in vain,
I blush'd and cry'd—I'll ne'er do so again:
But now no bugbears can my spirit tame,
I've conquer'd Fear—And almost conquer'd Shame;[1]
So much these Dear Instructors change and win us,
Without their light *we ne'er should know what's in us:*
Here we at once supply our childish wants—
NOVELS *are Hotbeds for your forward Plants.*[2]
Not only Sentiments refine the Soul,
But hence we learn to be the Smart and Drole;
Each awkward circumstance for laughter serves,
From Nurse's nonsense to my Mother's NERVES:
     Tho' Parents tell us, that our genius lies
In mending linnen and in making pies,
I set such formal precepts at defiance
That preach up prudence, neatness, and compliance:
Leap these old bounds, and boldly set the pattern,
To be a Wit, *Philosopher, and Slattern—*[3]

     O! did all Maids and Wives, my spirit feel,
We'd make this topsy-turvy world to reel:
Let us to arms!—Our Fathers, Husbands, dare!
NOVELS *will teach us all the Art of War:*
Our Tongues will serve for Trumpet and for Drum;
I'll be your Leader—General HONEYCOMBE!
     Too long has human nature gone astray,
Daughters should govern, Parents should obey;
Man shou'd submit, the moment that he weds,
And hearts of oak[4] *shou'd yield to wiser heads:*
I see you smile, bold Britons!*—But 'tis true—*
Beat You *the* French;*—But let your* Wives *beat* You.—

---

1 "Bugbears" are, in this context, sources of fear for which there is no
   foundation (like the prospect of shame?).
2 Cold frames (small greenhouses to help plants get started growing in
   advance—or "forward"—of their proper season).
3 A "slattern" is a woman who is untidy (in either appearance or habits).
4 "Heart of Oak" was a new and extremely popular song (with lyrics by
   David Garrick) in praise of the British naval victories of 1759 and early
   1760, which helped turn the tide of what would end up being called the
   Seven Years War—in the US, this is generally known as the French and
   Indian War. The "hearts of oak" here are presumably valiant sailors.

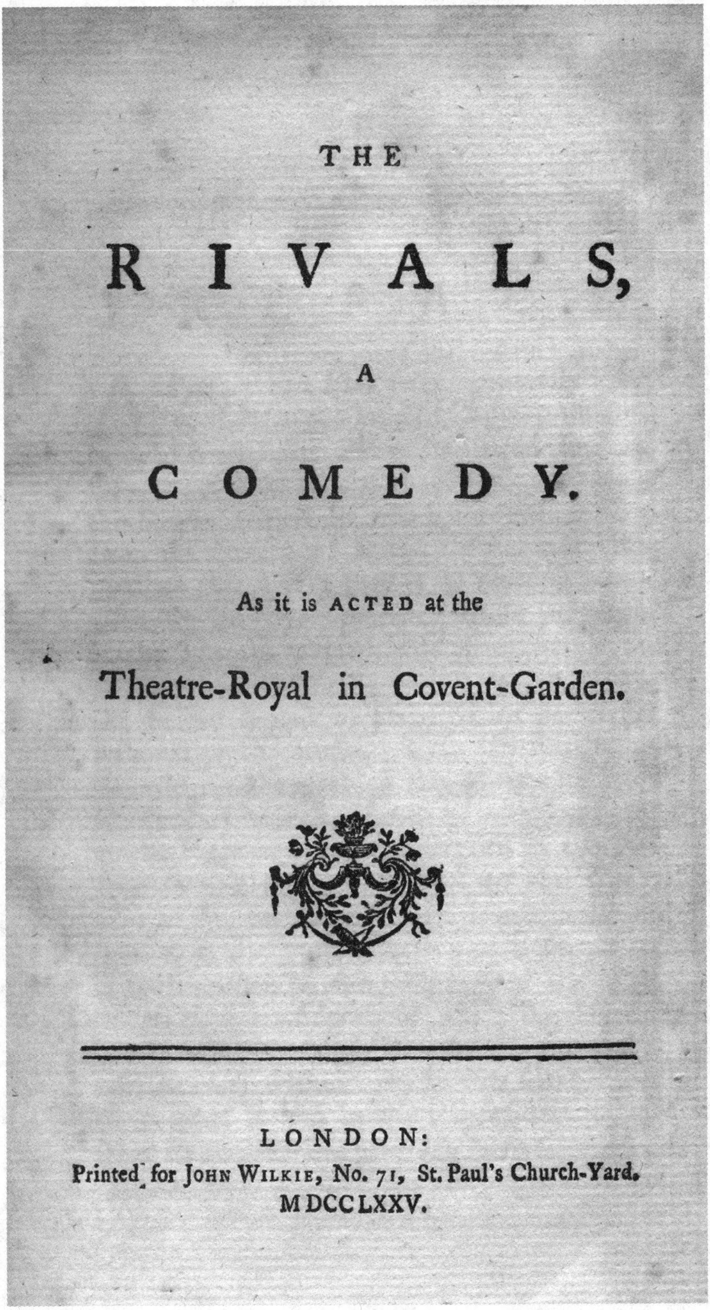

THE

RIVALS,

A

COMEDY.

As it is ACTED at the

Theatre-Royal in Covent-Garden.

LONDON:

Printed for JOHN WILKIE, No. 71, St. Paul's Church-Yard.

MDCCLXXV.

Figure 10: The title page for the first edition of *The Rivals*. Courtesy of The Ohio State University Rare Books and Manuscripts Library.

PREFACE

A Preface to a Play seems generally to be considered as a kind of Closet-prologue, in which—if his Piece has been successful—the Author solicits that indulgence from the Reader which he had before experienced from the Audience: But as the scope and immediate object of a Play is to please a mixed assembly in *Representation* (whose judgment in the Theatre at least is decisive) its degree of reputation is usually as determined as public, before it can be prepared for the cooler tribunal of the Study. Thus any farther solicitude on the part of the Writer becomes unnecessary at least, if not an intrusion: and if the Piece has been condemned in the Performance, I fear an Address to the Closet, like an Appeal to Posterity, is constantly regarded as the procrastination of a suit, from a consciousness of the weakness of the cause. From these considerations, the following Comedy would certainly have been submitted to the Reader, without any further introduction than what it had in the Representation, but that its success has probably been founded on a circumstance which the Author is informed has not before attended a theatrical trial, and which consequently ought not to pass unnoticed.

I need scarcely add, that the circumstance alluded to, was the withdrawing of the Piece, to remove those imperfections in the first Representation which were too obvious to escape reprehension, and too numerous to admit of a hasty correction.[1] There are few writers, I believe, who, even in the fullest consciousness of error, do not wish to palliate the faults which they acknowledge; and, however trifling the performance, to second their confession of its deficiencies, by whatever plea seems least disgraceful to their ability. In the present instance, it cannot be said to amount either to candour or modesty in me, to acknowledge an extreme

---

1   For more on the disastrous first night and Sheridan's subsequent withdrawal and revision of the play, see "A Note on the Texts." Sheridan's claim that such a thing had "not before attended a theatrical trial" is not quite accurate, though he may well have thought it was. After a mixed first night, Samuel Foote's *Taste* (1752) was withdrawn, and an advertisement was placed in a newspaper that "as the Entertainment ... was not quite so well receiv'd as was expected ... the Author has suspended its Representation [for the next eight days], by that time, some Alterations will be made, which, it is hop'd, will render the Piece more Palatable to the Publick" (diary of Richard Cross, the prompter for Drury Lane, quoted in Stone, 1:285).

inexperience and want of judgment on matters, in which, without guidance from practice, or spur from success, a young man should scarcely boast of being an adept. If it be said, that under such disadvantages no one should attempt to write a play—I must beg leave to dissent from the position, while the first point of experience that I have gained on the subject is, a knowledge of the candour and judgment with which an impartial Public distinguishes between the errors of inexperience and incapacity, and the indulgence which it shews even to a disposition to remedy the defects of either.[1]

It were unnecessary to enter into any farther extenuation of what was thought exceptionable in this Play, but that it has been said, that the Managers should have prevented some of the defects before its appearance to the Public—and in particular the uncommon length of the piece as represented the first night.—It were an ill return for the most liberal and gentlemanly conduct on their side, to suffer any censure to rest where none was deserved. Hurry in writing has long been exploded as an excuse for an Author;—however, in the dramatic line, it may happen, that both an Author and a Manager may wish to fill a chasm in the entertainment of the Public with a hastiness not altogether culpable. The season was advanced when I first put the play into Mr. Harris's hands:—it was at that time at least double the length of any acting comedy.—I profited by his judgment and experience in the curtailing of it—'till, I believe, his feeling for the vanity of a young Author got the better of his desire for correctness, and he left many excrescences remaining, because he had assisted in pruning so many more.[2] Hence, though I was not uninformed that the Acts were still too long, I flatter'd myself that, after the first trial, I might with safer judgment proceed to remove what should appear to have been most dissatisfactory.—Many other errors there were, which might in part have arisen from my being by no means conversant with plays in general,

---

1 In the eighteenth century, in addition to its modern meaning of speaking freely and frankly, "candor" (and related terms like "candid") often meant being kindly disposed and free from malice. The "candour" of "an impartial Public" is thus its predisposition to overlook a play's shortcomings, if possible.

2 Sheridan wrote to his father-in-law on 17 November 1774 that "there will be a *Comedy* of mine in rehearsal at Covent-Garden within a few days" and that "I had not written a line of it two months ago, except a scene or two" (*Letters*, 1:85). Thomas Harris was the manager of Covent Garden.

either in reading or at the theatre.—Yet I own that, in one respect, I did not regret my ignorance: for as my first wish in attempting a Play, was to avoid every appearance of plagiary, I thought I should stand a better chance of effecting this from being in a walk which I had not frequented, and where consequently the progress of invention was less likely to be interrupted by starts of recollection: for on subjects on which the mind has been much informed, invention is slow of exerting itself.—Faded ideas float in the fancy like half-forgotten dreams; and the imagination in its fullest enjoyments becomes suspicious of its offspring, and doubts whether it has created or adopted.[1]

With regard to some particular passages which on the First Night's Representation seemed generally disliked, I confess, that if I felt any emotion of surprise at the disapprobation, it was not that they were disapproved of, but that I had not before perceived that they deserved it. As some part of the attack on the Piece was begun too early to pass for the sentence of *Judgment*, which is ever tardy in condemning, it has been suggested to me, that much of the disapprobation must have arisen from virulence of Malice, rather than severity of Criticism: But as I was more apprehensive of there being just grounds to excite the latter, than conscious of having deserved the former, I continue not to believe that probable, which I am sure must have been unprovoked. However, if it was so, and I could even mark the quarter from whence it came, it would be ungenerous to retort; for no passion suffers more than malice from disappointment. For my own part, I see no reason why the Author of a Play should not regard a First Night's Audience, as a candid and judicious friend attending, in behalf of the Public, at his last Rehearsal. If he can dispense with flattery, he is sure at least of sincerity, and even though the annotation be rude, he may rely upon the justness of the comment. Considered in this light, that Audience, whose *fiat* is essential to the Poet's claim, whether his object be Fame or Profit, has surely a right to expect some deference to its opinion, from principles of Politeness at least, if not from Gratitude.[2]

---

1 A disingenuous series of claims at best: as the Introduction, pp. 40-41 suggests, *The Rivals* is chock-full of echoes of previous plays. Moreover, both of Sheridan's parents wrote successful plays, and his father was a celebrated, if controversial actor and teacher of oratory, who used to manage a theater in Dublin.

2 For more on this conception of first nights as what Colman, in the Preface to *Polly Honeycombe*, termed "Publick Rehearsal[s]" (*continued*)

As for the little puny Critics, who scatter their peevish strictures in private circles, and scribble at every Author who has the eminence of being unconnected with them, as they are usually spleen-swoln from a vain idea of increasing their consequence, there will always be found a petulance and illiberality in their remarks, which should place them as far beneath the notice of a Gentleman, as their original dulness had sunk them from the level of the most unsuccessful Author.

It is not without pleasure that I catch at an opportunity of justifying myself from the charge of intending any national reflection in the character of Sir *Lucius O'Trigger*. If any Gentlemen opposed the Piece from that idea, I thank them sincerely for their opposition; and if the condemnation of this Comedy (however misconceived the provocation,) could have added one spark to the decaying flame of national attachment to the country supposed to be reflected on, I should have been happy in its fate; and might with truth have boasted, that it had done more real service in its failure, than the successful morality of a thousand stage-novels[1] will ever effect.

It is usual, I believe, to thank the Performers in a new Play, for the exertion of their several abilities. But where (as in this instance) their merit has been so striking and uncontroverted, as to call for the warmest and truest applause from a number of judicious Audiences, the Poet's after-praise comes like the feeble acclamation of a child to close the shouts of a multitude. The conduct, however, of the Principals in a Theatre cannot be so apparent to the Public.—I think it therefore but justice to declare, that from this Theatre (the only one I can speak of from experience,) those Writers who wish to try the Dramatic Line, will meet with that candour and liberal attention, which are generally allowed to be better calculated to lead genius into excellence, than either the precepts of judgment, or the guidance of experience.

THE AUTHOR.

(p. 60), see "A Note on the Texts" and Stern, *Rehearsal*. "Rude" here means (at least primarily) "unpolished" or "inelegant," rather than intentionally ill-mannered. *Fiat* is Latin for "let it be done" and so means any sort of authorization.

1 "Stage-novels" are, presumably, sentimental comedies of the sort mocked in the Prologue "Spoken on the Tenth Night," which aim more to improve than to entertain their audiences.

PROLOGUE.[1]

BY THE AUTHOR.

Spoken by Mr. WOODWARD and Mr. QUICK.[2]

Enter Serjeant at Law, and Attorney.[3]

Serjeant. What's here!—a vile cramp hand! I cannot see
Without my spectacles.

                            Attorney. He means his fee.
Nay, Mr. Serjeant, good Sir, try again. [*Gives money.*

Serjeant. The scrawl improves [*more*] O come, 'tis pretty plain.
How's this! The Poet's Brief *again*! O ho!
Cast,[4] I suppose?

                            Attorney. O pardon me—No—No—
We found the Court, o'erlooking stricter laws,
Indulgent to the *merits* of the Cause;
By *Judges* mild, unus'd to harsh denial,
A Rule was granted for *another trial.*

---

1 This prologue was first spoken, in the form reproduced here, at the second performance of the play and dropped, as was customary, after the tenth performance (the ninth, if we omit the disastrous opening night). However, it was retained in most printed versions of the play. For the (somewhat, but not hugely different) text of the disastrous opening night, see Price, "The First Prologue."

2 Henry Woodward and John Quick, who played Captain Absolute and Bob Acres, respectively (see Appendix A).

3 A "serjeant" is an experienced lawyer belonging to an order from which judges were chosen. Serjeants, like other barristers, could argue cases in court, whereas mere "attorneys" could only prepare briefs for others to argue (usually in return for a substantial fee). Like Colman, Sheridan briefly trained to be a lawyer, although he never practiced. Most prologues were delivered by a single speaker, but a dialogue like this one would not have been particularly unusual.

4 If a case is "cast," it's been defeated.

Serjeant. Then heark'ee, *Dibble*,[1] did you *mend* your *Pleadings*,
Errors, no few, we've *found* in our *Proceedings*.

Attorney. Come, courage, Sir, we did *amend* our *Plea*,
Hence your *new Brief*, and this *refreshing Fee*.
Some Sons of Phoebus—in the Courts we meet,

Serjeant. And fifty Sons of Phoebus in the Fleet![2]

Attorney. Nor pleads he worse, who with a decent sprig
Of Bays—adorns his legal waste of wig.

Serjeant. Full-bottom'd Heroes thus, on signs, unfurl
A leaf of laurel—in a grove of curl!
Yet tell your Client, that, in adverse days,
This Wig is warmer than a bush of Bays.[3]

Attorney. Do you then, Sir, my Client's place supply,
Profuse of robe, and prodigal of tye——[4]
Do you, with all those blushing pow'rs of face, ⎫
And wonted bashful hesitating grace, ⎬
Rise in the Court, and flourish on the Case. ⎭ *[Exit.*

Serjeant. For practice then suppose—this Brief will shew it,——
Me, Serjeant *Woodward*,—Council for the Poet.
Us'd to the ground—I know 'tis hard to deal
With this dread *Court*, from whence there's *no appeal*;

---

1 A "dibble" is a stick used to make holes in the soil into which seeds will
   be planted. Presumably, the attorney is doing a similar kind of prepara-
   tory work for the serjeant.
2 "Phoebus" (a.k.a. Apollo) was, among other things, the God of Poetry.
   "The Fleet" was a debtors' prison in London. The poverty of poets and
   would-be poets was a never-ending source of amusement in the eighteenth century.
3 A wreath of bay laurel leaves ("bays") was used in antiquity to crown
   poets and military heroes. Such wreathes would be lost amidst the huge
   wigs worn by lawyers in court (their "legal waste of wig") and by military heroes on inn- and shop-signs. "Full-bottom'd" here refers to the
   heroes' wigs, rather than their bodies.
4 When arguing cases in court, barristers would wear long robes and
   bushy "tye-wigs."

No *Tricking* here, to blunt the edge of *Law*,
Or, damn'd in *Equity*—escape by *Flaw*:
But *Judgment* given—*your Sentence* must remain;
—No *Writ of Error* lies—to *Drury-lane!*[1]
      Yet when so kind you seem—'tis past dispute
We gain some favour, if not *Costs of Suit.*[2]
No spleen is here! I see no hoarded fury;
—I think I never fac'd a milder Jury!
Sad else our plight!—where frowns are transportation,
A hiss the gallows,—and a groan, damnation![3]
But such the public candour, without fear
My Client waves all *right of challenge* here.
No Newsman from *our* Session is dismiss'd,
Nor Wit nor Critic *we* scratch off the list;[4]
His faults can never hurt another's ease,
His crime at worst—a *bad attempt* to please:
Thus, all respecting, he appeals to all,
And by the general voice will *stand* or *fall.*

---

1 That is, unlike in the actual courts, the judgment of the audience could-
n't be appealed to a higher court (Drury Lane, the other patent theater,
wouldn't be interested in a play that failed at Covent Garden), or
evaded by any technicalities or procedural errors.

2 Legal expenses (and so, in this extended metaphor, the costs of preparing a new play, which would require several more nights of successful
performance to recoup).

3 "Transportation" was banishment to one of the colonies, either for a set
number of years or for life. It was a common punishment in the eighteenth century for crimes that required more than a fine or public
humiliation, but which didn't rise to the level of execution, much less
eternal damnation.

4 Unlike many prologues, which attempt to pit different segments of the
audience against one another (suggesting that one group's approval was
more important or reliable than another's), the serjeant here refuses to
exercise his right to exclude anyone from the theatrical jury, even if the
prospective juror was a scandal-seeking journalist ("newsman"), wit, or
critic.

PROLOGUE.

BY THE AUTHOR.

Spoken on the Tenth Night, by Mrs. BULKLEY.[1]

Granted our Cause, our suit and trial o'er,
The worthy Serjeant need appear no more:
In pleading I a different Client chuse,
He serv'd the Poet,—I would serve the Muse:
Like him, I'll try to merit your applause,
A female counsel in a female's cause.
Look on this form,*—where Humour quaint and sly,
Dimples the cheek, and points the beaming eye;
Where gay Invention seems to boast its wiles
In amorous hint, and half-triumphant smiles;
While her light mask or[2] covers Satire's strokes,
Or hides the conscious blush, her wit provokes.
—Look on her well—does she seem form'd to teach?
Shou'd you *expect* to hear this lady—preach?
Is grey experience suited to her youth?
Do solemn sentiments become that mouth?
Bid her be grave, those lips should rebel prove
To every theme that slanders mirth or love.
Yet thus adorn'd with every graceful art
To charm the fancy and yet reach the heart——
Must we displace her? And instead advance

---

* Pointing to the Figure of Comedy [Sheridan's note]. Covent Garden
had sculptures of Comedy and Tragedy on the pillars flanking the stage
(visible in Figure 7, p. 28). The Prologue suggests that the figure of
Comedy had a mask half-hiding her face, while the figure of Tragedy
apparently clutched a dagger (or "poignard").

---

1 Despite its title, this prologue was actually first spoken at the twelfth
night of the play (the eleventh night of the revised version). It was presumably part of the remaining three performances of the first season, but
wasn't included in the printed play until the third edition. Prologues
were generally spoken by men (whereas epilogues were the province of
women), but Mary Bulkley, who played Julia, was widely praised for her
performance of the Epilogue and so may have been given this assignment
as a special reward—or as an additional enticement to the audience.
2 The "or ... or" construction here works the same as "either ... or."

The Goddess of the woeful countenance—[1]
The sentimental Muse!—Her emblems view
The Pilgrim's progress, and a sprig of rue![2]
View her—too chaste to look like flesh and blood—
Primly portray'd on emblematic wood!
There fix'd in usurpation shou'd she stand,
She'll snatch the dagger from her sister's hand;
And having made her votaries *weep a flood*
Good Heav'n! she'll end her Comedies in blood—
Bid *Harry Woodward* break poor *Dunstall's* crown!
Imprison *Quick*—and knock *Ned Shuter* down;
While sad *Barsanti*—weeping o'er the scene,
Shall stab herself—or poison Mrs. *Green.*——[3]
  Such dire encroachments to prevent in time,
Demands the Critic's voice—the Poet's rhyme.
Can our light scenes add strength to holy laws!
Such puny patronage but hurts the cause:
Fair Virtue scorns our feeble aid to ask;
And moral Truth disdains the trickster's mask.
For here their fav'rite stands,* whose brow—severe
And sad—claims Youth's respect, and Pity's tear;
Who—when oppress'd by foes her worth creates—
Can point a poignard at the Guilt she hates.

---

*   Pointing to Tragedy [Sheridan's note].

---

1   Don Quijote was called "the Knight of the Woeful Countenance," which
   may suggest that pursuing the "sentimental Muse" is an equally self-
   deluding endeavor. The phrasing of the next three couplets suggests that
   Bulkley was pointing to a portrait or statue of "the Sentimental Muse"
   brought out on stage in order to drive home how "she" was usurping
   and illegitimately combining Comedy and Tragedy.
2   John Bunyan's *The Pilgrim's Progress* (1676-84), while still a best-seller
   among the pious and poor, was routinely sneered at in the later eighteenth century as ploddingly didactic. "Rue" is a bitter herb long associated with regret.
3   These are all actors in the initial cast of the play (see Appendix A).

Dramatis Personæ.[1]

MEN.

Sir Anthony Absolute,	Mr. SHUTER.
Capt. Absolute,	Mr. WOODWARD.
Faulkland,[2]	Mr. LEWES.
Acres,	Mr. QUICK.
Sir Lucius O'Trigger,	Mr. CLINCH.
Fag,[3]	Mr. LEE-LEWIS.
David,	Mr. DUNSTAL.
Coachman,	Mr. FEARON.

WOMEN.

Mrs. Malaprop,	Mrs. GREEN.
Lydia Languish,	Miss BARSANTI.
Julia,	Mrs. BULKLEY.
Lucy,	Mrs. LESSINGHAM.

Maid, Boy, Servants, &c.

SCENE, *Bath.*

TIME of ACTION, Five Hours.

---

1 For more on the particular talents and reputations of these performers (plus John Lee, who performed Sir Lucius on the first night), see Appendix A.

2 "Faulkland" is the name of the long-suffering (but also long-torment-ing) lover of the heroine in Frances Sheridan's *Memoirs of Miss Sidney Bidulph* (London, 1761-67). According to Sidney's brother, Faulkland's "ideas of love, honour, generosity, and gratitude, [were] so refined, that no hero in romance ever went beyond him" (1:28).

3 In the English public schools, a "fag" is a younger student who runs errands for or otherwise serves an older student, which may suggest something about Fag's social aspirations (i.e., he fancies himself more a junior gentleman than a servant). The term doesn't take on its modern associations with homosexuality until the twentieth century (and even then it's mostly a US phenomenon).

THE RIVALS.

ACT I.

SCENE I.[1]

A STREET *in* Bath.

Coachman *crosses the stage.*——*Enter* Fag, *looking after him.*

FAG.
What!—Thomas!—Sure 'tis he?—What!—Thomas!—Thomas!

COACHMAN.
Hay!—Odd's life!—Mr. Fag!—give us your hand, my old fellow-servant.

FAG.
Excuse my glove,[2] Thomas:—I'm dev'lish glad to see you, my lad: why, my prince of charioteers, you look as hearty!—but who the deuce thought of seeing you in Bath!

COACHMAN.
Sure, Master, Madam Julia, Harry, Mrs. Kate, and the postillion[3] be all come!

FAG.
Indeed!

COACHMAN.
Aye! Master thought another fit of the gout was coming to make him a visit:—so he'd a mind to gi't the slip, and whip we were all off at an hour's warning.

---

1 According to an early nineteenth-century promptbook, "this Scene [was] generally left out," once the play passed into the repertory.
2 Meaning "excuse my not removing my glove to shake your hand," as a social equal should do: one of several signs that Fag feels superior to the other servants.
3 A servant who rides on a coach-horse (generally when there are only two horses pulling a small carriage and so nowhere for a coachman to sit).

FAG.
Aye, aye! hasty in every thing, or it would not be Sir Anthony
Absolute!

COACHMAN.
But tell us, Mr. Fag, how does young Master? Odd! Sir
Anthony will stare to see the Captain here!

FAG.
I do not serve Captain Absolute now.—

COACHMAN.
Why sure!

FAG.
At present I am employ'd by Ensign Beverley.

COACHMAN.
I doubt,[1] Mr. Fag, you ha'n't changed for the better.

FAG.
I have not changed, Thomas.

COACHMAN.
No! why didn't you say you had left young Master?

FAG.
No——Well, honest Thomas, I must puzzle you no farther:—
briefly then—Captain Absolute and Ensign Beverley are one
and the same person.

COACHMAN.
The devil they are!

FAG.
So it is indeed, Thomas; and the *Ensign* half of my master being
on guard at present—the Captain has nothing to do with me.

---

1 "Doubt" here means, as it often does in the eighteenth century,
"suspect."

COACHMAN.
So, so!—what, this is some freak, I warrant!—Do, tell us, Mr. Fag, the meaning o't—you know I ha' trusted you.

FAG.
You'll be secret, Thomas.

COACHMAN.
As a coach-horse.

FAG.
Why then the cause of all this is—LOVE,—Love, Thomas, who (as you may get read to you) has been a masquerader ever since the days of Jupiter.[1]

COACHMAN.
Aye, aye;—I guessed there was a lady in the case:—but pray, why does your Master pass only for *Ensign*?—now if he had shamm'd *General*[2] indeed———

FAG.
Ah! Thomas, there lies the mystery o'the matter.—Hark'ee, Thomas, my Master is in love with a lady of a very singular taste: a lady who likes him better as a *half-pay Ensign* than if she knew he was son and heir to Sir Anthony Absolute, a baronet with three thousand a-year![3]

---

1 In performance, "LOVE" was apparently spelled out by Fag in order to further drive home the difference between him and the apparently illiterate Coachman. "Jupiter" may be a private joke: in 1771, Sheridan revised a burlesque, written by a friend, in which Jupiter seduces the wife of a theater manager. However, they were unable to get it staged and so the personal significance of the line, if such there was, would have passed unnoticed by most audience members.
2 Ensign was the lowest rank of officer in the infantry. General was the highest.
3 When military officers were not on active duty, they only received half pay. A half-pay ensign's salary was about £33 a year—far less than was necessary to maintain a gentlemanly lifestyle. Indeed, Captain Absolute's full pay of about £180-275 a year (depending on what regiment he was in), plus the £50 a year which Sir Anthony gives him as an allowance, would be just barely enough to make genteel ends meet. For more on money and the comparative costs of things, see Introduction, pp. 20-22 and 33-34.

COACHMAN.
That is an odd taste indeed!—but has she got the stuff, Mr. Fag; is she rich, hey?

FAG.
Rich!—why, I believe she owns half the stocks!—Z——ds![1] Thomas, she could pay the national debt as easy as I could my washerwoman!—She has a lap-dog that eats out of gold,—she feeds her parrot with small pearls,—and all her thread-papers[2] are made of bank-notes!

COACHMAN.
Bravo!—faith!——Odd! I warrant she has a set of thousands[3] at least:—but does she draw kindly with the Captain?

FAG.
As fond as pigeons.[4]

COACHMAN.
May one hear her name?

FAG.
Miss Lydia Languish—But there is an old tough aunt in the way;—though by the bye—she has never seen my Master—for he got acquainted with Miss while on a visit in Gloucestershire.

COACHMAN.
Well—I wish they were once harness'd together in matrimony.— But pray, Mr. Fag, what kind of a place is this Bath?—I ha' heard a deal of it—here's a mort[5] o' merry-making—hey?

---

1 A mild oath (it's a contraction of "By God's Wounds!").
2 Strips of paper folded into creases, around each of which could be wrapped a different skein of thread. They were a convenient way of carrying thread in an age before disposable spools.
3 A "set" of horses is a team of six (enough to draw a carriage in style). Apparently, the Coachman can only comprehend Lydia's reported wealth by imagining what sort of luxurious transportation it would yield.
4 Fag presumably means "turtle doves" (proverbial for their devotion and constancy, and in the same family as pigeons).
5 A large amount. Along with some of his pronunciations, this term marks the Coachman as rural.

FAG.
Pretty well, Thomas, pretty well—'tis a good lounge. Though at
present we are, like other great assemblies, divided into
parties—High-roomians and Low-roomians; however, for my
part, I have resolved to stand neuter; and so I told Bob Brush at
our last committee.[1]

COACHMAN.
But what do the folks do here?

FAG.
Oh! there are little amusements enough—in the morning we go
to the pump-room (though neither my Master nor I drink the
waters); after breakfast we saunter on the parades or play
a game at billiards; at night we dance: but d—n the place, I'm
tired of it: their regular hours stupify me—not a fiddle nor a
card after eleven!—however Mr. Faulkland's gentleman and I
keep it up a little in private parties;—I'll introduce you there,
Thomas—you'll like him much.[2]

COACHMAN.
Sure I know Mr. Du-Peigne[3]—you know his Master is to marry
Madam Julia.

FAG.
I had forgot.—But Thomas you must polish a little—indeed you
must:—here now—this wig!—what the devil do you do with a
wig, Thomas?—none of the London whips of any degree of Ton
wear *wigs* now.[4]

---

1 "High-roomians" and "Low-roomians" are, it would seem, partisans of
   the two Assembly Rooms in Bath, which had a fierce rivalry with one
   another (indeed, in 1769 there was a small riot between the two fac-
   tions). Bob Brush is presumably another valet with social pretensions
   (he and Fag meet as a "committee").
2 For more on these amusements and the social life of Bath, see Introduction, pp. 39-40 and Appendix D. The Assembly Rooms closed promptly
   at 11 p.m., whether or not the patrons were ready for their evenings to
   end.
3 *Du Peigne* is French for "of the comb," which further suggests the kind
   of self-important company Fag has been keeping.
4 "Whips," in this context, are coachmen. To have "ton" is to be fashionable. As the next few lines suggest, men's long-standing   (*continued*)

COACHMAN.
More's the pity! more's the pity, I say.—Odd's life! when I
heard how the lawyers and doctors had took to their own hair, I
thought how 'twould go next:—Odd rabbit it! when the fashion
had got foot on the Bar, I guess'd 'twould mount to the Box![1]—
but 'tis all out of character, believe me, Mr. Fag: and look'ee,
I'll never gi' up mine—the lawyers and doctors may do as they
will.

FAG.
Well, Thomas, we'll not quarrel about that.

COACHMAN.
Why, bless you, the gentlemen of they professions ben't all of a
mind—for in our village now tho'ff *Jack Gauge* the *exciseman*,
has ta'en to his carrots, there's little Dick the farrier swears he'll
never forsake his *bob*, tho' all the college[2] should appear with
their own heads!

FAG.
Indeed! well said Dick! but hold—mark! mark! Thomas.

COACHMAN.
Zooks! 'tis the Captain—Is that the lady with him?

FAG.
No! no! that is Madam Lucy—my Master's mistress's maid.—
They lodge at that house—but I must after him to tell him the
news.

---

practice of shaving their heads and wearing wigs (which started out as a
mark of gentility and gradually trickled down to tradesmen and servants) was beginning to fade away in the later 1760s and 1770s, in favor
of wearing one's own hair—sometimes with powder in it.
1 In this context, the seat on top of a coach where the driver sits (not, in
general, as prestigious a venue as the Bar).
2 The "they" here probably indicates a rural pronunciation. Excisemen
calculated ("gauged") the capacity of casks and barrels in order to
determine the proper tax on their contents. Jack Gauge's taking "to his
carrots" means wearing his own red hair, rather than a wig. A "bob" is a
short wig (cheaper and less formal than other styles). "All the college" is
a grandiose way of saying "all the other farriers" (doctors and surgeons
often referred to themselves as a college; farriers, who shoed and otherwise cared for horses, not so much).

COACHMAN.
Odd! he's giving her money!—well, Mr. Fag——

FAG.
Good bye, Thomas.—I have an appointment in Gydes' Porch[1] this evening at eight; meet me there, and we'll make a little party. [*Exeunt severally.*]

SCENE II.

A Dressing-room in Mrs. Malaprop's lodgings.

Lydia *sitting on a sopha with a book in her hand.—*
Lucy, *as just returned from a message.*

LUCY.
Indeed, Ma'am, I transferr'd[2] half the town in search of it:—I don't believe there's a circulating library in Bath I ha'n't been at.

LYDIA.
And could not you get *The Reward of Constancy*?[3]

LUCY.
No, indeed, Ma'am.

LYDIA.
Nor *The Fatal Connection*?

---

1 Presumably the entrance to the Lower Assembly Rooms (which were run by a man named Cam Gyde).
2 In the third edition, "transferr'd" was changed to "travers'd." Cecil Price, the editor of the standard scholarly edition of Sheridan, suspects that the word spoken on stage was actually the more ordinary "traips'd." In the mid-1770s, Bath had at least six circulating libraries, including the ones operated by Lewis Bull and William Frederick which Lucy mentions.
3 All the titles mentioned in this scene until *The Whole Duty of Man* are novels (except for *The Memoirs of a Lady of Quality*, which is a substantial—and detachable—chunk of a novel, *Peregrine Pickle*, which Lucy also rents in its entirety). For details, see Brewer and Whitehead, and Nettleton.

LUCY.
No, indeed, Ma'am.

LYDIA.
Nor *The Mistakes of the Heart?*

LUCY.
Ma'am, as ill-luck would have it, Mr. Bull said Miss Sukey
Saunter had just fetch'd it away.

LYDIA.
Heigh-ho!—Did you inquire for *The Delicate Distress?*——

LUCY.
——Or *The Memoirs of Lady Woodford?* Yes indeed, Ma'am.—I
ask'd every where for it; and I might have brought it from Mr.
Frederick's, but Lady Slattern Lounger, who had just sent it
home, had so soiled and dog's-ear'd it, it wa'n't fit for a christian to read.

LYDIA.
Heigh-ho!—Yes, I always know when Lady Slattern has been
before me.—She has a most observing thumb; and I believe
cherishes her nails for the convenience of making marginal
notes.[1]—Well, child, what *have* you brought me?

LUCY.
Oh! here Ma'am. [*Taking books from under her cloke, and from her
pockets.*[2]]
This is *The Gordian Knot,*—and this *Peregrine Pickle.* Here are
The Tears of Sensibility and *Humphry Clinker.* This is *The Memoirs
of a Lady of Quality, written by herself,*—and here the second
volume of *The Sentimental Journey.*

LYDIA.
Heigh-ho!—What are those books by the glass?

---

1 Lady Slattern's habit of scratching marginalia into a page with her
   thumbnail seems to have been a real practice of some readers.
2 A woman's "pockets" were actually a bag tied around her waist beneath
   her dress, with access through slits in the seams.

LUCY.
The great one is only *The whole Duty of Man*——where I press a few blonds,[1] Ma'am.

LYDIA.
Very well—give me the *sal volatile.*

LUCY.
Is it in a blue cover, Ma'am?

LYDIA.
My smelling bottle, you simpleton!

LUCY.
O, the drops!—here Ma'am.

LYDIA.
No note, Lucy?

LUCY.
No indeed, Ma'am—but I have seen a certain person——

LYDIA.
What, my Beverley!—well Lucy?

LUCY.
O Ma'am! he looks so desponding and melancholic!

LYDIA.
Hold Lucy!—here's some one coming—quick, see who it is.—— [*Exit* Lucy.
Surely I heard my cousin Julia's voice!

[*Re-enter* Lucy.]

LUCY.
Lud! Ma'am, here is Miss Melville.[2]

---

1   *The Whole Duty of Man* (1659) was a tremendously popular devotional work. "Blondes" are pieces of unbleached silk lace.
2   Presumably Lucy exits here, so that she can reenter "in a hurry" later in the scene, but none of the printed texts of the play record such an exit.

LYDIA.
Is it possible!———

Enter Julia.

LYDIA.
My dearest Julia, how delighted am I!—*(Embrace)* How unexpected was this happiness!

JULIA.
True, Lydia—and our pleasure is the greater;—but what has
been the matter?—you were denied[1] to me at first!

LYDIA.
Ah! Julia, I have a thousand things to tell you!—but first inform
me, what has conjur'd you to Bath?—Is Sir Anthony here?

JULIA.
He is—we are arrived within this hour—and I suppose he will
be here to wait on Mrs. Malaprop as soon as he is dress'd.

LYDIA.
Then before we are interrupted, let me impart to you some of
my distress!—I know your gentle nature will sympathize with
me, tho' your prudence may condemn me!—My letters have
inform'd you of my whole connexion with Beverley;—but I have
lost him, Julia!—my aunt has discover'd our intercourse by a
note she intercepted, and has confin'd me ever since!——Yet,
would you believe it? she has fallen absolutely in love with a tall
Irish baronet she met one night since we have been here, at
Lady Macshuffle's rout.[2]

JULIA.
You jest, Lydia!

---

1   People who moved in the fashionable world often instructed their ser-
    vants to "deny" them (i.e., tell unexpected visitors that their employers
    were "not at home"), even if lights were blazing, conversation or music
    was audible, etc. In Lydia's case, though, the denial is the result of
    Mrs. Malaprop's having "confin'd" her (presumably to her room).
2   A "rout" was a large fashionable evening party, often involving
    gambling.

LYDIA.
No, upon my word.—She absolutely carries on a kind of correspondence with him, under a feigned name though, till she
chuses to be known to him;——but it is a *Delia* or a *Celia*,[1]
I assure you.

JULIA.
Then, surely, she is now more indulgent to her niece.

LYDIA.
Quite the contrary. Since she has discovered her own frailty, she
is become more suspicious of mine. Then I must inform you of
another plague!—That odious Acres is to be in Bath to-day; so
that I protest I shall be teased out of all spirits!

JULIA.
Come, come, Lydia, hope the best.—Sir Anthony shall use his
interest with Mrs. Malaprop.

LYDIA.
But you have not heard the worst. Unfortunately I had quarrel-
l'd with my poor Beverley, just before my aunt made the discovery, and I have not seen him since, to make it up.

JULIA.
What was his offence?

LYDIA.
Nothing at all!—But, I don't know how it was, as often as we
had been together, we had never had a quarrel!—And,
somehow I was afraid he would never give me an opportunity.—So, last Thursday, I wrote a letter to myself, to inform
myself that Beverley was at that time paying his addresses to
another woman.—I sign'd it *your Friend unknown*, shew'd it to
Beverley, charg'd him with his falsehood, put myself in a violent
passion, and vow'd I'd never see him more.

JULIA.
And you let him depart so, and have not seen him since?

---

1   "Delia" and "Celia" are stock poetic names for young women being
     courted. Sheridan addressed Elizabeth Linley as "Delia" in some poetry
     written while their parents were keeping them apart.

LYDIA.
'Twas the next day my aunt found the matter out. I intended
only to have teased him three days and a half, and now I've lost
him for ever.

JULIA.
If he is as deserving and sincere as you have represented him to
me, he will never give you up so. Yet consider, Lydia, you tell
me he is but an ensign, and you have thirty thousand pounds!

LYDIA.
But you know I lose most of my fortune, if I marry without my
aunt's consent, till of age;[1] and that is what I have determin'd to
do, ever since I knew the penalty.—Nor could I love the man,
who would wish to wait a day for the alternative.

JULIA.
Nay, this is caprice!

LYDIA.
What, does Julia tax me with caprice?—I thought her lover
Faulkland had enured her to it.

JULIA.
I do not love even *his* faults.

LYDIA.
But a-propos—you have sent to him, I suppose?

JULIA.
Not yet, upon my word—nor has he the least idea of my being
in Bath.—Sir Anthony's resolution was so sudden, I could not
inform him of it.

LYDIA.
Well, Julia, you are your own mistress,[2] (though under the pro-

---

1 Lydia will come "of age" (i.e., be able to marry without her guardian's
   consent or any penalty imposed by her parents' will) at twenty-one.
   She's currently seventeen.
2 Being her "own mistress" means that Julia does not need anyone else's
   permission to marry. Sir Anthony does not have legal power over her in
   the way that Mrs. Malaprop has over Lydia.

tection of Sir Anthony) yet have you, for this long year, been the slave to the caprice, the whim, the jealousy of this ungrateful Faulkland, who will ever delay assuming the right of a husband, while you suffer him to be equally imperious as a lover.

JULIA.
Nay, you are wrong entirely.—We were contracted before my father's death.—*That*, and some consequent embarrassments, have delay'd what I know to be my Faulkland's most ardent wish.—He is too generous to trifle on such a point.—And for his character, you wrong him there too.—No, Lydia, he is too proud, too noble to be jealous; if he is captious, 'tis without dissembling; if fretful, without rudeness.—Unus'd to the foppery of love, he is negligent of the little duties expected from a lover—but being unhackney'd in the passion, his love is ardent and sincere; and as it engrosses his whole soul, he expects every thought and emotion of his mistress to move in unison with his.—Yet, though his pride calls for this full return—his humility makes him undervalue those qualities in him, which should entitle him to it; and not feeling why he should be lov'd to the degree he wishes, he still suspects that he is not lov'd enough:— This temper, I must own, has cost me many unhappy hours; but I have learn'd to think myself his debtor, for those imperfections which arise from the ardour of his love.[1]

LYDIA.
Well, I cannot blame you for defending him.—But tell me candidly, Julia, had he never sav'd your life, do you think you should have been attach'd to him as you are?—Believe me, the rude blast that overset your boat was a prosperous gale of love to him.

JULIA.
Gratitude may have strengthened my attachment to Mr. Faulkland, but I lov'd him before he had preserv'd me; yet surely that alone were an obligation sufficient.

---

1 Sheridan later claimed that this was "the only Speech in the Play that cannot be omitted!" (anecdote recorded in an early nineteenth-century promptbook, quoted in Purdy, li).

LYDIA.
Obligation!—Why a water-spaniel would have done as much.—
Well, I should never think of giving my heart to a man because
he could swim![1]

JULIA.
Come, Lydia, you are too inconsiderate.

LYDIA.
Nay, I do but jest.——What's here?

Enter Lucy *in a hurry.*

LUCY.
O Ma'am, here is Sir Anthony Absolute just come home with
your aunt.

LYDIA.
They'll not come here.—Lucy do you watch. [*Exit* Lucy.

JULIA.
Yet I must go.—Sir Anthony does not know I am here, and if
we meet, he'll detain me, to shew me the town.—I'll take
another opportunity of paying my respects to Mrs. Malaprop,
when she shall treat me, as long as she chooses, with her select
words so ingeniously *misapplied*, without being *mispronounced*.

Re-enter Lucy.

LUCY.
O Lud! Ma'am, they are both coming up stairs.

LYDIA.
Well, I'll not detain you Coz.—Adieu, my dear Julia, I'm sure
you are in haste to send to Faulkland.——There—through my
room you'll find another stair-case.

JULIA.
Adieu.—*(Embrace.)* [*Exit* Julia.

---

1 A "water-spaniel" is a breed of spaniel used by hunters to retrieve ducks
  or other water-fowl that have been shot down. It was fairly rare for
  people in the eighteenth century (even sailors) to know how to swim.

LYDIA.
Here, my dear Lucy, hide these books.—Quick, quick.—Fling
Peregrine Pickle under the toilet—throw *Roderick Random* into
the closet—put *the Innocent Adultery* into *The Whole Duty of
Man*—thrust *Lord Aimworth* under the sopha—cram *Ovid*
behind the bolster—there—put *the Man of Feeling* into your
pocket—so, so, now lay *Mrs. Chapone* in sight, and leave
Fordyce's Sermons[1] open on the table.

LUCY.
O burn it, Ma'am, the hair-dresser has torn away as far as
Proper Pride.[2]

LYDIA.
Never mind—open at *Sobriety*.—Fling me *Lord Chesterfield's
Letters*.[3]——Now for 'em.

   Enter Mrs. Malaprop *and Sir* Anthony Absolute.

Mrs. MALAPROP.
There, Sir Anthony, there sits the deliberate Simpleton, who
wants to disgrace her family, and lavish herself on a fellow not
worth a shilling!

LYDIA.
Madam, I thought you once——

---

1 The "toilet" here is a dressing table. Like the earlier titles mentioned,
 these are mostly novels. "Ovid" is, presumably, one or more works by
 the ancient Roman poet (often regarded as too erotically frank for
 women to read). Hester Chapone and James Fordyce were widely read
 moralists who condemned novel-reading (and Chapone's *Letters on the
 Improvement of the Mind* [1773] take the form of instructions from an
 aunt to her teenage niece)—for excerpts, see Appendix B, items 7 and 8.
2 Hairdressers used torn-out pages from unwanted books as rollers to
 help hold curls in place.
3 Philip Dormer Stanhope, Earl of Chesterfield, wrote a series of (posthu-
 mously published) *Letters ... to his Son* (1774) which focused on how to
 conduct oneself in polite society, regardless of sincerity. Presumably the
 display value of the *Letters* for Lydia is connected to Chesterfield's insis-
 tence that his son had no choice in the matter: he *was* going to be
 trained this way and resistance would only make it more painful.

Mrs. MALAPROP.
You thought, Miss!—I don't know any business you have to think at all—thought does not become a young woman; the point we would request of you is, that you will promise to forget this fellow—to illiterate him, I say, quite from your memory.[1]

LYDIA.
Ah! Madam! our memories are independent of our wills.—It is not so easy to forget.

Mrs. MALAPROP.
But I say it is, Miss; there is nothing on earth so easy as to *forget*, if a person chooses to set about it.—I'm sure I have as much forgot your poor dear uncle as if he had never existed—and I thought it my duty so to do; and let me tell you, Lydia, these violent memories don't become a young woman.

Sir ANTHONY.
Why sure she won't pretend to remember what she's order'd not!—aye, this comes of her reading!

LYDIA.
What crime, Madam, have I committed to be treated thus?

Mrs. MALAPROP.
Now don't attempt to extirpate yourself from the matter; you know I have proof controvertible of it.—But tell me, will you promise to do as you're bid?—Will you take a husband of your friends' choosing?

LYDIA.
Madam, I must tell you plainly, that had I no preference for any one else, the choice you have made would be my aversion.

---

1 Unlike most other editors of *The Rivals*, I am deliberately not attempting to "translate" Mrs. Malaprop's verbal strayings, both because they often make a sly sort of sense that would be obscured by "correcting" them, and because (as Leigh Hunt put it in 1830) "one of the pleasant things in being present at this comedy is to see how *Mrs. Malaprop*'s blunders are hailed by the persons around you. It furnishes a curious insight into the respective amounts of their reading and education" (308).

Mrs. MALAPROP.
What business have you, Miss, with *preference* and *aversion*?
They don't become a young woman; and you ought to know,
that as both always wear off, 'tis safest in matrimony to begin
with a little *aversion*. I am sure I hated your poor dear uncle
before marriage as if he'd been a black-a-moor—and yet, Miss,
you are sensible what a wife I made!—and when it pleas'd
Heav'n to release me from him, 'tis unknown what tears I
shed!—But suppose we were going to give you another choice,
will you promise us to give up this Beverley?

LYDIA.
Could I belie my thoughts so far, as to give that promise, my
actions would certainly as far belie my words.

Mrs. MALAPROP.
Take yourself to your room.—You are fit company for nothing
but your own ill-humours.

LYDIA.
Willingly, Ma'am—I cannot change for the worse. [*Exit* Lydia.

Mrs. MALAPROP.
There's a little intricate hussy for you!

Sir ANTHONY.
It is not to be wonder'd at, Ma'am—all this is the natural consequence of teaching girls to read.—Had I a thousand daughters,
by Heavens! I'd as soon have them taught the black-art as their
alphabet![1]

Mrs. MALAPROP.
Nay, nay, Sir Anthony, you are an absolute misanthropy.

---

1 The "black-art" is witchcraft, especially that which involves conjuring up
evil spirits or the dead. This line may have had private significance for
Sheridan: his maternal grandfather was only "with difficulty prevailed
on to allow his daughter to learn to read; and to write, he affirmed to be
perfectly superfluous in the education of a female," as he "considered
the possession of this art, as tending to nothing but the multiplication of
love letters, or the scarcely less dangerous interchange of sentiment in
the confidential effusions of female correspondence" (Alicia LeFanu,
Memoirs of the Life and Writings of Mrs. Frances Sheridan [London, 1824],
4).

Sir ANTHONY.
In my way hither, Mrs. Malaprop, I observed your niece's maid
coming forth from a circulating library!—She had a book in
each hand—they were half-bound volumes, with marbled
covers![1]—From that moment I guess'd how full of duty I should
see her mistress!

Mrs. MALAPROP.
Those are vile places, indeed!

Sir ANTHONY.
Madam, a circulating library in a town is, as an ever-green tree,
of diabolical knowledge!—It blossoms through the year!—And
depend on it, Mrs. Malaprop, that they who are so fond of han-
dling the leaves, will long for the fruit at last.

Mrs. MALAPROP.
Well, but Sir Anthony, your wife, Lady Absolute, was fond of
books.

Sir ANTHONY.
Aye—and injury sufficient they were to her, Madam.—But were
I to chuse another helpmate, the extent of her erudition should
consist in her knowing her simple letters, without their mischievous combinations;—and the summit of her science be—her
ability to count as far as twenty.—The first, Mrs. Malaprop,
would enable her to work *A. A.* upon my linen;—and the latter
would be quite sufficient to prevent her giving me a shirt, No.
1. and a stock, No. 2.[2]

Mrs. MALAPROP.
Fie, fie, Sir Anthony, you surely speak laconically!

---

1 Books from circulating libraries were typically half-bound with marbled
   covers (i.e., they had leather spines and marbled paper boards). Given
   the libraries' reputation for stocking little or nothing but fiction, such a
   binding would visually mark a book as being most likely a novel. For a
   photo of such a binding, see Figure 11, p. 262.
2 A "stock" is a tight, stiff cloth that buckled around the neck and was
   worn beneath an open shirt collar. Apparently Sir Anthony has his shirts
   and stocks numbered to indicate their proper combinations.

Sir ANTHONY.
Why, Mrs. Malaprop, in moderation, now, what would you have
a woman know?

Mrs. MALAPROP.
Observe me, Sir Anthony.—I would by no means wish a daughter of mine to be a progeny of learning; I don't think so much
learning becomes a young woman; for instance—I would never
let her meddle with Greek, or Hebrew, or Algebra, or Simony,
or Fluxions,[1] or Paradoxes, or such inflammatory branches of
learning—neither would it be necessary for her to handle any of
your mathematical, astronomical, diabolical instruments;—But,
Sir Anthony, I would send her, at nine years old, to a boarding-
school, in order to learn a little ingenuity and artifice.—Then,
Sir, she should have a supercilious knowledge in accounts;—and
as she grew up, I would have her instructed in geometry, that
she might know something of the contagious countries;—but
above all, Sir Anthony, she should be mistress of orthodoxy, that
she might not mis-spell, and mis-pronounce words so shame-
fully as girls usually do; and likewise that she might reprehend
the true meaning of what she is saying.—This, Sir Anthony, is
what I would have a woman know;—and I don't think there is a
superstitious article in it.

Sir ANTHONY.
Well, well, Mrs. Malaprop, I will dispute the point no further
with you; though I must confess, that you are a truly moderate
and polite arguer, for almost every third word you say is on my
side of the question.—But, Mrs. Malaprop, to the more important point in debate,—you say, you have no objection to my
proposal.

Mrs. MALAPROP.
None, I assure you.—I am under no positive engagement with
Mr. Acres, and as Lydia is so obstinate against him, perhaps
your son may have better success.

Sir ANTHONY.
Well, Madam, I will write for the boy directly.—He knows not a

---

1   "Simony" is the sale of positions in the Church. "Fluxions" is Sir Isaac
    Newton's term for what we know as differential calculus.

syllable of this yet, though I have for some time had the proposal in my head. He is at present with his regiment.

Mrs. MALAPROP.
We have never seen your son, Sir Anthony; but I hope no objection on his side.

Sir ANTHONY.
Objection!—let him object if he dare!—No, no, Mrs. Malaprop, Jack knows that the least demur puts me in a frenzy directly.— My process was always very simple—in their younger days, 'twas "Jack, do this";—if he demur'd—I knock'd him down— and if he grumbled at that—I always sent him out of the room.

Mrs. MALAPROP.
Aye, and the properest way, o' my conscience!—nothing is so conciliating to young people as severity.—Well, Sir Anthony, I shall give Mr. Acres his discharge, and prepare Lydia to receive your son's invocations;—and I hope you will represent *her* to the Captain as an object not altogether illegible.

Sir ANTHONY.
Madam, I will handle the subject prudently.—Well, I must leave you—and let me beg you, Mrs. Malaprop, to enforce this matter roundly to the girl;—take my advice—keep a tight hand—if she rejects this proposal—clap her under lock and key:—and if you were just to let the servants forget to bring her dinner for three or four days, you can't conceive how she'd come about! [*Exit Sir* Anthony.

Mrs. MALAPROP.
Well, at any rate I shall be glad to get her from under my intuition.—She has somehow discovered my partiality for Sir Lucius O'Trigger—sure, Lucy can't have betray'd me!—No, the girl is such a simpleton, I should have made her confess it.—Lucy!— Lucy!—*(calls)* Had she been one of your artificial[1] ones, I should never have trusted her.

Enter Lucy.

---

1 "Artificial" here is not a malapropism, but simply an eighteenth-century way of saying "cunning" or "full of artifice."

LUCY.
Did you call, Ma'am?

Mrs. MALAPROP.
Yes, girl.—Did you see Sir Lucius while you was out?

LUCY.
No, indeed, Ma'am, not a glimpse of him.

Mrs. MALAPROP.
You are sure, Lucy, that you never mention'd————

LUCY.
O Gemini![1] I'd sooner cut my tongue out.

Mrs. MALAPROP.
Well, don't let your simplicity be impos'd on.

LUCY.
No, Ma'am.

Mrs. MALAPROP.
So, come to me presently, and I'll give you another letter to Sir
Lucius;—but mind Lucy—if ever you betray what you are
entrusted with—(unless it be other people's secrets to me) you
forfeit my malevolence for ever:—and your being a simpleton
shall be no excuse for your locality. [*Exit Mrs.* Malaprop.

LUCY.
Ha! ha! ha!—So, my dear *simplicity*, let me give you a little
respite—
(altering her manner)—let girls in my station be as fond as they
please of appearing expert, and knowing in their trusts;—
commend me to a mask of *silliness*, and a pair of sharp eyes for
my own interest under it!—Let me see to what account I have
turn'd my *simplicity* lately—*(looks at a paper)*
For *abetting Miss Lydia Languish in a design of running away with
an Ensign!—in money—sundry times—twelve pound twelve—gowns,
five—hats, ruffles, caps,* &c. &c.—*numberless!—From the said*

---

1 A mild oath (possibly a contraction of *Jesu domine* [Latin for "Lord
   Jesus"]), now usually spelled "Jiminy."

Ensign, within this last month, six guineas and a half.—About a quarter's pay!—Item, *from Mrs. Malaprop, for betraying the young people to her*—when I found matters were likely to be discovered—*two guineas, and a black paduasoy.*—Item, *from Mr. Acres, for carrying divers letters*—which I never deliver'd—*two guineas, and a pair of buckles.*—Item, *from Sir Lucius O'Trigger—three crowns—two gold pocket-pieces—and a silver snuff-box!*——Well done, *simplicity!*—yet I was forced to make my Hibernian[1] believe, that he was corresponding, not with the *Aunt*, but with the *Niece*: for, though not over rich, I found he had too much pride and delicacy to sacrifice the feelings of a gentleman to the necessities of his fortune. [*Exit.*

ACT II.

SCENE I.

Captain Absolute*'s Lodgings.*

Captain Absolute *and* Fag.

FAG.
Sir, while I was there, Sir Anthony came in: I told him, you had sent me to inquire after his health, and to know if he was at leisure to see you.

Capt. ABSOLUTE.
And what did he say, on hearing I was at Bath?

FAG.
Sir, in my life I never saw an elderly gentleman more astonished! He started back two or three paces, rapt out a dozen interjectoral oaths, and asked, what the devil had brought you here!

Capt. ABSOLUTE.
Well, Sir, and what did you say?

---

1 A "paduasoy" is a dress made of corded or embossed silk. "Pocket-pieces" are coins carried as good-luck charms. A "Hibernian" is an Irishman.

FAG.

O, I lied, Sir—I forgot the precise lie, but you may depend on't; he got no truth from me. Yet, with submission, for fear of blunders in future, I should be glad to fix what *has* brought us to Bath: in order that we may lie a little consistently.—Sir Anthony's servants were curious, Sir, very curious indeed.

Capt. ABSOLUTE.

You have said nothing to them————?

FAG.

O, not a word, Sir—not a word.—Mr. Thomas, indeed, the coachman (whom I take to be the discreetest of whips)—

Capt. ABSOLUTE.

S'death![1]—you rascal! you have not trusted him!

FAG.

O, *no*, Sir—no—no—not a syllable, upon my veracity!—He was, indeed, a little inquisitive; but I was sly, Sir—devilish sly!—My Master (said I) honest Thomas (you know, Sir, one says *honest* to one's inferiors) is come to Bath to *recruit*—Yes, Sir—I said, *to recruit*—and whether for men, money, or constitution, you know, Sir, is nothing to him, nor any one else.

Capt. ABSOLUTE.

Well—*recruit* will do—let it be so—

FAG.

O, Sir, recruit will do surprisingly—indeed, to give the thing an air, I told Thomas, that your Honour had already inlisted, five disbanded chairmen, seven minority waiters, and thirteen billiard markers.[2]

---

1 A mild oath (a contraction of "By God's Death!").

2 "Chairmen" are the men who carry sedan chairs. If they are "disbanded," then they've been dismissed (for insolence? for weakness?), and so are as dubious candidates to become soldiers as the underage food servers and billiards scorekeepers whom Fag also invents. A former waiter and billiard marker, Robert Mackreth, was, somewhat scandalously, made a Member of Parliament in October 1774 (as an aristocrat's way of paying off his gambling debts), and so this line may have had some topical resonance for its initial audiences.

Capt. ABSOLUTE.
You blockhead, never say more than is necessary.

FAG.
I beg pardon, Sir—I beg pardon—But with submission, a lie is
nothing unless one supports it.—Sir, whenever I draw on my
invention for a good current lie, I always forge *indorsements*, as
well as the bill.[1]

Capt. ABSOLUTE.
Well, take care you don't hurt your credit, by offering too much
security.—Is Mr. Faulkland returned?

FAG.
He is above, Sir, changing his dress.

Capt. ABSOLUTE.
Can you tell whether he has been informed of Sir Anthony's
and Miss Melville's arrival?

FAG.
I fancy not, Sir; he has seen no one since he came in, but his
gentleman, who was with him at Bristol.—I think, Sir, I hear
Mr. Faulkland coming down—

Capt. ABSOLUTE.
Go, tell him, I am here.

FAG.
Yes, Sir—*(going)* I beg pardon, Sir, but should Sir Anthony call,
you will do me the favour to remember, that we are *recruiting*, if
you please.

Capt. ABSOLUTE.
Well, well.

FAG.
And in tenderness to my character, if your Honour could bring

---

1 The writer of a bill of exchange—a precursor to a modern check—was
called its "drawer." A bill was not payable, or transferable as "current"
to a third party, until its original payee "endorsed" it (wrote his signa-
ture on the back as a guarantee of its value).

in the chairmen and waiters, I shall esteem it as an obligation;—for though I never scruple a lie to serve my Master, yet it
hurts one's conscience, to be found out. [*Exit.*

Capt. ABSOLUTE.
Now for my whimsical friend—if he does not know that his
mistress is here, I'll tease him a little before I tell him———

Enter Faulkland.

Faulkland, you're welcome to Bath again; you are punctual in
your return.

FAULKLAND.
Yes; I had nothing to detain me, when I had finished the business I went on. Well, what news since I left you? How stand
matters between you and Lydia?

Capt. ABSOLUTE.
Faith, much as they were; I have not seen her since our quarrel,
however I expect to be recalled every hour.

FAULKLAND.
Why don't you persuade her to go off with you at once?

Capt. ABSOLUTE.
What, and lose two thirds of her fortune? You forget that my
friend.—No, no, I could have brought her to that long ago.

FAULKLAND.
Nay then, you trifle too long—if you are sure of *her*, propose to
the aunt *in your own character*, and write to Sir Anthony for his
consent.

Capt. ABSOLUTE.
Softly, softly, for though I am convinced my little Lydia would
elope with me as Ensign Beverley, yet am I by no means
certain that she would take me with the impediment of our
friends' consent, a regular humdrum wedding, and the reversion of a good fortune on my side;[1] no, no, I must prepare her

---

1 Having the "reversion" of a fortune means being next in line to inherit
  it.

gradually for the discovery, and make myself necessary to her, before I risk it.——Well, but Faulkland, you'll dine with us to-day at the Hotel?

FAULKLAND.
Indeed I cannot: I am not in spirits to be of such a party.

Capt. ABSOLUTE.
By Heavens! I shall forswear your company. You are the most teasing, captious, incorrigible lover!—Do love like a man.

FAULKLAND.
I own I am unfit for company.

Capt. ABSOLUTE.
Am not *I* a lover; aye, and a romantic one too? Yet do I carry every where with me such a confounded farago[1] of doubts, fears, hopes, wishes, and all the flimsy furniture of a country Miss's brain!

FAULKLAND.
Ah! Jack, your heart and soul are not, like mine, fixed immutably on one only object.—You throw for a large stake, but losing—you could stake, and throw again:—but I have set my sum of happiness on this cast, and not to succeed, were to be stript of all.

Capt. ABSOLUTE.
But for Heaven's sake! what grounds for apprehension can your whimsical brain conjure up at present? Has Julia miss'd writing this last post? or was her last too tender, or too cool; or too grave, or too gay; or——

FAULKLAND.
Nay, nay, Jack.

Capt. ABSOLUTE.
Why, her love—her honour—her prudence, you cannot doubt.

---

1 "Romantic" here means fantastic or extravagant (i.e., behaving as if he were a character in one of the novels which Lydia reads). A "farrago" is a confused mixture of things.

FAULKLAND.

O! upon my soul, I never have;—but what grounds for apprehension did you say? Heavens! are there not a thousand! I fear for her spirits—her health—her life.—My absence may fret her; her anxiety for my return, her fears for me, may oppress her gentle temper. And for her health—does not every hour bring me cause to be alarmed? If it rains, some shower may even then have chilled her delicate frame!—If the wind be keen, some rude blast may have affected her! The heat of noon, the dews of the evening, may endanger the life of her, for whom only I value mine. O! Jack, when delicate and feeling souls are separated, there is not a feature in the sky, not a movement of the elements; not an aspiration of the breeze, but hints some cause for a lover's apprehension!

Capt. ABSOLUTE.

Aye, but we may choose whether we will take the hint or no.—Well then, Faulkland, if you were convinced that Julia was well and in spirits, you would be entirely content.

FAULKLAND.

I should be happy beyond measure—I'm anxious only for that.

Capt. ABSOLUTE.

Then to cure your anxiety at once—Miss Melville is in perfect health, and is at this moment in Bath.

FAULKLAND.

Nay Jack—don't trifle with me.

Capt. ABSOLUTE.

She is arrived here with my father within this hour.

FAULKLAND.

Can you be serious?

Capt. ABSOLUTE.

I thought you knew Sir Anthony better than to be surprised at a sudden whim of this kind.—Seriously then, it is as I tell you—upon my honour.

FAULKLAND.

My dear friend!——Hollo, Du-Peigne! my hat—my dear Jack—*now nothing on earth can give me a moment's uneasiness.*

Enter Fag.

FAG.
Sir, Mr. Acres just arrived is below.

Capt. ABSOLUTE.
Stay, Faulkland, this Acres lives within a mile of Sir Anthony,
and he shall tell you how your mistress has been ever since you
left her.—Fag, shew the gentleman up. [*Exit* Fag.

FAULKLAND.
What, is he much acquainted in the family?

Capt. ABSOLUTE.
O, very intimate: I insist on your not going: besides, his character will divert you.

FAULKLAND.
Well, I should like to ask him a few questions.

Capt. ABSOLUTE.
He is likewise a rival of mine—that is of my *other self*'s, for he
does not think his friend Captain Absolute ever saw the lady in
question;—and it is ridiculous enough to hear him complain to
me of *one Beverley* a concealed sculking rival, who——

FAULKLAND.
Hush!—He's here.

Enter Acres.

ACRES.
Hah! my dear friend, noble captain, and honest Jack, how do'st
thou? just arrived faith, as you see.—Sir, your humble servant.
Warm work on the roads Jack—Odds, whips and wheels, I've
travelled like a Comet, with a tail of dust all the way as long as
the Mall.[1]

---

1 "The Mall" was a fashionable walk along the edge of St. James's Park in
   London. It ran a scant two-thirds of a mile.

Capt. ABSOLUTE.
Ah! Bob, you are indeed an excentric Planet,[1] but we know your attraction hither—give me leave to introduce Mr. Faulkland to you; Mr. Faulkland, Mr. Acres.

ACRES.
Sir, I am most heartily glad to see you: Sir, I solicit your connections.—Hey Jack—what this is Mr. Faulkland, who———

Capt. ABSOLUTE.
Aye, Bob, Miss Melville's Mr. Faulkland.

ACRES.
Od'so! she and your father can be but just arrived before me—I suppose you have seen them.——Ah! Mr. Faulkland, you are indeed a happy man.

FAULKLAND.
I have not seen Miss Melville yet, Sir—I hope she enjoyed full health and spirits in Devonshire.

ACRES.
Never knew her better in my life, Sir,—never better.—Odd's Blushes and Blooms! she has been as healthy as the German Spa.[2]

FAULKLAND.
Indeed!—I did hear that she had been a little indisposed.

ACRES.
False, false, Sir—only said to vex you: quite the reverse I assure you.

FAULKLAND.
There, Jack, you see she has the advantage of me; I had almost fretted myself ill.

---

1 An "eccentric planet" is one whose orbit is not circular (which presumably suggests something about Acres's "attraction" to Lydia).
2 The town of Spa (in present-day Belgium) was a popular hot springs resort.

Capt. ABSOLUTE.

Now are you angry with your mistress for not having been sick.

FAULKLAND.

No, no, you misunderstand me:—yet surely a little trifling indisposition is not an unnatural consequence of absence from those we love.—Now confess—isn't there something unkind in this violent, robust, unfeeling health?

Capt. ABSOLUTE.

O, it was very unkind of her to be well in your absence to be sure!

ACRES.

Good apartments, Jack.

FAULKLAND.

Well Sir, but you were saying that Miss Melville has been so *exceedingly* well—what then she has been merry and gay I suppose?—Always in spirits—hey?

ACRES.

Merry, Odds Crickets! she has been the bell and spirit of the company wherever she has been—so lively and entertaining! so full of wit and humour!

FAULKLAND.

There, Jack, there.—O, by my soul! there is an innate levity in woman, that nothing can overcome.—What! happy and I away!

Capt. ABSOLUTE.

Have done: how foolish this is! just now you were only apprehensive for your mistress's *spirits*.

FAULKLAND.

Why Jack, have I been the joy and spirit of the company?

Capt. ABSOLUTE.

No indeed, you have not.

FAULKLAND.

Have I been lively and entertaining?

Capt. ABSOLUTE.
O, upon my word, I acquit you.

FAULKLAND.
Have I been full of wit and humour?

Capt. ABSOLUTE.
No, faith, to do you justice, you have been confounded stupid indeed.

ACRES.
What's the matter with the gentleman?

Capt. ABSOLUTE.
He is only expressing his great satisfaction at hearing that Julia has been so well and happy—that's all—hey, Faulkland?

FAULKLAND.
Oh! I am rejoiced to hear it—yes, yes, she has a *happy* disposition!

ACRES.
That she has indeed—then she is so accomplished—so sweet a voice—so expert at her Harpsichord—such a mistress of flat and sharp, squallante, rumblante, and quiverante!—there was this time month—Odds Minnums and Crotchets! how she did chirup[1] at Mrs. Piano's Concert.

FAULKLAND.
There again, what say you to this? you see she has been all mirth and song—not a thought of me!

Capt. ABSOLUTE.
Pho! man, is not music the food of love?[2]

---

1 "Squallante, rumblante, and quiverante" are all made-up musical terms. "This time month" means "this time a month ago." A "minum" is a half-note. A "crotchet" is a quarter-note. To "chirup" is to chirp.

2 Cf. the opening line of Shakespeare's *Twelfth Night*: "If music be the food of love, play on" (I.i.1).

FAULKLAND.
Well, well, it may be so.—Pray Mr.——what's his d—d name?—
Do you remember what Songs Miss Melville sung?

ACRES.
Not I, indeed.

Capt. ABSOLUTE.
Stay now, they were some pretty, melancholy, purling stream
airs, I warrant; perhaps you may recollect:—did she sing—"*When
absent from my soul's delight?*"

ACRES.
No, that wa'n't it.

Capt. ABSOLUTE.
Or—"*Go, gentle Gales!*——*Go, gentle Gales!*" (sings.)

ACRES.
O no! nothing like it.—Odds slips? now I recollect one of
them—"*My heart's my own, my will is free.*" (sings)[1]

FAULKLAND.
Fool! fool that I am! to fix all my happiness on such a trifler!
S'death! to make herself the pipe and ballad-monger of a circle!
to sooth her light heart with catches and glees!—What can you
say to this, Sir?

Capt. ABSOLUTE.
Why, that I should be glad to hear my mistress had been so
merry, *Sir.*

FAULKLAND.
Nay, nay, nay—I am not sorry that she has been happy—no, no,
I am glad of that—I would not have had her sad or sick—yet
surely a sympathetic heart would have shewn itself even in the
choice of a song—she might have been temperately healthy, and
somehow, plaintively gay;—but she has been dancing too, I
doubt not!

---

1   The songs that Captain Absolute suggests are both plaintive laments
    that the singer is separated from her beloved. The song that Julia actu-
    ally sang is far jauntier and insists upon the singer's independence.

ACRES.
What does the gentleman say about dancing?

Capt. ABSOLUTE.
He says the lady we speak of dances as well as she sings.

ACRES.
Aye truly, does she—there was at our last race-ball———[1]

FAULKLAND.
Hell and the devil! There! there!—I told you so! I told you so!
Oh! she thrives in my absence!—Dancing!—but her whole feelings have been in opposition with mine!—I have been anxious,
silent, pensive, sedentary—my days have been hours of care, my
nights of watchfulness.—She has been all Health! Spirit! Laugh!
Song! Dance!—Oh! d—n'd, d—n'd levity!

Capt. ABSOLUTE.
For Heaven's sake! Faulkland, don't expose yourself so.—
Suppose she has danced, what then?—does not the ceremony of
society often oblige——

FAULKLAND.
Well, well, I'll contain myself—perhaps, as you say—for form
sake.—What, Mr. Acres, you were praising Miss Melville's
manner of dancing a *minuet*—hey?

ACRES.
O I dare insure her for that—but what I was going to speak of
was her *country dancing*:—Odds swimmings! she has such an air
with her!—[2]

---

1 A "race ball" is a ball held around the time of a major horse race (which
   would attract gentry from the surrounding area).

2 The "minuet" is an elegant dance for just two partners, done while all
   the other ball guests watch. "Country dances" are more vigorous and
   involve a large group of dancers, who frequently change partners, and
   touch—i.e., "palm"—one another's hands. A "cotillion" is, as Faulkland
   suggests, more energetic and likely to involve bodily contact than a
   minuet, yet more restrained than a country dance. Mary Bulkley, the
   original actress playing Julia, was known both for her dancing and her
   "amorous" activities (see Appendix A).

FAULKLAND.
Now disappointment on her!—defend this, Absolute, why don't
you defend this?—Country-dances! jiggs, and reels! am I to
blame now? A Minuet I could have forgiven—I should not have
minded that—I say I should not have regarded a Minuet—but
Country-dances! Z——ds! had she made one in a *Cotillon*—I
believe I could have forgiven even that—but to be monkey-led
for a night!—to run the gauntlet thro' a string of amorous
palming puppies!—to shew paces like a managed filly!—O Jack,
there never can be but *one* man in the world, whom a truly
modest and delicate woman ought to pair with in a *Country-
dance*; and even then, the rest of the couples should be her great
uncles and aunts!

Capt. ABSOLUTE.
Aye, to be sure!—grand-fathers and grand-mothers!

FAULKLAND.
If there be but one vicious mind in the Set, 'twill spread like a
contagion—the action of their pulse beats to the lascivious
movement of the jigg—their quivering, warm-breath'd sighs
impregnate the very air—the atmosphere becomes electrical to
love, and each amorous spark darts thro' every link of the
chain!—I must leave you—I own I am somewhat flurried—and
that confounded looby[1] has perceived it. [*Going.*

Capt. ABSOLUTE.
Aye, aye, you are in a hurry to throw yourself at Julia's feet.

FAULKLAND.
I'm not in a humour to be trifled with—I shall see her only to
upbraid her. [*Going.*

Capt. ABSOLUTE.
Nay, but stay Faulkland, and thank Mr. Acres for his good
news.

FAULKLAND.
D—n his news! [*Exit* Faulkland.

---

1 An awkward stupid person (generally a country bumpkin).

Capt. ABSOLUTE.
Ha! ha! ha! poor Faulkland five minutes since—"nothing on earth could give him a moment's uneasiness!"

ACRES.
The gentleman wa'n't angry at my praising his mistress, was he?

Capt. ABSOLUTE.
A little jealous, I believe, Bob.

ACRES.
You don't say so? Ha! ha! jealous of me—that's a good joke.

Capt. ABSOLUTE.
There's nothing strange in that, Bob: let me tell you, that sprightly grace and insinuating manner of yours will do some mischief among the girls here.

ACRES.
Ah! you joke—ha! ha! mischief—ha! ha! but you know I am not my own property, my dear Lydia, has forestalled me.——She could never abide me in the country, because I used to dress so badly—but odds frogs and tambours! I shan't take matters so here—now ancient Madam has no voice in it—I'll make my old clothes know who's master—I shall straitway cashier the hunting-frock—and render my leather breeches incapable—My hair has been in training some time.[1]

Capt. ABSOLUTE.
Indeed!

ACRES.
Aye—and tho'ff the side-curls are a little restive, my hind-part takes to it very kindly.

---

1 A "frog" is an ornamental loop and button on a military-style coat. A "tambour" is here something embroidered. "Ancient Madam" is presumably Acres's mother. To "cashier" something is to get rid of it (it's primarily a military term for getting rid of unwanted soldiers). To render something "incapable" is to make it unable to serve. In performance, Acres's hair seems to have been rolled up in curl papers in order to emphasize how awkward his attempts at foppery were.

Capt. ABSOLUTE.
O, you'll polish, I doubt not.

ACRES.
Absolutely I propose so—then if I can find out this Ensign Beverley, odds triggers and flints! I'll make him know the difference o't.

Capt. ABSOLUTE.
Spoke like a man——but pray, Bob, I observe you have got an odd kind of a new method of swearing——

ACRES.
Ha! ha! you've taken notice of it—'tis genteel, isn't *it?*—I didn't invent it myself though; but a commander in our militia—a great scholar, I assure you—says that there is no meaning in the common oaths, and that nothing but their antiquity makes them respectable;—because, he says, the ancients would never stick to an oath or two, but would say By Jove! or by Bacchus! or by Mars! or by Venus! or by Pallas! according to the sentiment—so that to swear with propriety, says my little Major, the "oath should be an echo to the sense"; and this we call the *oath referential*, or *sentimental*[1] *swearing*—ha! ha! ha! 'tis genteel, isn't it?

Capt. ABSOLUTE.
Very genteel, and very new indeed—and I dare say will supplant all other figures of imprecation.

ACRES.
Aye, aye, the best terms will grow obsolete——D—ns have had their day.

Enter Fag.

FAG.
Sir, there is a gentleman below, desires to see you—shall I shew him into the parlour?

---

1 Alexander Pope's *An Essay on Criticism* (London, 1711) argued that, in verse, "'Tis not enough no Harshness gives Offence, / The *Sound* must seem an *Eccho* to the *Sense*" (22). "Sentimental" here simply means epigrammatic or sententious, rather than anything involving an appeal to emotion.

Capt. ABSOLUTE.
Aye—you may.

ACRES.
Well, I must be gone———

Capt. ABSOLUTE.
Stay; who is it, Fag?

FAG.
Your father, Sir.

Capt. ABSOLUTE.
You puppy, why didn't you shew him up directly? [*Exit* Fag.

ACRES.
You have business with Sir Anthony.—I expect a message from
Mrs. Malaprop at my lodgings—I have sent also to my dear
friend Sir Lucius O'Trigger.—Adieu, Jack, we must meet at
night—Odds bottles and glasses! you shall give me a dozen
bumpers[1] to little Lydia.

Capt. ABSOLUTE.
That I will with all my heart. [*Exit* Acres.

Capt. ABSOLUTE.
Now for a parental lecture—I hope he has heard nothing of the
business that has brought me here.—I wish the gout had held
him fast in Devonshire, with all my soul!

Enter Sir Anthony.

Capt. ABSOLUTE.
Sir, I am delighted to see you here; and looking so well!—your
sudden arrival at Bath made me apprehensive for your health.

Sir ANTHONY.
Very apprehensive, I dare say, Jack.—What, you are recruiting
here, hey?

---

1 Full glasses of wine drunk in a single gulp as a toast.

Capt. ABSOLUTE.
Yes, Sir, I am on duty.

Sir ANTHONY.
Well, Jack, I am glad to see you, tho' I did not expect it, for I
was going to write to you on a little matter of business.—Jack, I
have been considering that I grow old and infirm, and shall
probably not trouble you long.

Capt. ABSOLUTE.
Pardon me, Sir, I never saw you look more strong and hearty;
and I pray frequently that you may continue so.

Sir ANTHONY.
I hope your prayers may be heard with all my heart. Well then,
Jack, I have been considering that I am so strong and hearty,
I may continue to plague you a long time.—Now, Jack, I am
sensible that the income of your commission, and what I have
hitherto allowed you, is but a small pittance for a lad of your
spirit.

Capt. ABSOLUTE.
Sir, you are very good.

Sir ANTHONY.
And it is my wish, while yet I live, to have my Boy make some
figure in the world.—I have resolved, therefore, to fix you at
once in a noble independence.

Capt. ABSOLUTE.
Sir, your kindness overpowers me—such generosity makes the
gratitude of reason more lively than the sensations even of filial
affection.

Sir ANTHONY.
I am glad you are so sensible of my attention—and you shall be
master of a large estate in a few weeks.

Capt. ABSOLUTE.
Let my future life, Sir, speak my gratitude: I cannot express the
sense I have of your munificence.——Yet, Sir, I presume you
would not wish me to quit the army?

Sir ANTHONY.
O, that shall be as your wife chooses.

Capt. ABSOLUTE.
My wife, Sir!

Sir ANTHONY.
Aye, aye, settle that between you—settle that between you.

Capt. ABSOLUTE.
A *wife*, Sir, did you say?

Sir ANTHONY.
Aye, a wife—why; did not I mention her before?

Capt. ABSOLUTE.
Not a word of it, Sir.

Sir ANTHONY.
Odd so!—I mustn't forget *her* tho'.—Yes, Jack, the independence I was talking of is by a marriage—the fortune is saddled
with a wife—but I suppose that makes no difference.

Capt. ABSOLUTE.
Sir! Sir!—you amaze me!

Sir ANTHONY.
Why, what the d——l's the matter with the fool? Just now you
were all gratitude and duty.

Capt. ABSOLUTE.
I was, Sir,—you talked to me of independence and a fortune,
but not a word of a wife.

Sir ANTHONY.
Why—what difference does that make? Odd's life, Sir! if you
have the estate, you must take it with the live stock on it, as it
stands.

Capt. ABSOLUTE.
If my happiness is to be the price, I must beg leave to decline
the purchase.——Pray, Sir, who is the lady?

Sir ANTHONY.
What's that to you, Sir?—Come, give me your promise to love,
and to marry her directly.

Capt. ABSOLUTE.
Sure, Sir, this is not very reasonable, to summon my affections
for a lady I know nothing of!

Sir ANTHONY.
I am sure, Sir, 'tis more unreasonable in you to *object* to a lady
you know nothing of.

Capt. ABSOLUTE.
Then, Sir, I must tell you plainly, that my inclinations are fix'd
on another.

Sir ANTHONY.
They are, are they? well, that's lucky—because you will have
more merit in your obedience to me.

Capt. ABSOLUTE.
Sir, my heart is engaged to an Angel.

Sir ANTHONY.
Then pray let it send an excuse.——It is very sorry—but *business* prevents its waiting on her.

Capt. ABSOLUTE.
But my vows are pledged to her.

Sir ANTHONY.
Let her foreclose, Jack; let her foreclose; they are not worth
redeeming: besides, you have the Angel's vows in exchange, I
suppose; so there can be no loss there.[1]

Capt. ABSOLUTE.
You must excuse me, Sir, if I tell you, once for all, that in this
point I cannot obey you.

---

1 A "pledge" is something pawned or otherwise given as security for a
   debt. If one could pay back the debt, the pledge would be "redeemed."
   Otherwise, the lender could "foreclose" and seize it.

Sir ANTHONY.
Hark'ee Jack;—I have heard you for some time with patience—I
have been cool,—quite cool;—but take care—you know I am
compliance itself—when I am not thwarted;—no one more
easily led—when I have my own way;—but don't put me in a
phrenzy.

Capt. ABSOLUTE.
Sir, I must repeat it—in this I cannot obey you.

Sir ANTHONY.
Now, d—n me! if ever I call you *Jack* again while I live!

Capt. ABSOLUTE.
Nay, Sir, but hear me.

Sir ANTHONY.
Sir, I won't hear a word—not a word! not one word! so give me
your promise by a nod—and I'll tell you what, Jack—I mean,
you Dog—if you don't, by———

Capt. ABSOLUTE.
What, Sir, promise to link myself to some mass of ugliness!
to———

Sir ANTHONY.
Z———ds! sirrah! the lady shall be as ugly as I choose: she
shall have a hump on each shoulder; she shall be as crooked as
the Crescent; her one eye shall roll like the Bull's in Coxe's
musæum—she shall have a skin like a mummy, and the beard of
a Jew[1]—she shall be all this, sirrah!—yet I'll make you ogle her
all day, and sit up all night to write sonnets on her beauty.

Capt. ABSOLUTE.
This is reason and moderation indeed!

Sir ANTHONY.
None of your sneering, puppy! no grinning, jackanapes!

---

1   "The Crescent" was a new real estate development in Bath (see the
    map in Figure 15, p. 298). James Cox exhibited automata in both Bath
    and London. Eighteenth-century Englishmen were generally clean-
    shaven, which made (the typically bearded) Jews stand out all the more.

Capt. ABSOLUTE.
Indeed, Sir, I never was in a worse humour for mirth in my
life.

Sir ANTHONY.
'Tis false, Sir! I know you are laughing in your sleeve: I know
you'll grin when I am gone, sirrah!

Capt. ABSOLUTE.
Sir, I hope I know my duty better.

Sir ANTHONY.
None of your passion, Sir! none of your violence! if you
please.—It won't do with me, I promise you.

Capt. ABSOLUTE.
Indeed, Sir, I never was cooler in my life.

Sir ANTHONY.
'Tis a confounded lie!—I know you are in a passion in your
heart; I know you are, you hypocritical young dog! but it won't
do.

Capt. ABSOLUTE.
Nay, Sir, upon my word.

Sir ANTHONY.
So you will fly out! can't you be cool, like me? What the devil
good can *Passion* do!—*Passion* is of no service, you impudent,
insolent, over-bearing Reprobate!—There you sneer again!—
don't provoke me!—but you rely upon the mildness of my
temper—you do, you Dog! you play upon the meekness of my
disposition! Yet take care—the patience of a saint may be overcome at last!—but mark! I give you six hours and a half to
consider of this: if you then agree, without any condition, to
do every thing on earth that I choose, why—confound you! I
may in time forgive you——If not, z——ds! don't enter the
same hemisphere with me! don't dare to breathe the same air,
or use the same light with me; but get an atmosphere and sun
of your own! I'll strip you of your commission; I'll lodge a
five-and-three-pence in the hands of trustees, and you shall
live on the interest.—I'll disown you, I'll disinherit you, I'll

unget you! and—d—n me, if ever I call you Jack again![1] [*Exit Sir* Anthony.

Captain Absolute, *solus.*

Capt. ABSOLUTE.
Mild, gentle, considerate father—I kiss your hands.—What a tender method of giving his opinion in these matters Sir Anthony has! I dare not trust him with the truth.—I wonder what old, wealthy Hag it is that he wants to bestow on me!—yet he married himself for love! and was in his youth a bold Intriguer, and a gay[2] Companion!

Enter Fag.

FAG.
Assuredly, Sir, our Father is wrath to a degree; he comes down stairs eight or ten steps at a time—muttering, growling, and thumping the bannisters all the way: I, and the Cook's dog, stand bowing at the door—rap! he gives me a stroke on the head with his cane; bids me carry that to my master, then kicking the poor Turnspit into the area,[3] d—ns us all, for a puppy triumvirate!——Upon my credit, Sir, were I in your place, and found my father such very bad company, I should certainly drop his acquaintance.

Capt. ABSOLUTE.
Cease your impertinence, Sir, at present.—Did you come in for

---

1 Leaving the income from a ridiculously small amount of capital to one's heir was a way to effectively disinherit that person without opening up one's estate to legal challenge (leaving nothing could sometimes be taken as a sign of forgetfulness, rather than deliberate exclusion). In a similar scene in William Congreve's *Love for Love* (London, 1695), Sir Sampson Legend berates his son, "Did not I beget you? And might not I have chosen whether I would have begot you or no?" (25). Sir Anthony seems to want to go even further and reverse time itself.

2 "Gay" here means wild or hedonistic. The word doesn't acquire its associations with homosexuality until the twentieth century.

3 A "turnspit" is a dog who turns a roasting spit by running on a treadmill. The "area," in this context, is a small sunken courtyard by the basement door.

nothing more?——Stand out of the way! [*Pushes him aside, and Exit.*

Fag, solus.

FAG.
Soh! Sir Anthony trims my Master; He is afraid to reply to his Father—then vents his spleen on poor Fag!——When one is vexed by one person, to revenge one's self on another, who happens to come in the way—is the vilest injustice! Ah! it shews the worst temper—the basest——

Enter Errand-Boy.

BOY.
Mr. Fag! Mr. Fag! your Master calls you.

FAG.
Well, you little, dirty puppy, you need not baul so!——The meanest disposition! the——

BOY.
Quick, quick, Mr. Fag.

FAG.
Quick, quick, you impudent Jackanapes! am I to be commanded by you too? you little, impertinent, insolent, kitchen-bred—— [*Exit, kicking and beating him.*

SCENE II.

The North Parade.[1]

Enter Lucy.

LUCY.
So—I shall have another Rival to add to my mistress's list— Captain Absolute.——However, I shall not enter his name till

---

1 For the North and South Parades (both popular places to promenade), see the map in Figure 15 (p. 298) and the etching in Figure 16 (p. 319). After the first performance of the play in Bath in March 1775, Mary Linley wrote to her sister that "there was a new scene of the N. Parade

my purse has received notice in form. Poor Acres is dismissed!—Well, I have done him a last friendly office, in letting him know that Beverley was here before him.—Sir Lucius is generally more punctual, when he expects to hear from his *dear Dalia*, as he calls her:—I wonder he's not here!—I have a little scruple of conscience from this deceit; tho' I should not be paid so well, if my hero knew that *Delia* was near fifty, and her own mistress.—I could not have thought he would have been so nice, when there's a golden egg in the case, as to care whether he has it from a pullet[1] or an old hen!

Enter Sir Lucius O'Trigger.

Sir LUCIUS.
Hah! my little embassadress—upon my conscience I have been looking for you; I have been on the South Parade this half-hour.

LUCY. (*Speaking simply*)
O gemini! and I have been waiting for your worship here on the North.

Sir LUCIUS.
Faith!—may be, that was the reason we did not meet; and it is very comical too, how you could go out and I not see you—for I was only taking a nap at the Parade-Coffee-house, and I chose the *window* on purpose that I might not miss you.

LUCY.
My stars! Now I'd wager a six-pence I went by while you were asleep.

Sir LUCIUS.
Sure enough it must have been so——and I never dreamt it was so late, till I waked. Well, but my little girl, have you got nothing for me?

... and a most delightful one it is, I assure you. Every body says, ... that yours in town is not so good" (quoted in Thomas Moore, *Memoirs of the Life of the Right Honourable Richard Brinsley Sheridan* [London, 1825], 103). The Theatre Royal in Bath was on Orchard Street, about 400 feet from the North Parade.

1 A young hen.

LUCY.
Yes, but I have:——I've got a letter for you in my pocket.

Sir LUCIUS.
O faith! I guessed you weren't come empty-handed—well—let me see what the dear creature says.

LUCY.
There, Sir Lucius. *(Gives him a letter.)*

Sir LUCIUS. (Reads)
"Sir—there is often a sudden incentive impulse in love, that has a greater induction than years of domestic combination: such was the commotion I felt at the first superfluous view of Sir Lucius O'Trigger." Very pretty, upon my word. *"As my motive is interested, you may be assured my love shall never be miscellaneous."* Very well. *"Female punctuation forbids me to say more; yet let me add, that it will give me joy infallible to find Sir Lucius worthy the last criterion of my affections.——Yours, while meretricious.——* DELIA.*"*
Upon my conscience! Lucy, your lady is a great mistress of language.—Faith, she's quite the queen of the dictionary!—for the devil a word dare refuse coming at her call—tho' one would think it was quite out of hearing.

LUCY.
Aye, Sir, a lady of her experience.

Sir LUCIUS.
Experience! what, at seventeen?

LUCY.
O true, Sir—but then she reads so——my stars! how she will read off-hand!

Sir LUCIUS.
Faith, she must be very deep read to write this way—tho' she is rather an arbitrary writer too—for here are a great many poor words pressed into the service of this note, that would get their *habeas corpus* from any court in Christendom.[1]——However,

---

1 To be "pressed into" service was, effectively, to be kidnapped and forcibly enlisted in the military. A writ of *habeas corpus* [Latin for "you shall have the body"] was the only way in which to get someone who

when affection guides the pen, Lucy, he must be a brute who finds fault with the style.

LUCY.
Ah! Sir Lucius, if you were to hear how she talks of you!

Sir LUCIUS.
O tell her, I'll make her the best husband in the world, and Lady O'Trigger into the bargain!—But we must get the old gentlewoman's consent—and do every thing fairly.

LUCY.
Nay, Sir Lucius, I thought you wa'n't rich enough to be so nice![1]

Sir LUCIUS.
Upon my word, young woman, you have hit it:—I am so poor that I can't afford to do a dirty action.—If I did not want money I'd steal your mistress and her fortune with a great deal of pleasure.—However, my pretty girl, *(gives her money)* here's a little something to buy you a ribband; and meet me in the evening, and I'll give you an answer to this. So, hussy, take a kiss before-hand, to put you in mind. *(Kisses her.)*

LUCY.
O lud! Sir Lucius——I never seed such a gemman! My lady won't like you if you're so impudent.

Sir LUCIUS.
Faith she will, Lucy—that same——pho! what's the name of it?——*Modesty!*——is a quality in a lover more praised by the women than liked; so, if your mistress asks you whether Sir Lucius ever gave you a kiss, tell her *fifty*—my dear.

LUCY.
What, would you have me tell her a lie?

---

had been "pressed" released. It required the person who was restricting the liberty of the subject of the writ (e.g., a jailor or the captain of a ship full of "pressed" sailors) to produce him in court, so that the legality of his detention could be investigated.

1 "Nice" here (and elsewhere in the play) means scrupulous, perhaps to the point of being fastidious or over-refined.

Sir LUCIUS.
Ah then, you baggage! I'll make it a truth presently.

LUCY.
For shame now; here is some one coming.

Sir LUCIUS.
O faith, I'll quiet your conscience! [*Sees* Fag.—*Exit, humming a Tune.*

Enter Fag.

FAG.
So, so, Ma'am. I humbly beg pardon.

LUCY.
O lud!—now, Mr. Fag—you flurry one so.

FAG.
Come, come, Lucy, here's no one bye—so a little less simplicity, with a grain or two more sincerity, if you please.——You play false with us, Madam.——I saw you give the Baronet a letter. ——My Master shall know this—and if he don't call him out[1]— I will.

LUCY.
Ha! ha! ha! you gentlemen's gentlemen are so hasty.——That letter was from Mrs. Malaprop, simpleton.——She is taken with Sir Lucius's address.[2]

FAG.
What tastes some people have!——Why I suppose I have walked by her window an hundred times.——But what says our young lady? Any message to my master?

LUCY.
Sad news! Mr. Fag.—A worse Rival than Acres!—Sir Anthony Absolute has proposed his son.

---

1 To "call someone out" is to challenge him to a duel.
2 "Address" here means appearance or general bearing.

FAG.
What, Captain Absolute?

LUCY.
Even so.—I overheard it all.

FAG.
Ha! ha! ha!—very good, faith.—Goodbye, Lucy, I must away
with this news.

LUCY.
Well—you may laugh—but it is true, I assure you. *(Going.)*
But—Mr. Fag—tell your master not to be cast down by this.

FAG.
O he'll be so disconsolate!

LUCY.
And charge him not to think of quarrelling with young Absolute.

FAG.
Never fear!—never fear!

LUCY.
Be sure—bid him keep up his spirits.

FAG.
We will—we will. [*Exeunt severally.*

ACT III.

SCENE I.

The North Parade.

Enter Captain Absolute.

Capt. ABSOLUTE.
'Tis just as Fag told me, indeed.—Whimsical enough, faith! My
Father wants to *force* me to marry the very girl I am plotting to
run away with!——He must not know of my connection with

her yet a-while.——He has too summary a method of proceeding in these matters—and Lydia shall not yet lose her hopes of
an elopement.——However, I'll read my recantation instantly.
——My conversion is something sudden indeed—but I can
assure him it is very *sincere*.——So, so—here he comes.—He
looks plaguy gruff. [*Steps aside.*

Enter Sir Anthony.

Sir ANTHONY.
No—I'll die sooner than forgive him.—*Die*, did I say? I'll live
these fifty years to plague him.——At our last meeting, his
impudence had almost put me out of temper.—An obstinate,
passionate, self-willed boy!—Who can he take after? This is my
return for getting him before all his brothers and sisters!—for
putting him, at twelve years old, into a marching regiment, and
allowing him fifty pounds a-year, beside his pay ever since!—
But I have done with him;—he's any body's son for me.——I
never will see him more,—never—never—never—never.[1]

Capt. ABSOLUTE.
Now for a penitential face.

Sir ANTHONY.
Fellow, get out of my way.

Capt. ABSOLUTE.
Sir, you see a penitent before you.

Sir ANTHONY.
I see an impudent scoundrel before me.

Capt. ABSOLUTE.
A sincere penitent.——I am come, Sir, to acknowledge my
error, and to submit entirely to your will.

Sir ANTHONY.
What's that?

---

1 Cf. King Lear's exclamation at the death of Cordelia: "Thou'lt come no
   more. / Never, never, never, never, never" (V.iii.283 in the Folio text).

Capt. ABSOLUTE.
I have been revolving, and reflecting, and considering on your
past goodness, and kindness, and condescension[1] to me.

Sir ANTHONY.
Well, Sir?

Capt. ABSOLUTE.
I have been likewise weighing and balancing what you were
pleased to mention concerning duty, and obedience, and
authority.

Sir ANTHONY.
Well, Puppy?

Capt. ABSOLUTE.
Why then, Sir, the result of my reflections is—a resolution to
sacrifice every inclination of my own to your satisfaction.

Sir ANTHONY.
Why now, you talk sense—absolute sense—I never heard any
thing more sensible in my life.——Confound you; you shall be
Jack again.

Capt. ABSOLUTE.
I am happy in the appellation.

Sir ANTHONY.
Why, then, Jack, my dear Jack, I will now inform you—who the
lady really is.——Nothing but your passion and violence, you
silly fellow, prevented my telling you at first. Prepare, Jack, for
wonder and rapture—prepare.——What think you of Miss
Lydia Languish?

Capt. ABSOLUTE.
Languish! What, the Languishes of Worcestershire?

Sir ANTHONY.
Worcestershire! No. Did you never meet Mrs. Malaprop and

---

1 In the eighteenth century, "condescension" meant a social superior's
  voluntarily coming down to the level of his inferior as an act of courtesy
  in order to put him at ease.

her Niece, Miss Languish, who came into our country[1] just before you were last ordered to your regiment?

Capt. ABSOLUTE.
Malaprop! Languish! I don't remember ever to have heard the names before. Yet, stay—I think I do recollect something.—— *Languish! Languish!* She squints, don't she?——A little, red-haired girl?[2]

Sir ANTHONY.
Squints?——A red-haired girl!——Z——ds, no.

Capt. ABSOLUTE.
Then I must have forgot; it can't be the same person.

Sir ANTHONY.
Jack! Jack! what think you of blooming, love-breathing seventeen?

Capt. ABSOLUTE.
As to that, Sir, I am quite indifferent.—If I can please you in the matter, 'tis all I desire.

Sir ANTHONY.
Nay, but Jack, such eyes! such eyes! so innocently wild! so bashfully irresolute! Not a glance but speaks and kindles some thought of love! Then, Jack, her cheeks! her cheeks, Jack! so deeply blushing at the insinuations of her tell-tale eyes! Then, Jack, her lips!—O Jack, lips smiling at their own discretion; and if not smiling, more sweetly pouting; more lovely in sullenness!

Capt. ABSOLUTE.
That's she indeed.—Well done, old gentleman![3]

Sir ANTHONY.
Then, Jack, her neck.[4]——O Jack! Jack!

---

1 "Country" here means area or neighborhood.
2 Red hair was often regarded as ugly in eighteenth-century England.
3 Presumably this entire line is an aside, though none of the printed texts of the play mark it as such.
4 Lydia's "neck" here presumably extends, as it often did in eighteenth-century usage, all the way down to her cleavage.

Capt. ABSOLUTE.

And which is to be mine, Sir, the Niece or the Aunt?

Sir ANTHONY.

Why, you unfeeling, insensible Puppy, I despise you. When I was of your age, such a description would have made me fly like a rocket! The *Aunt*, indeed!—Odds life! when I ran away with your mother, I would not have touched anything old or ugly to gain an empire.

Capt. ABSOLUTE.

Not to please your father, Sir?

Sir ANTHONY.

To please my father!——Z——ds! not to please———O my father!——Oddso!——yes—yes! if my father indeed had desired——that's quite another matter.——Tho' he wa'n't the indulgent father that I am, Jack.

Capt. ABSOLUTE.

I dare say not, Sir.

Sir ANTHONY.

But, Jack, you are not sorry to find your mistress is so beautiful.

Capt. ABSOLUTE.

Sir, I repeat it; if I please you in this affair, 'tis all I desire. Not that I think a woman the worse for being handsome; but, Sir, if you please to recollect, you before hinted something about a hump or two, one eye, and a few more graces of that kind— now, without being very nice, I own I should rather chuse a wife of mine to have the usual number of limbs, and a limited quantity of back: and tho' *one* eye may be very agreeable, yet as the prejudice has always run in favour of *two*, I would not wish to affect a singularity in that article.

Sir ANTHONY.

What a phlegmatic sot it is! Why, sirrah, you're an anchorite! ——a vile insensible stock.—You a soldier!—you're a walking block, fit only to dust the company's regimentals on![1]——Odds life! I've a great mind to marry the girl myself!

---

1   A "phlegmatic sot" is a fool who is not easily excited. An "anchorite" is a hermit. A "stock" is here a stump or other large chunk of wood (such as a roughly human-shaped "block" on which a uniform could be draped for dusting).

Capt. ABSOLUTE.

I am entirely at your disposal, Sir; if you should think of
addressing Miss Languish yourself, I suppose you would have
me marry the *Aunt*; or if you should change your mind, and
take the old lady—'tis the same to me—I'll marry the *Niece*.

Sir ANTHONY.

Upon my word, Jack, thou'rt either a very great hypocrite, or
————but, come, I know your indifference on such a subject
must be all a lie—I'm sure it must—come, now—d—n your
demure face!——come, confess, Jack—you have been lying—
ha'n't you? You have been lying, hey? I'll never forgive you, if
you ha'n't:—so now, own, my dear Jack, you have been playing
the hypocrite, hey!—I'll never forgive you, if you ha'n't been
lying and playing the hypocrite.

Capt. ABSOLUTE.

I'm sorry, Sir, that the respect and duty which I bear to you
should be so mistaken.

Sir ANTHONY.

Hang your respect and duty! But, come along with me, I'll
write a note to Mrs. Malaprop, and you shall visit the lady
directly.

Capt. ABSOLUTE.

Where does she lodge, Sir?

Sir ANTHONY.

What a dull question!—only on the Grove[1] here.

Capt. ABSOLUTE.

O! then I can call on her in my way to the coffee-house.

Sir ANTHONY.

In your way to the coffee-house! You'll set your heart down in
your way to the coffee-house, hey? Ah! you leaden-nerv'd,
wooden-hearted dolt! But come along, you shall see her

---

1 For the Orange Grove (another popular place to promenade), see the
 map in Figure 15, p. 298.

directly; her eyes shall be the Promethian torch[1] to you—come along, I'll never forgive you, if you don't come back, stark mad with rapture and impatience—if you don't, egad, I'll marry the girl myself! [*Exeunt.*

SCENE II.

Julia's *Dressing-room.*

Faulkland, *solus.*

FAULKLAND.
They told me Julia would return directly; I wonder she is not yet come!—How mean does this captious, unsatisfied temper of mine appear to my cooler judgment! Yet I know not that I indulge it in any other point:—but on this one subject, and to this one object, whom I think I love beyond my life, I am ever ungenerously fretful, and madly capricious!—I am conscious of it—yet I cannot correct myself! What tender, honest joy sparkled in her eyes when we met!—How delicate was the warmth of her expressions!——I was ashamed to appear less happy—though I had come resolved to wear a face of coolness and upbraiding. Sir Anthony's presence prevented my proposed expostulations:—yet I must be satisfied that she has not been so *very* happy in my absence.—She is coming!—Yes!—I know the nimbleness of her tread, when she thinks her impatient Faulkland counts the moments of her stay.

Enter Julia.

JULIA.
I had not hop'd to see you again so soon.

FAULKLAND.
Could I, Julia, be contented with my first welcome—restrained as we were by the presence of a third person?

---

1 In Greek mythology, Prometheus stole fire from the gods and gave it to mankind, thereby kindling civilization (and presumably for the purposes of this metaphor, love and all the other things which set us apart from "leaden-nerv'd" brutes).

JULIA.

O Faulkland, when your kindness can make me thus happy, let me not think that I discovered more coolness in your first salutation than my long-hoarded joy could have presaged.[1]

FAULKLAND.

'Twas but your fancy, Julia.—I *was* rejoiced to see you—to see you in such health—Sure I had no cause for coldness?

JULIA.

Nay then, I see you have taken something ill.—You must not conceal from me what it is.

FAULKLAND.

Well then—shall I own to you—but you will despise me, Julia—nay, I despise myself for it.——Yet I *will* own, that my joy at hearing of your health and arrival here, by your neighbour Acres, was something damped, by his dwelling much on the high spirits you had enjoyed in Devonshire—on your mirth—your singing—dancing, and I know not what!—For such is my temper, Julia, that I should regard every mirthful moment in your absence as a treason to constancy:—The mutual tear that steals down the cheek of parting lovers is a compact, that no smile shall live there till they meet again.

JULIA.

Must I never cease to tax my Faulkland with this teasing minute caprice?—Can the idle reports of a silly boor[2] weigh in your breast against my tried affection?

FAULKLAND.

They have no weight with me, Julia: no, no—I am happy if you have been so—yet only say, that you did not sing with *mirth*—say that you *thought* of Faulkland in the dance.

JULIA.

I never can be happy in your absence.——If I wear a countenance of content, it is to shew that my mind holds no doubt of my Faulkland's truth.——If I seem'd sad—it were to make malice triumph; and say, that I had fixed my heart on one, who

---

1 To "presage" something is to predict it, especially on the basis of omens.
2 A country bumpkin.

left me to lament his roving, and my own credulity.——Believe me, Faulkland, I mean not to upbraid you, when I say, that I have often dressed sorrow in smiles, lest my friends should guess whose unkindness had caused my tears.

FAULKLAND.
You were ever all goodness to me.—O, I am a brute, when I but admit a doubt of your true constancy!

JULIA.
If ever, without such cause from you, as I will not suppose possible, you find my affections veering but a point, may I become a proverbial scoff[1] for levity, and base ingratitude.

FAULKLAND.
Ah! Julia, that *last* word is grating to me. I would I had no title to your *gratitude*! Search your heart, Julia; perhaps what you have mistaken for Love, is but the warm effusion of a too thankful heart!

JULIA.
For what quality must I love you?

FAULKLAND.
For no quality! To regard me for any quality of mind or understanding, were only to *esteem* me. And for person—I have often wish'd myself deformed, to be convinced that I owed no obligation *there* for any part of your affection.

JULIA.
Where Nature has bestowed a shew of nice attention in the features of a man, he should laugh at it, as misplaced. I have seen men, who in *this* vain article perhaps might rank above you; but my heart has never asked my eyes if it were so or not.

FAULKLAND.
Now this is not well from *you*, Julia—I despise person in a man——Yet if you lov'd me as I wish, though I were an Æthiop, you'd think none so fair.

---

1 An object of contempt.

JULIA.
I see you are determined to be unkind.—The *contract* which my
poor father bound us in gives you more than a lover's privilege.

FAULKLAND.
Again, Julia, you raise ideas that feed and justify my doubts.
——I would not have been more free—no—I am proud of my
restraint.——Yet—yet—perhaps your high respect alone for this
solemn compact has fettered your inclinations, which else had
made a worthier choice.—How shall I be sure, had you
remained unbound in thought and promise, that I should still
have been the object of your persevering love?

JULIA.
Then try me now.—Let us be free as strangers as to what is
past:—*my* heart will not feel more liberty!

FAULKLAND.
There now! so hasty, Julia! so anxious to be free!—If your love
for me were fixed and ardent, you would not loose your hold,
even tho' I wish'd it!

JULIA.
O, you torture me to the heart!—I cannot bear it.

FAULKLAND.
I do not mean to distress you.—If I lov'd you less, I should
never give you an uneasy moment.—But hear me.—All my
fretful doubts arise from this—Women are not used to weigh,
and separate the motives of their affections:—the cold dictates
of prudence, gratitude, or filial duty, may sometimes be mistaken for the pleadings of the heart.——I would not boast—yet
let me say, that I have neither age, person, or character, to
found dislike on;—my fortune such as few ladies could be
charged with *indiscretion* in the match.—O Julia! when *Love*
receives such countenance from *Prudence*, nice minds will be
suspicious of its *birth*.

JULIA.
I know not whither your insinuations would tend:—as they
seem pressing to insult me—I will spare you the regret of
having done so.—I have given you no cause for this! [*Exit in
Tears.*

FAULKLAND.
In Tears! stay, Julia: stay but for a moment.————The door is fastened!—Julia!—my soul—but for one moment:—I hear her sobbing!—'Sdeath! what a brute am I to use her thus! Yet stay.—Aye—she is coming now:—how little resolution there is in woman!—how a few soft words can turn them!————No, faith!—she is *not* coming either.————Why, Julia—my love—say but that you forgive me—come but to tell me that—now, this is being *too* resentful:—stay! she *is* coming too—I thought she would—no *steadiness* in any thing! her going away must have been a mere trick then—she sha'n't see that I was hurt by it.— I'll affect indifference——*(hums a tune: then listens)*————No— Z—ds! she's *not* coming!—nor don't intend it, I suppose.—This is not *steadiness*, but *obstinacy*! Yet I deserve it.—What, after so long an absence, to quarrel with her tenderness!—'twas bar- barous and unmanly!——I should be ashamed to see her now.—I'll wait till her just resentment is abated—and when I distress her so again, may I lose her for ever! and be linked instead to some antique virago, whose knawing passions, and long-hoarded spleen, shall make me curse my folly half the day, and all the night! [*Exit.*

SCENE III.

Mrs. Malaprop's *Lodgings.*

Mrs. Malaprop, *and Captain* Absolute.

Mrs. MALAPROP.
Your being Sir Anthony's son, Captain, would itself be a suffi- cient accommodation;—but from the ingenuity of your appear- ance, I am convinced you deserve the character here given of you.

Capt. ABSOLUTE.
Permit me to say, Madam, that as I never yet have had the pleasure of seeing Miss Languish, my principal inducement in this affair at present, is the honour of being allied to Mrs. Mala- prop; of whose intellectual accomplishments, elegant manners, and unaffected learning, no tongue is silent.

Mrs. MALAPROP.
Sir, you do me infinite honour!—I beg, Captain, you'll be

seated.—*(Sit)*—Ah! few gentlemen, now a days, know how to value the ineffectual qualities in a woman! few think how a little knowledge becomes a gentlewoman! Men have no sense now but for the worthless flower, beauty!

Capt. ABSOLUTE.
It is but too true indeed, Ma'am;—yet I fear our ladies should share the blame—they think our admiration of *beauty* so great, that *knowledge* in *them* would be superfluous. Thus, like garden-trees, they seldom shew fruits, till time has robb'd them of the more specious blossom.—Few, like Mrs. Malaprop and the Orange-tree, are rich in both at once!

Mrs. MALAPROP.
Sir—you overpower me with good-breeding.—He is the very Pine-apple of politeness![1] You are not ignorant, Captain, that this giddy girl has somehow contrived to fix her affections on a beggarly, strolling, eve's-dropping Ensign, whom none of us have seen, and nobody knows any thing of.

Capt. ABSOLUTE.
O, I have heard the silly affair before.—I'm not at all prejudiced against her on *that* account.

Mrs. MALAPROP.
You are very good, and very considerate, Captain.—I am sure I have done every thing in my power since I exploded the affair! long ago I laid my positive conjunctions on her never to think on the fellow again;—I have since laid Sir Anthony's preposition before her;—but I'm sorry to say she seems resolved to decline every particle that I enjoin her.

Capt. ABSOLUTE.
It must be very distressing indeed, Ma'am.

Mrs. MALAPROP.
It gives me the hydrostatics[2] to such a degree!—I thought she had persisted from corresponding with him; but behold this

---

1 This phrase is, presumably, an aside, though it is not marked as such in any of the printed texts of the play.
2 The study of the pressure of liquids not in motion.

very day, I have interceded another letter from the fellow! I believe I have it in my pocket.

Capt. ABSOLUTE.
O the devil! my last note. [*Aside.*

Mrs. MALAPROP.
Aye, here it is.

Capt. ABSOLUTE.
Aye, my note indeed! O the little traitress Lucy. [*Aside.*

Mrs. MALAPROP.
There, perhaps you may know the writing. [*Gives him the letter.*

Capt. ABSOLUTE.
I think I have seen the hand before—yes, I *certainly must* have seen this hand before:——

Mrs. MALAPROP.
Nay, but read it, Captain.

Capt. ABSOLUTE. *(Reads)*
"*My soul's idol, my ador'd Lydia!*"—Very tender indeed!

Mrs. MALAPROP.
Tender! aye, and prophane too, o' my conscience!

Capt. ABSOLUTE.
"*I am excessively alarmed at the intelligence you send me, the more so as my new rival*"——

Mrs. MALAPROP.
That's *you*, Sir.

Capt. ABSOLUTE.
"*has universally the character of being an accomplished gentle-man, and a man of honour.*"——Well, that's handsome enough.

Mrs. MALAPROP.
O, the fellow had some design in writing so——

Capt. ABSOLUTE.
That he had, I'll answer for him, Ma'am.

Mrs. MALAPROP.
But go on, Sir—you'll see presently.

Capt. ABSOLUTE.
"*As for the old weather-beaten she-dragon who guards you,*"—Who
can he mean by that?

Mrs. MALAPROP.
Me, Sir—*me*—he means *me* there—what do you think now?—
but go on a little further.

Capt. ABSOLUTE.
Impudent scoundrel!—"*it shall go hard but I will elude her vigilance, as I am told that the same ridiculous vanity, which makes her
dress up her coarse features, and deck her dull chat with hard words
which she don't understand*"———

Mrs. MALAPROP.
There, Sir! an attack upon my language! what do you think of
that?—an aspersion upon my parts of speech! was ever such a
brute! Sure if I reprehend any thing in this world, it is the use of
my oracular tongue, and a nice derangement of epitaphs!

Capt. ABSOLUTE.
He deserves to be hang'd and quartered! let me see—"*same
ridiculous vanity*"——

Mrs. MALAPROP.
You need not read it again, Sir.

Capt. ABSOLUTE.
I beg pardon, Ma'am "*does also lay her open to the grossest decep-
tions from flattery and pretended admiration*"—an impudent
coxcomb! "*so that I have a scheme to see you shortly with the old
Harridan's consent, and even to make her a go between in our interviews.*"——Was ever such assurance.

Mrs. MALAPROP.
Did you ever hear any thing like it?—he'll elude my vigilance,

will he?—yes, yes! ha! ha! he's very likely to enter these doors!—
we'll try who can plot best!

Capt. ABSOLUTE.
Ha! ha! ha! a conceited puppy, ha! ha! ha!——Well, but Mrs.
Malaprop, as the girl seems so infatuated by this fellow, suppose
you were to wink at her corresponding with him for a little time—
let her even plot an elopement with him—then do you connive at
her escape—while *I*, just in the nick, will have the fellow laid by
the heels,[1] and fairly contrive to carry her off in his stead.

Mrs. MALAPROP.
I am delighted with the scheme, never was any thing better per-
petrated!

Capt. ABSOLUTE.
But, pray, could not I see the lady for a few minutes now?—I
should like to try her temper a little.

Mrs. MALAPROP.
Why, I don't know——I doubt she is not prepared for a first
visit of this kind.——There is a decorum in these matters.

Capt. ABSOLUTE.
O Lord! she won't mind *me*—only tell her Beverley——

Mrs. MALAPROP.
Sir!——

Capt. ABSOLUTE.
Gently, good tongue. [*Aside.*

Mrs. MALAPROP.
What did you say of Beverley?

Capt. ABSOLUTE.
O, I was going to propose that you should tell her, by way of
jest, that it was Beverley who was below—she'd come down fast
enough then—ha! ha! ha!

---

1 To be "laid by the heels" is to be arrested or otherwise removed from
action.

Mrs. MALAPROP.
'Twould be a trick she well-deserves—besides you know the
fellow tells her he'll get my consent to see her—ha! ha!—Let
him if he can, I say again.—Lydia, come down here! [*Calling.*
—He'll make me a *go-between in their interviews!*—ha! ha! ha!
Come down, I say, Lydia!—I don't wonder at your laughing, ha!
ha! ha! his impudence is truly ridiculous.

Capt. ABSOLUTE.
'Tis very ridiculous, upon my soul, Ma'am, ha! ha! ha!

Mrs. MALAPROP.
The little hussy won't hear.—Well, I'll go and tell her at once
who it is—she shall know that Captain Absolute is come to wait
on her.—And I'll make her behave as becomes a young woman.

Capt. ABSOLUTE.
As you please, Ma'am.

Mrs. MALAPROP.
For the present, Captain, your servant—Ah! you've not done
laughing yet, I see—*elude my vigilance!* yes, yes, ha! ha! ha! [*Exit.*

Capt. ABSOLUTE.
Ha! ha! ha! one would think now that I might throw off all dis-
guise at once, and seize my prize with security—but such is
Lydia's caprice, that to undeceive were probably to lose her.—
I'll see whether she knows me. [*Walks aside, and seems engaged in
looking at the pictures.*

Enter Lydia.

LYDIA.
What a scene am I now to go thro'! surely nothing can be more
dreadful than to be obliged to listen to the loathsome addresses
of a stranger to one's heart.—I have heard of girls persecuted as
I am, who have appealed in behalf of their favoured lover to the
generosity of his rival: suppose I were to try it—there stands the
hated rival—an officer too!—but O how unlike my Beverley!—I
wonder he don't begin—truly he seems a very negligent
wooer!—quite at his ease, upon my word! I'll speak first—Mr.
Absolute.

Capt. ABSOLUTE.
Madam. [*Turns round.*

LYDIA.
O Heav'ns! Beverley!

Capt. ABSOLUTE.
Hush!—hush, my life!—softly! be not surprised!

LYDIA.
I am so astonished! and so terrified! and so overjoy'd!—for
Heav'n's sake! how came you here?

Capt. ABSOLUTE.
Briefly—I have deceived your Aunt—I was informed that my
new rival was to visit here this evening, and contriving to have
him kept away, have passed myself on *her* for Captain Absolute.

LYDIA.
O, charming!—And she really takes you for young Absolute?

Capt. ABSOLUTE.
O, she's convinced of it.

LYDIA.
Ha! ha! ha! I can't forbear laughing to think how her sagacity is
over-reached!

Capt. ABSOLUTE.
But we trifle with our precious moments—such another opportunity may not occur—then let me now conjure my kind, my
condescending angel, to fix the time when I may rescue her
from undeserved persecution, and with a licensed warmth[1]
plead for my reward.

LYDIA.
Will you then, Beverley, consent to forfeit that portion of my
paltry wealth?—that burthen[2] on the wings of love?

---

1 "A licensed warmth" would be one within wedlock.
2 An alternate spelling of "burden."

Capt. ABSOLUTE.

O come to me—rich only thus—in loveliness—Bring no portion
to me but thy love—'twill be generous in you, Lydia—for well
you know, it is the only dower your poor Beverley can repay.

LYDIA.

How persuasive are his words!——how charming will poverty
be with him!

Capt. ABSOLUTE.

Ah! my soul, what a life will we then live? Love shall be our idol
and support! we will worship him with a monastic strictness;
abjuring all worldly toys, to center every thought and action
there.—Proud of calamity, we will enjoy the wreck of wealth;
while the surrounding gloom of adversity shall make the flame
of our pure love show doubly bright.—By Heav'ns! I would
fling all goods of fortune from me with a prodigal hand to enjoy
the scene where I might clasp my Lydia to my bosom, and say,
the world affords no smile to me—but here—— [*Embracing her.*
If she holds out now the devil is in it! [*Aside.*

LYDIA.

Now could I fly with him to the Antipodes! but my persecution
is not yet come to a crisis.[1]

       Enter Mrs. Malaprop, *listening.*

Mrs. MALAPROP.

I'm impatient to know how the little huzzy[2] deports herself.
[*Aside.*

Capt. ABSOLUTE.

So pensive, Lydia!—is then your warmth abated?

Mrs. MALAPROP.

Warmth abated!—so!—she has been in a passion, I suppose.

---

1 The "Antipodes" are the other side of the earth. A "crisis" is here a peak
   or turning point.
2 In the eighteenth century, "hussy" could simply mean "bold, impudent
   girl" (i.e., it didn't have to have the sexual connotations it now pos-
   sesses).

LYDIA.
No—nor ever can while I have life.

Mrs. MALAPROP.
An ill-temper'd little devil!—She'll be *in a passion all her life*—will she?

LYDIA.
Think not the idle threats of my ridiculous aunt can ever have any weight with me.

Mrs. MALAPROP.
Very dutiful, upon my word!

LYDIA.
Let her choice be *Captain Absolute*, but Beverley is mine.

Mrs. MALAPROP.
I am astonished at her assurance!—*to his face—this to his face!*

Capt. ABSOLUTE.
Thus then let me enforce my suit. [*Kneeling.*

Mrs. MALAPROP.
Aye—poor young man!—down on his knees entreating for pity!—I can contain no longer.——Why, huzzy! huzzy!—I have overheard you.

Capt. ABSOLUTE.
O confound her vigilance! [*Aside.*

Mrs. MALAPROP.
Captain Absolute—I know not how to apologize for her shocking rudeness.

Capt. ABSOLUTE.
So—all's safe, I find. [*Aside.*
I have hopes, Madam, that time will bring the young lady———

Mrs. MALAPROP.
O, there's nothing to be hoped for from her! she's as headstrong as an allegory on the banks of Nile.

LYDIA.
Nay, Madam, what do you charge me with now?

Mrs. MALAPROP.
Why, thou unblushing rebel—didn't you tell this gentleman to
his face that you loved another better?—didn't you say you
never would be his?

LYDIA.
No, Madam—I did not.

Mrs. MALAPROP.
Good Heav'ns! what assurance!—Lydia, Lydia, you ought to
know that lying don't become a young woman!—Didn't you
boast that Beverley—that stroller[1] Beverley, possessed your
heart?—Tell me that, I say.

LYDIA.
'Tis true, Ma'am, and none but Beverley—

Mrs. MALAPROP.
Hold;—hold Assurance!—you shall not be so rude.

Capt. ABSOLUTE.
Nay, pray Mrs. Malaprop, don't stop the young lady's speech:—
she's very welcome to talk thus—it does not hurt *me* in the
least, I assure you.

Mrs. MALAPROP.
You are *too* good, Captain—*too* amiably patient—but come with
me, Miss—let us see you again soon, Captain—remember what
we have fixed.

Capt. ABSOLUTE.
I shall, Ma'am.

Mrs. MALAPROP.
Come, take a graceful leave of the gentleman.

LYDIA.
May every blessing wait on my Beverley, my lov'd Bev———

---

1 A vagabond.

Mrs. MALAPROP.
Huzzy! I'll choak the word in your throat!—come along—come along. [*Exeunt severally. Captain* Absolute *kissing his hand to* Lydia—*Mrs.* Malaprop *stopping her from speaking.*

SCENE IV.

Acres's lodgings.

Acres *and* David.

Acres *as just dress'd.*

ACRES.
Indeed, David—do you think I become it so?

DAVID.
You are quite another creature, believe me Master, by the Mass! an' we've any luck we shall see the Devon monkeyrony[1] in all the print-shops in Bath!

ACRES.
Dress *does* make a difference, David.

DAVID.
'Tis all in all, I think—difference! why, an' you were to go now to Clod-Hall, I am certain the old lady wouldn't know you: Master Butler wouldn't believe his own eyes, and Mrs. Pickle would cry, "Lard presarve me!" our dairy-maid would come giggling to the door, and I warrant Dolly Tester, your Honour's favourite, would blush like my waistcoat.—Oons! I'll hold a gallon, there an't a dog in the house but would bark, and I question whether *Phillis* would wag a hair of her tail![2]

---

1 Engraved caricatures of various celebrities and social types, including the "macaroni" (extravagantly dressed young men—so called because they had been to Italy or "aped" Italian fashions), were routinely sold or rented at print shops. Acres is presumably now "just dress'd" like a foppish macaroni, rather than the country bumpkin with his "hair ... in training" of Act Two, Scene One.
2 Presumably "the old lady" is Acres's mother, and Mrs. Pickle is his cook. A "tester" is both a canopy over a bed and a sixpence, (*continued*)

ACRES.
Aye, David, there's nothing like *polishing*.

DAVID.
So I says of your Honour's boots; but the boy never heeds me!

ACRES.
But, David, has Mr. De-la-Grace been here? I must rub up my balancing, and chasing, and boring.[1]

DAVID.
I'll call again, Sir.

ACRES.
Do—and see if there are any letters for me at the post-office.

DAVID.
I will.——By the Mass, I can't help looking at your head!—if I hadn't been by at the cooking, I wish I may die if I should have known the dish again myself! [*Exit.* Acres *comes forward, practising a dancing step.*

ACRES.
Sink, slide—coupee—Confound the first inventors of cotillons! say I—they are as bad as algebra to us country gentlemen—I can walk a Minuet easy enough when I'm forced!—and I have been accounted a good stick in a Country-dance.—Odd's jigs and tabors!--I never valued your cross-over two couple—figure in—right and left—and I'd foot it with e'er a captain in the county!—but these outlandish heathen Allemandes and Cotillons are quite beyond me!—I shall never prosper at 'em, that's sure—mine are true-born English legs—they don't understand

---

which may suggest that Acres has been paying his "favourite" chambermaid for her company. "Oons!" is a variant of "Zounds!" David would seem to be wearing a scarlet waistcoat, if Dolly can "blush like" it. "I'll hold a gallon" means "I'll wager a gallon" (perhaps of ale?). Phillis is apparently Acres's pet (since she is implicitly opposed to the dogs kept for hunting).

1 *De la Grâce* is French for "of grace" (a good name for a dancing master). Acres is mispronouncing various French terms for dance steps: *balancé* (swaying from one foot to the other), *chassé* (gliding along with one foot behind the other), and *bourrée* (stepping sideways with one foot crossing behind the other).

their curst French lingo!—their *Pas* this, and *Pas* that, and *Pas* t'other!—d—n me, my feet don't like to be called Paws! no, 'tis certain I have most Antigallican[1] Toes!

Enter Servant.

SERVANT.
Here is Sir Lucius O'Trigger to wait on you, Sir.

ACRES.
Shew him in.

Enter Sir Lucius.

Sir LUCIUS.
Mr. Acres, I am delighted to embrace you.

ACRES.
My dear Sir Lucius, I kiss your hands.

Sir LUCIUS.
Pray, my friend, what has brought you so suddenly to Bath?

ACRES.
Faith! I have followed Cupid's Jack-a-Lantern,[2] and find myself in a quagmire at last.—In short, I have been very ill-used, Sir Lucius.—I don't choose to mention names, but look on me as on a very ill-used gentleman.

Sir LUCIUS.
Pray, what is the case?—I ask no names.

---

1   A *coupé* is another dance step (moving one foot diagonally forward or back, while keeping the other stationary; it's often part of a bow). A "tabor" is a drum. An "allemande" is a French dance that involved supposedly German arm movements (*allemande* is French for "German"). *Pas*—French for "step"—is the first word in several phrases related to dancing (e.g., *pas de deux*), but it also means "no" or "not," which, presumably, the dancing master has repeatedly had to say to Acres. To be "anti-Gallican" is to be anti-French (the Anti-Gallican Society, formed around 1745, championed the consumption of English-made goods and denounced all things French).
2   A "Jack-a-lantern" is, in this context, a will-o'-the-wisp (which were often thought to lead travelers into swamps).

ACRES.
Mark me, Sir Lucius, I fall as deep as need be in love with a
young lady——her friends take my part—I follow her to Bath—
send word of my arrival; and receive answer, that the lady is to
be otherwise disposed of.—This, Sir Lucius, I call being ill-
used.

Sir LUCIUS.
Very ill, upon my conscience—Pray, can you divine the cause of
it?

ACRES.
Why, there's the matter: she has another lover, one *Beverley*,
who, I am told, is now in Bath.—Odds slanders and lies! he
must be at the bottom of it.

Sir LUCIUS.
A rival in the case, is there?—and you think he has supplanted
you unfairly.

ACRES.
Unfairly!—to be sure he has.—He never could have done it
fairly.

Sir LUCIUS.
Then sure you know what is to be done!

ACRES.
Not I, upon my soul!

Sir LUCIUS.
We wear no swords[1] here, but you understand me.

ACRES.
What! fight him!

Sir LUCIUS.
Aye, to be sure: what can I mean else?

---

1 The wearing of swords had been forbidden in Bath since the early
   eighteenth century (in an attempt to curtail dueling).

ACRES.
But he has given me no provocation.

Sir LUCIUS.
Now, I think he has given you the greatest provocation in the
world.——Can a man commit a more heinous offence against
another than to fall in love with the same woman? O, by my
soul, it is the most unpardonable breach of friendship!

ACRES.
Breach of *friendship*! Aye, aye; but I have no acquaintance with
this man. I never saw him in my life.

Sir LUCIUS.
That's no argument at all—he has the less right then to take
such a liberty.

ACRES.
'Gad that's true—I grow full of anger, Sir Lucius!—I fire apace!
Odds hilts and blades! I find a man may have a deal of valour in
him, and not know it! But couldn't I contrive to have a little
right of my side?

Sir LUCIUS.
What the d——l signifies *right*, when your *honour* is concerned?
Do you think *Achilles*, or my little *Alexander the Great* ever
inquired where the right lay?[1] No, by my soul, they drew their
broad-swords, and left the lazy sons of peace to settle the justice
of it.

ACRES.
Your words are a grenadier's march to my heart! I believe
courage must be catching!—I certainly do feel a kind of valour
rising as it were———a kind of courage, as I may say———
Odds flints, pans, and triggers! I'll challenge him directly.

Sir LUCIUS.
Ah, my little friend! if we had *Blunderbuss-Hall* here—I could

---

1 Perhaps a theatrical in-joke? Lawrence Clinch, who played Sir Lucius
   for the first season (except on the disastrous opening night), was known
   for his over-the-top performance of Alexander the Great in Nathaniel
   Lee's *The Rival Queens* (1677). "Little" is here a term of endearment.

shew you a range of ancestry, in the O'Trigger line, that would furnish the new room; every one of whom had killed his man! ——For though the mansion-house and dirty acres have slipt through my fingers, I thank God our honour, and the family-pictures, are as fresh as ever.[1]

ACRES.
O Sir Lucius! I have had ancestors too! every man of 'em colonel or captain in the militia!——Odds balls and barrels! say no more—I'm brac'd for it—my nerves are become catgut! my sinews wire! and my heart Pinchbeck! The thunder of your words has soured the milk of human kindness in my breast!—— Z—ds! as the man in the play says, "I could do such deeds!"[2]

Sir LUCIUS.
Come, come, there must be no passion at all in the case—these things should always be done civilly.

ACRES.
I must be in a passion, Sir Lucius——I must be in a rage—— Dear Sir Lucius let me be in a rage, if you love me.——Come, here's pen and paper. (Sits down to write)
I would the ink were red!——Indite, I say, indite!—How shall I begin? Odds bullets and blades! I'll write a good *bold hand*, however.

---

1   A "blunderbuss" is a precursor to the modern shotgun, which may suggest something about how precisely Sir Lucius's family tends to choose their opponents. The "New Room" is presumably the Upper Assembly Rooms in Bath (which opened in 1771 and were often called the "New Rooms"). See the map in Figure 15, p. 298.

2   "Catgut" (dried and twisted animal intestines) was used for violin strings, which can be kept under tension more easily than ordinary nerves. "Pinchbeck" is a copper-zinc alloy which looks like gold (the idea is that Acres has substituted such a compound for his usual heart of gold). Lady Macbeth fears that her husband's nature "is too full o'th' milk of human kindness" to murder their King (I.v.15). "The man in the play" is probably a slightly misremembered King Lear, who threatens his daughters: "I will do such things— / What they are, yet I know not; but they shall be / The terrors of the earth" (II.ii.446-48 in the Folio text).

Sir LUCIUS.
Pray compose yourself.

ACRES.
Come—now shall I begin with an oath? Do, Sir Lucius, let me
begin with a damme.

Sir LUCIUS.
Pho! pho! do the thing *decently* and like a Christian. Begin
now,——"*Sir*"———

ACRES.
That's too civil by half.

Sir LUCIUS.
"*To prevent the confusion that might arise.*"

ACRES.
Well———

Sir LUCIUS.
"*From our both addressing the same lady.*"

ACRES.
Aye—there's the reason—"*same lady*"—Well———

Sir LUCIUS.
"*I shall expect the honour of your company*"———

ACRES.
Z——ds! I'm not asking him to dinner.

Sir LUCIUS.
Pray be easy.

ACRES.
Well then, "*honour of your company*"

Sir LUCIUS.
"*To settle our pretensions.*"

ACRES.
Well.

Sir LUCIUS.
Let me see, aye, *King's Mead-fields*[1] will do.——"*In King's Mead fields.*"

ACRES.
So that's done.——Well, I'll fold it up presently; my own crest—a hand and dagger shall be the seal.

Sir LUCIUS.
You see now this little explanation will put a stop at once to all confusion or misunderstanding that might arise between you.

ACRES.
Aye, we fight to prevent any misunderstanding.

Sir LUCIUS.
Now, I'll leave you to fix your own time.—take my advice, and you'll decide it this evening if you can; then let the worst come of it, 'twill be off your mind to-morrow.

ACRES.
Very true.

Sir LUCIUS.
So I shall see nothing more of you, unless it be by letter, till the evening.——I would do myself the honour to carry your message; but, to tell you a secret, I believe I shall have just such another affair on my own hands. There is a gay captain here, who put a jest on me lately, at the expence of my country, and I only want to fall in with the gentleman, to call him out.

ACRES.
By my valour, I should like to see you fight first! Odds life! I should like to see you kill him, if it was only to get a little lesson.

Sir LUCIUS.
I shall be very proud of instructing you.——Well for the present ——but remember now, when you meet your antagonist, do

---

1 For King's Mead (an undeveloped area at the edge of the city), see the map in Figure 15, p. 298. Most late eighteenth-century duels were fought in such places (which allowed for privacy, but weren't too far from medical attention, should it become necessary).

every thing in a mild and agreeable manner.——Let your
courage be as keen, but at the same time as polished as your
sword. [*Exeunt severally.*

ACT IV.

SCENE I.

Acres's Lodgings.

Acres *and* David.

DAVID.
Then, by the Mass, Sir! I would do no such thing—ne'er a Sir
Lucius O'Trigger in the kingdom should make me fight, when I
wa'n't so minded. Oons! what will the old lady say, when she
hears o't!

ACRES.
Ah! David, if you had heard Sir Lucius!—Odds sparks and
flames! he would have rous'd your valour.

DAVID.
Not he, indeed. I hates such blood-thirsty cormorants. Look'ee,
Master, if you'd wanted a bout at boxing, quarter-staff, or
short-staff, I should never be the man to bid you cry off: But
for your curst sharps and snaps,[1] I never knew any good come
of 'em.

ACRES.
But my *honour*, David, my *honour*! I must be very careful of my
honour.

DAVID.
Aye, by the Mass! and I would be very careful of it; and I think in
return my *honour* couldn't do less than to be very careful of *me*.

---

1 "Cormorants" are notoriously voracious birds (and so a good metaphor
   for any sort of greed). "Quarter-staff" and "short-staff" are types of
   (generally non-lethal) fighting—using long poles and short clubs,
   respectively. "Sharps and snaps" are swords and pistols.

ACRES.
Odds blades! David, no gentleman will ever risk the loss of his
honour!

DAVID.
I say then, it would be but civil in *honour* never to risk the loss
of the *gentleman*.——Lookee, Master, this *honour* seems to me
to be a marvelous false friend; aye, truly, a very courtier-like
servant.——Put the case, I was a gentleman (which, thank God,
no one can say of me); well—my honour makes me quarrel with
another gentleman of my acquaintance.—So—we fight. (Pleasant enough that) Boh!—I kill him—(the more's my luck.) Now,
pray who gets the profit of it?—Why, my *honour*.——But put
the case that he kills me!——by the Mass! I go to the worms,
and my honour whips over to my enemy![1]

ACRES.
No, David—in that case!—Odds crowns and laurels! your
honour follows you to the grave.

DAVID.
Now, that's just the place where I could make a shift to do
without it.

ACRES.
Z——ds, David! you're a coward!—It doesn't become my
valour to listen to you.——What, shall I disgrace my ancestors?—Think of that, David—think what it would be to disgrace
my ancestors!

DAVID.
Under favour, the surest way of not disgracing them, is to keep
as long as you can out of their company. Look'ee now, Master,
to go to them in such haste—with an ounce of lead in your
brains—I should think might as well be let alone. Our ancestors
are very good kind of folks; but they are the last people I should
choose to have a visiting acquaintance with.

---

1 David loosely echoes Falstaff's meditation on the emptiness of honor in
   Shakespeare's *1 Henry IV*, which closes with "Who hath it? He that died
   o'Wednesday? Doth he feel it? No. Doth he hear it? No. 'Tis insensible
   then? Yea, to the dead.... Therefore I'll none of it. Honour is a mere
   scutcheon" (V.i.134-38).

ACRES.
But David, now, you don't think there is such very, very, *very* great danger, hey?——Odds life! people often fight without any mischief done!

DAVID.
By the Mass, I think 'tis ten to one against you!——Oons! here to meet some lion-headed fellow, I warrant, with his d——n'd double-barrell'd swords, and cut and thrust pistols! Lord bless us! it makes me tremble to think o't!——Those be such desperate bloody-minded weapons! Well, I never could abide 'em!— from a child I never could fancy 'em!—I suppose there a'n't so merciless a beast in the world as your loaded pistol![1]

ACRES.
Z——ds! I *won't* be afraid—Odds fire and fury! you shan't make me afraid.——Here is the challenge, and I have sent for my dear friend Jack Absolute to carry it for me.

DAVID.
Aye, i'the name of mischief, let *him* be the messenger.—For my part, I wouldn't lend a hand to it for the best horse in your stable. By the Mass! it don't look like another letter!—It is, as I may say, a designing and malicious-looking letter!—and I warrant smells of gunpowder like a soldier's pouch!—Oons! I wouldn't swear it mayn't go off!

ACRES.
Out, you poltroon!—you ha'n't the valour of a grass-hopper.

DAVID.
Well, I say no more—'twill be sad news, to be sure, at Clod-Hall!—but I ha' done.—How Phyllis will howl when she hears of it!—Aye, poor bitch, she little thinks what shooting her

---

1 The odds against Acres aren't quite as bad as David makes them out to be, although the risk varied considerably, depending on the choice of weapons. Shoemaker has calculated that close to half of the eighteenth-century duels with swords that he studied ended in injury or death, while only a scant third of the duels with pistols produced any casualties—largely because "it was ... considered bad form consciously to aim the pistol, or to practice beforehand," and most pistol duels ended after only one or two exchanges of fire (533).

Master's going after!—And I warrant old Crop,[1] who has carried your honour, field and road, these ten years, will curse the hour he was born. *(Whimpering.)*

ACRES.
It won't do, David—I am determined to fight—so get along, you Coward, while I'm in the mind.

Enter Servant.

SERVANT.
Captain Absolute, Sir.

ACRES.
O! shew him up. [*Exit* Servant.]

DAVID.
Well, Heaven send we be all alive this time to-morrow.

ACRES.
What's that!—Don't provoke me, David!

DAVID.
Good bye, Master. *(Whimpering.)*

ACRES.
Get along, you cowardly, dastardly, croaking raven.[2] [*Exit* David.

Enter Captain Absolute.

Capt. ABSOLUTE.
What's the matter, Bob?

---

1   "Phyllis" (who was also mentioned in Act Three, Scene Four) is apparently Acres's pet dog. "Crop" (named after a short whip used in hunting) is presumably his horse.
2   People given to making gloomy predictions were often called ravens or croakers.

ACRES.
A vile, sheep-hearted blockhead!—If I hadn't the valour of St.
George and the dragon to boot———

Capt. ABSOLUTE.
But what did you want with me, Bob?

ACRES.
O!—There— *(Gives him the challenge.)*

Capt. ABSOLUTE.
"*To Ensign Beverley.*" So—what's going on now! [*Aside.*
Well, what's this?

ACRES.
A challenge!

Capt. ABSOLUTE.
Indeed!——Why, you won't fight him; will you, Bob?

ACRES.
'Egad but I will, Jack.——Sir Lucius has wrought me to it. He
has left me full of rage—and I'll fight this evening, that so much
good passion mayn't be wasted.

Capt. ABSOLUTE.
But what have I to do with this?

ACRES.
Why, as I think you know something of this fellow, I want you
to find him out for me, and give him this mortal *defiance.*

Capt. ABSOLUTE.
Well, give it to me, and trust me he gets it.

ACRES.
Thank you, my dear friend, my dear Jack; but it is giving you a
great deal of trouble.

Capt. ABSOLUTE.
Not in the least—I beg you won't mention it.—No trouble in
the world, I assure you.

ACRES.
You are very kind.——What it is to have a friend!——You couldn't be my second[1]—could you, Jack?

Capt. ABSOLUTE.
Why no, Bob—not in *this* affair—it would not be quite so proper.

ACRES.
Well then I must fix on my friend Sir Lucius. I shall have your good wishes, however, Jack.

Capt. ABSOLUTE.
Whenever he meets you, believe me.

Enter Servant.

SERVANT.
Sir Anthony Absolute is below, inquiring for the Captain.

Capt. ABSOLUTE.
I'll come instantly.——Well, my little hero, success attend you. *(Going.)*

ACRES.
Stay—stay, Jack.——If Beverly should ask you what kind of a man your friend Acres is, do, tell him I am a devil of a fellow—will you, Jack?

Capt. ABSOLUTE.
To be sure I shall.——I'll say you are a determined dog—hey, Bob!

ACRES.
Aye, do, do—and if that frightens him, 'egad perhaps he mayn't come. So tell him I generally kill a man a week; will you, Jack!

---

1 "Seconds" in a duel were friends and supporters of the men who were fighting. Their role was to arrange the details of the fight (e.g., how many paces apart the duelists would stand, if using pistols), to make sure the duel was conducted fairly, and—usually—to try to reconcile the parties as soon as they had each demonstrated their courage.

Capt. ABSOLUTE.
I will, I will; I'll say you are call'd in the country "*Fighting Bob!*"

ACRES.
Right, right—'tis all to prevent mischief; for I don't want to take his life if I clear my honour.

Capt. ABSOLUTE.
No!—that's very kind of you.

ACRES.
Why, you don't wish me to kill him—do you, Jack?

Capt. ABSOLUTE.
No, upon my soul, I do not.—But a devil of a fellow, hey? *(Going.)*

ACRES.
True, true—but stay—stay, Jack—you may add that you never saw me in such a rage before—a most devouring rage!

Capt. ABSOLUTE.
I will, I will.

ACRES.
Remember, Jack——a determined dog!

Capt. ABSOLUTE.
Aye, aye, "*Fighting Bob!*" [*Exeunt severally.*

SCENE II.

Mrs. Malaprop's *Lodgings.*

Mrs. Malaprop *and* Lydia.

Mrs. MALAPROP.
Why, thou perverse one!—tell me what you can object to him?——Isn't he a handsome man?—tell me that.—A genteel man? a pretty figure of a man?

LYDIA.
She little thinks whom she is praising! *(aside)*
—So is Beverley, Ma'am.

Mrs. MALAPROP.
No caparisons,[1] Miss, if you please!—Caparisons don't become
a young woman.—No! Captain Absolute is indeed a fine gentleman!

LYDIA.
Aye, the Captain Absolute *you* have seen. [*Aside.*

Mrs. MALAPROP.
Then he's *so* well bred;—*so* full of alacrity, and adulation!—and
has *so much* to say for himself:—in such good language too!—
His physiognomy so grammatical!—Then his presence is so
noble!—I protest, when I saw him, I thought of what Hamlet
says in the Play:—"Hesperian curls!—the front of *Job* himself!—
an eye, like *March*, to threaten at command!—a Station, like
Harry Mercury, new—" Something about kissing—on a hill—
however, the similitude struck me directly.[2]

LYDIA.
How enraged she'll be presently when she discovers her
mistake! [*Aside.*

Enter Servant.

SERVANT.
Sir Anthony, and Captain Absolute are below Ma'am.

Mrs. MALAPROP.
Shew them up here. [*Exit* Servant.
Now, Lydia, I insist on your behaving as becomes a young
woman.—Shew your good breeding at least, though you have
forgot your duty.

LYDIA.
Madam, I have told you my resolution;—I shall not only give

---

1 Fancy cloths draped over a horse, either for ornament or protection.
2 Cf. Hamlet's description of his murdered father: "See what a grace was
   seated on this brow— / Hyperion's curls, the front of Jove himself, /
   An eye like Mars, to threaten or command, / A station like the herald
   Mercury / New lighted on a heaven-kissing hill; / A combination and a
   form indeed / Where every god did seem to set his seal / To give the
   world assurance of a man" (III.iv.54-61).

him no encouragement, but I won't even speak to, or look at him. [*Flings herself into a chair, with her face from the door.*]

Enter Sir Anthony *and Captain* Absolute.

Sir ANTHONY.
Here we are, Mrs. Malaprop; come to mitigate the frowns of unrelenting beauty—and difficulty enough I had to bring this fellow.—I don't know what's the matter; but if I hadn't held him by force, he'd have given me the slip.

Mrs. MALAPROP.
You have infinite trouble, Sir Anthony, in the affair.—I am ashamed for the cause! Lydia, Lydia, rise I beseech you!—pay your respects! [*Aside to her.*]

Sir ANTHONY.
I hope, Madam, that Miss Languish has reflected on the worth of this gentleman, and the regard due to her Aunt's choice, and *my* alliance.—Now, Jack, speak to her! [*Aside to him.*]

Capt. ABSOLUTE.
What the d—l shall I do!—*(Aside)*—You see, Sir, she won't even look at me, whilst you are here.—I knew she wouldn't!—I told you so—Let me intreat you, Sir, to leave us together! [*Captain* Absolute *seems to expostulate with his Father.*]

LYDIA. *(aside.)*
I wonder I ha'n't heard my Aunt exclaim yet! sure she can't have look'd at him!—perhaps their regimentals are alike, and she is something blind.

Sir ANTHONY.
I say, Sir, I won't stir a foot yet.

Mrs. MALAPROP.
I am sorry to say, Sir Anthony, that my affluence over my Niece is very small.—Turn round Lydia, I blush for you! [*Aside to her.*]

Sir ANTHONY.
May I not flatter myself that Miss Languish will assign what cause of dislike she can have to my son!—Why don't you begin, Jack?—Speak, you puppy—speak [*Aside to him.*]

Mrs. MALAPROP.
It is impossible, Sir Anthony, she can have any.—She will not *say* she has.———Answer, hussy! why don't you answer? [*Aside to her.*

Sir ANTHONY.
Then, Madam, I trust that a childish and hasty predilection will be no bar to Jack's happiness.—Z—ds! sirrah! why don't you speak? [*Aside to him.*

LYDIA. *(aside)*
I think my lover seems as little inclined to conversation as myself.—How strangely blind my Aunt is!

Capt. ABSOLUTE.
Hem! hem!—Madam—hem! *(Captain* Absolute *attempts to speak, then returns to Sir* Anthony*)*—Faith! Sir, I am so confounded!—and so--so--confused!—I told you I should be so, Sir,—I knew it—The-the-tremor of my passion, entirely takes away my presence of mind.

Sir ANTHONY.
But it don't take away your voice, fool, does it?—Go up, and speak to her directly!

[*Captain* Absolute *makes signs to Mrs.* Malaprop *to leave them together.*

Mrs. MALAPROP.
Sir Anthony, shall we leave them together?—Ah! you stubborn, little vixen! [*Aside to her.*

Sir ANTHONY.
Not yet, Ma'am, not yet!—what the d—l are you at? unlock your jaws, sirrah, or— [*Aside to him.*

[*Captain* Absolute *draws near* Lydia.]

Capt. ABSOLUTE.
Now Heav'n send she may be too sullen to look round!—I must disguise my voice—*(Aside)*—
[*Speaks in a low hoarse tone.*
—Will not Miss Languish lend an ear to the mild accents of true love?—Will not———

Sir ANTHONY.
What the d—l ails the fellow?—Why don't you speak out?—not
stand croaking like a frog in a quinsey!¹

Capt. ABSOLUTE.
The–the--excess of my awe, and my--my--my modesty, quite
choak me!

Sir ANTHONY.
Ah! your *modesty* again!—I'll tell you what, Jack; if you don't
speak out directly, and glibly too, I shall be in such a rage!—
Mrs. Malaprop, I wish the lady would favour us with something
more than a side-front!² [*Mrs.* Malaprop *seems to chide* Lydia.

Capt. ABSOLUTE.
So!—all will out I see!³
[*Goes up to* Lydia, *speaks softly.*
Be not surprised, my Lydia, suppress all surprise at present.

LYDIA. *(aside)*
Heav'ns! 'tis Beverley's voice!—Sure he can't have impos'd on
Sir Anthony too!— [*Looks round by degrees, then starts up.*
Is this possible!—my Beverley!—how can this be?—my Bever-
ley?

Capt. ABSOLUTE.
Ah! 'tis all over. [*Aside.*

Sir ANTHONY.
Beverley!—the devil—Beverley!——What can the girl mean?—
This is my son, Jack Absolute!

Mrs. MALAPROP.
For shame, hussy! for shame!—your head runs so on that
fellow, that you have him always in your eyes!—beg Captain
Absolute's pardon directly.

---

1 A swollen throat.
2 A side-view.
3 Presumably this is an aside, though none of the printed texts of the play
   mark it as such.

LYDIA.
I see no Captain Absolute, but my lov'd Beverley!

Sir ANTHONY.
Z—ds! the girl's mad!—her brain's turn'd by reading!

Mrs. MALAPROP.
O' my conscience, I believe so!—what do you mean by Beverley,
hussy?—You saw Captain Absolute before to-day; there he is—
your husband that shall be.

LYDIA.
With all my soul, Ma'am—when I refuse my Beverley———

Sir ANTHONY.
O! she's as mad as Bedlam![1]—or has this fellow been playing us
a rogue's trick!—Come here, sirrah! who the d—l are you?

Capt. ABSOLUTE.
Faith, Sir, I am not quite clear myself; but I'll endeavour to recollect.

Sir ANTHONY.
Are you my son, or not?—answer for your mother, you dog, if
you won't for me.

Mrs. MALAPROP.
Aye, Sir, who are you? O mercy! I begin to suspect!—

Capt. ABSOLUTE.
Ye Powers of Impudence befriend me! *(aside)* Sir Anthony,
most assuredly I am your wife's son; and that I sincerely believe
myself to be *yours* also, I hope my duty has always shewn.—
Mrs. Malaprop, I am your most respectful admirer—and shall
be proud to add *affectionate nephew*.—I need not tell my Lydia,
that she sees her faithful Beverley, who, knowing the singular
generosity of her temper, assum'd that name, and a station,
which has proved a test of the most disinterested love, which he
now hopes to enjoy in a more elevated character.

---

1 "Bedlam" was the popular nickname of Bethlem Hospital, London's
   insane asylum. See the map in Figure 9, p. 58.

LYDIA.
So!—there will be no elopement after all! *(sullenly.)*

Sir ANTHONY.
Upon my soul, Jack, thou art a very impudent fellow! to do you justice, I think I never saw a piece of more consummate assurance!

Capt. ABSOLUTE.
O, you flatter me, Sir—you compliment—'tis my *modesty* you know, Sir—my *modesty* that has stood in my way.

Sir ANTHONY.
Well, I am glad you are not the dull, insensible varlet you pretended to be, however!—I'm glad you have made a fool of your father, you dog—I am.———So this was your *penitence,* your *duty,* and *obedience!*—I thought it was d—n'd sudden!—You *never heard their names before,* not you!—*What, Languishes of Worcestershire,* hey?—*if you could please me in the affair, 'twas all you desired!*—Ah! you dissembling villain!—What! *(pointing to* Lydia*)* she squints, *don't she?—a little red-hair'd girl!*—hey?—Why, you hypocritical young rascal—I wonder you a'n't asham'd to hold up your head!

Capt. ABSOLUTE.
'Tis with difficulty, Sir—I *am* confus'd—very much confus'd, as you must perceive.

Mrs. MALAPROP.
O Lud! Sir Anthony!—a new light breaks in upon me!—hey! how! what! Captain, did *you* write the letters then?—What!—I am to thank *you* for the elegant compilation of "*an old weatherbeaten she-dragon*"—hey?—O mercy!—was it *you* that reflected on my parts of speech?

Capt. ABSOLUTE.
Dear Sir! my modesty will be overpower'd at last, if you don't assist me.—I shall certainly not be able to stand it!

Sir ANTHONY.
Come, come, Mrs. Malaprop, we must forget and forgive;— odds' life![1] matters have taken so clever a turn all of a sudden,

---

1 A mild oath (a contraction of "By God's Life!")

that I could find in my heart, to be so good humour'd! and so gallant!—hey! Mrs. Malaprop!

Mrs. MALAPROP.
Well, Sir Anthony, since *you* desire it, we will not anticipate the past;—so mind young people—our retrospection will now be all to the future.

Sir ANTHONY.
Come, we must leave them together; Mrs. Malaprop, they long to fly into each other's arms, I warrant!—Jack—is'n't the *cheek* as I said, hey?—and the eye, you dog!—and the lip---hey? Come, Mrs. Malaprop, we'll not disturb their tenderness--- theirs is the time of life for happiness!———"*Youth's the season made for joy*"---*(sings)*---hey!---Odds' life! I'm in such spirits,---I don't know what I couldn't do!---Permit me, Ma'am---*(gives his hand to Mrs. Malaprop.) (sings)* Tol-de-rol---'gad I should like a little fooling myself---Tol-de-rol! de-rol! [*Exit singing, and handing*[1] *Mrs. Malaprop.*

(Lydia *sits sullenly in her chair.*)

Capt. ABSOLUTE.
So much thought bodes me no good *(aside)* ---So grave, Lydia!

LYDIA.
Sir!

Capt. ABSOLUTE.
So!----egad! I thought as much!----that d—n'd monosyllable has froze me! *(aside)* —What, Lydia, now that we are as happy in our *friends' consent*, as in our *mutual vows*———

LYDIA.
Friends' consent, indeed! *(peevishly)*

---

1 "Youth's the Season" is a *carpe diem* song sung, in a tavern, by a glamorous highwayman and several prostitutes in John Gay's phenomenally successful *The Beggar's Opera* (1728). To "hand" someone is to lead her by the hand (usually in or out of something).

Capt. ABSOLUTE.
Come, come, we must lay aside some of our romance—a little
wealth and *comfort* may be endur'd after all. And for your
fortune, the lawyers shall make such settlements as————

LYDIA.
Lawyers! I *hate* lawyers!

Capt. ABSOLUTE.
Nay then, we will not wait for their lingering forms, but
instantly procure the licence, and—

LYDIA.
The *licence!*—I *hate* licence!

Capt. ABSOLUTE.
O my Love! *be* not so unkind!—thus let me intreat————
[*Kneeling.*

LYDIA.
Pshaw!—what signifies kneeling, when you know I *must* have you?

Capt. ABSOLUTE. *(rising)*
Nay, Madam, there shall be no constraint upon your inclinations, I promise you.—If I have lost your *heart,*—I resign the
rest.—'Gad, I must try what a little *spirit* will do. [*Aside.*

LYDIA. *(rising)*
Then, Sir, let me tell you, the interest you had there was
acquired by a mean, unmanly imposition, and deserves the punishment of fraud.—What, you have been treating *me* like a
child!—humouring my romance! and laughing, I suppose, at
your success!

Capt. ABSOLUTE.
You wrong me, Lydia, you wrong me—only hear————

LYDIA.
So, while *I* fondly imagined we were deceiving my relations, and
flatter'd myself that I should outwit and incense them *all*—
behold! my hopes are to be crush'd at once, by my Aunt's
consent and approbation!—and *I* am *myself*, the only dupe at
last! [*Walking about in heat.*

Capt. ABSOLUTE.
Nay, but hear me—

LYDIA.
No, Sir, you could not think that such paltry artifices could
please me, when the mask was thrown off!—But I suppose since
your tricks have made you secure of my *fortune*, you are little
solicitous about my *affections*.—But here, Sir, here is the
picture—Beverley's picture! *(taking a miniature from her bosom)*
which I have worn, night and day, in spite of threats and
entreaties!—There, Sir, *(flings it to him)* and be assured I throw
the original from my heart as easily!

Capt. ABSOLUTE.
Nay, nay, Ma'am, we will not differ as to that.—Here, *(taking
out a picture) here* is Miss Lydia Languish.—What a difference!—aye, *there* is the heav'nly assenting smile, that first gave
soul and spirit to my hopes!—those are the lips which seal'd a
vow, as yet scarce dry in Cupid's calendar!—and *there* the *half*
resentful blush, that *would* have check'd the ardour of my
thanks—Well, all that's past!—all over indeed!—There,
Madam—in *beauty*, that copy is not equal to you, but in my
mind its merit over the original, in being still the same, is
such—that—I cannot find in my heart to *part with* it. [*Puts it up
again.*

LYDIA. *(Softening)*
'Tis *your own* doing, Sir—I, I, I suppose you are perfectly satisfied.

Capt. ABSOLUTE.
O, most certainly—sure now this is much better than being in
love!—ha! ha! ha!—there's some spirit in *this*!—What signifies
breaking some scores of solemn promises, half an hundred
vows, under one's hand, with the marks of a dozen or two
angels to witness—all that's of no consequence you know.—To
be sure people will say, that Miss didn't know her own mind—
but never mind that:—or perhaps they may be ill-natured
enough to hint, that the gentleman grew tired of the lady and
forsook her—but don't let that fret you.

LYDIA.
There's no bearing his insolence. [*Bursts into tears.*

Enter Mrs. Malaprop *and Sir* Anthony.

Mrs. MALAPROP. *(Entering)*
Come, we must interrupt your billing and cooing a while.

LYDIA.
This is *worse* than your treachery and deceit, you base ingrate!
[*Sobbing.*

Sir ANTHONY.
What the devil's the matter now!—Z—ds! Mrs. Malaprop, this
is the *oddest billing* and *cooing* I ever heard!—but what the deuce
is the meaning of it?—I'm quite astonish'd!

Capt. ABSOLUTE.
Ask the lady, Sir.

Mrs. MALAPROP.
O mercy!—I'm quite analys'd for my part!—why, Lydia, what is
the reason of this?

LYDIA.
Ask the *gentleman*, Ma'am.

Sir ANTHONY.
Z—ds! I shall be in a phrenzy!—why Jack, you scoundrel, you
are not come out to be any one else, are you?

Mrs. MALAPROP.
Aye, Sir, there's no more *trick*, is there?—you are not like Cerberus,[1] *three* Gentlemen at once, are you?

Capt. ABSOLUTE.
You'll not let me speak—I say the *lady* can account for *this*
much better than I can.

LYDIA.
Ma'am, you once commanded me never to think of Beverley
again—*there* is the man—I now obey you:—for, from this
moment, I renounce him for ever. [*Exit* Lydia.

---

1 In Greek mythology, Cerberus was a three-headed dog that guarded the
   entrance to Hades.

Mrs. MALAPROP.
O mercy! and miracles! what a turn here is—why sure, Captain, you haven't behaved disrespectfully to my Niece.

Sir ANTHONY.
Ha! ha! ha!---ha! ha! ha!—now I see it—Ha! ha! ha!—now I see it—you have been too lively, Jack.

Capt. ABSOLUTE.
Nay, Sir, upon my word———

Sir ANTHONY.
Come, no lying, Jack—I'm sure *'twas* so.

Mrs. MALAPROP.
O Lud! Sir Anthony!———O fie, Captain!

Capt. ABSOLUTE.
Upon my soul, Ma'am———

Sir ANTHONY.
Come, no excuses, Jack;—why, your father, you rogue, was so before you:—the blood of the Absolutes was always impatient.—Ha! ha! ha! poor little Lydia!—why, you've frighten'd her, you Dog, you have.

Capt. ABSOLUTE.
By all that's good, Sir——

Sir ANTHONY.
Z—ds! say no more, I tell you.——Mrs. Malaprop shall make your peace.—You must make his peace, Mrs. Malaprop;—you must tell her 'tis Jack's way—tell her 'tis all our ways—it runs in the blood of our family!—Come, get on, Jack,—ha! ha! ha! Mrs. Malaprop—a young villain! [*Pushing him out.*

Mrs. MALAPROP.
O! Sir Anthony!—O fie, Captain! [*Exeunt severally.*

SCENE III.

The North-Parade.

Enter Sir Lucius O'Trigger.

Sir LUCIUS.
I wonder where this Captain Absolute hides himself.—Upon my
conscience!—these officers are always in one's way in love-
affairs:—I remember I might have married Lady Dorothy
Carmine, if it had not been for a little rogue of a Major, who
ran away with her before she could get a sight of me!—And I
wonder too what it is the ladies can see in them to be so fond
of them—unless it be a touch of the old serpent in 'em, that
makes the little creatures be caught, like vipers with a bit of
red cloth.—Hah!—isn't this the Captain coming?—faith it is!—
There is a probability of succeeding about that fellow, that is
mighty provoking!—Who the devil is he talking to?[1]
[*Steps aside.*

Enter Captain Absolute.

Capt. ABSOLUTE.
To what fine purpose I have been plotting! a noble reward for
all my schemes, upon my soul!—a little gypsey!—I did not think
her romance could have made her so d—n'd absurd either—
S'death, I never was in a worse humour in my life!—I could cut
my own throat, or any other person's, with the greatest pleasure
in the world!

---

1 "Carmine" is crimson, so the lady's name suggests a predisposition
   toward the army (the uniform coats of which were that color). "The old
   serpent" is presumably Satan (who tempted Eve in the form of a snake).
   This passage seems to be a vestige of the conception of Sir Lucius that
   so annoyed the audience at the disastrous first performance (remember
   that in Act Three, Scene Four, Sir Lucius said that the cause of his
   quarrel with Captain Absolute was the patriotic one of his having "put a
   jest on me lately, at the expence of my country," rather than his being a
   rival for the hand of the woman he thinks of as "Delia"). Cf. the similarly vestigial passage in Act Five, Scene Three, where Sir Lucius
   instructs his sword to "ask the gentleman, whether he will resign the
   lady, without forcing you to proceed against him?"

Sir LUCIUS.

O, faith! I'm in the luck of it—I never could have found him in a sweeter temper for my purpose—to be sure I'm just come in the nick! now to enter into conversation with him, and so quarrel genteelly. [*Sir* Lucius *goes up to Captain* Absolute.

——With regard to that matter, Captain, I must beg leave to differ in opinion with you.

Capt. ABSOLUTE.

Upon my word then, you must be a very subtle disputant:— because, Sir, I happen'd just then to be giving no opinion at all.

Sir LUCIUS.

That's no reason.—For give me leave to tell you, a man may *think* an untruth as well as *speak* one.[1]

Capt. ABSOLUTE.

Very true, Sir, but if the man never utters his thoughts, I should think they *might* stand a *chance* of escaping controversy.

Sir LUCIUS.

Then, Sir, you differ in opinion with me, which amounts to the same thing.

Capt. ABSOLUTE.

Hark'ee, Sir Lucius,—if I had not before known you to be a gentleman, upon my soul, I should not have discovered it at this interview:—for what you can drive at, unless you mean to quarrel with me, I cannot conceive!

Sir LUCIUS.

I humbly thank you, Sir, for the quickness of your apprehen-sion, [*Bowing.*

—you have nam'd the very thing I would be at.

---

1 The easiest way to provoke a duel was to publicly accuse a gentleman of lying (since to do so suggested that he lacked the courage to speak truthfully, and so didn't deserve the honor that his social status had granted him). The alleged liar would then be likely to feel duty-bound to defend his honor, regardless of the veracity of what he had said.

Capt. ABSOLUTE.
Very well, Sir—I shall certainly not baulk your inclinations:——
but I should be glad you would please to explain your motives.

Sir LUCIUS.
Pray, Sir, be easy—the quarrel is a very pretty quarrel as it
stands—we should only spoil it, by trying to explain it.—
However, your memory is very short—or you could not have
forgot an affront you pass'd on me within this week.—So no
more, but name your time and place.[1]

Capt. ABSOLUTE.
Well, Sir, since you are so bent on it, the sooner the better;—let
it be this evening—here, by the Spring-Gardens.[2]—We shall
scarcely be interrupted.

Sir LUCIUS.
Faith! that same interruption in affairs of this nature, shews
very great ill-breeding.——I don't know what's the reason, but
in England, if a thing of this kind gets wind, people make such
a pother,[3] that a gentleman can never fight in peace and quiet-
ness.—However, if it's the same to you, Captain, I should take it
as a particular kindness, if you'd let us meet in King's-Mead-
Fields, as a little business will call me there about six o'clock,
and I may dispatch both matters at once.

Capt. ABSOLUTE.
'Tis the same to me exactly.—A little after six, then we will
discuss this matter more seriously.

Sir LUCIUS.
If you please, Sir, there will be very pretty small-sword[4] light,
tho' it won't do for a long shot.—So that matter's settled! and
my mind's at ease. [*Exit Sir* Lucius.

Enter Faulkland, *meeting* Absolute.

---

1 The recipient of a challenge to a duel had the right to choose the time
   and place of the fight (and often the weapons to be employed).
2 For the Spring Gardens, see the map in Figure 15, p. 298.
3 A fuss or commotion.
4 A "small-sword" was the standard sword carried by gentlemen (and
   used for dueling) in the eighteenth century.

Capt. ABSOLUTE.
Well met.—I was going to look for you.—O, Faulkland! all the
Dæmons of spite and disappointment have conspired against
me! I'm so vex'd, that if I had not the prospect of a resource in
being knock'd o'the head[1] by and bye, I should scarce have
spirits to tell you the cause.

FAULKLAND.
What can you mean?——Has Lydia chang'd her mind?—I
should have thought her duty and inclination would now have
pointed to the same object.

Capt. ABSOLUTE.
Aye, just as the eyes do of a person who squints:—when her
love-eye was fix'd on *me*——t'other—her *eye* of *duty*, was finely
obliqued:—but when duty bid her point *that* the same way—
off t'other turn'd on a swivel, and secured its retreat with a
frown![2]

FAULKLAND.
But what's the resource you——

Capt. ABSOLUTE.
O, to wind up the whole, a good natured Irishman here has
(*mimicking Sir* Lucius) beg'd leave to have the pleasure of
cutting my throat—and I mean to indulge him—that's all.

FAULKLAND.
Prithee, be serious.

Capt. ABSOLUTE.
'Tis fact, upon my soul.——Sir Lucius O'Trigger—you know
him by sight—for some affront, which I am sure I never
intended, has obliged me to meet him this evening at six
o'clock:—'tis on that account I wish'd to see you—you must go
with me.

---

1 To be "knocked on the head" was to be killed, particularly in a quick
   way.
2 The metaphors here are all military (to "oblique" is to turn 45 degrees
   and then march forward).

FAULKLAND.
Nay, there must be some mistake, sure.—Sir Lucius shall explain himself—and I dare say matters may be accommodated:—but this evening, did you say?—I wish it had been any other time.

Capt. ABSOLUTE.
Why?—there will be light enough:——there will (as Sir Lucius says) "be very pretty small-sword light, tho' it won't do for a long shot."—Confound his long shots!

FAULKLAND.
But I am myself a good deal ruffled, by a difference I have had with Julia—my vile tormenting temper has made me treat her so cruelly, that I shall not be myself till we are reconciled.

Capt. ABSOLUTE.
By Heav'ns, Faulkland, you don't deserve her.

Enter Servant, *gives* Faulkland *a letter.*

FAULKLAND.
O Jack! this is from Julia—I dread to open it—I fear it may be to take a last leave—perhaps to bid me return her letters—and restore——O! how I suffer for my folly!

Capt. ABSOLUTE.
Here—let me see. [*Takes the letter and opens it.*
Aye, a final sentence indeed!—'tis all over with you, faith!

FAULKLAND.
Nay, Jack—don't keep me in suspence.

Capt. ABSOLUTE.
Hear then.—"*As I am convinced that my dear Faulkland's own reflections have already upbraided him for his last unkindness to me, I will not add a word on the subject.—I wish to speak with you as soon as possible.—Yours ever and truly,* Julia."
—There's stubbornness and resentment for you! [*Gives him the letter.*
Why, man, you don't seem one whit the happier at this.

FAULKLAND.
O, yes, I am—but—but——

Capt. ABSOLUTE.

Confound your *buts*.—You never hear any thing that would make another man bless himself, but you immediately d—n it with a *but*.

FAULKLAND.

Now, Jack, as you are my friend, own honestly—don't you think there is something forward—something indelicate in this haste to forgive?—Women should never sue for reconciliation:—*that* should *always* come from us.—*They* should retain their coldness till *woo'd* to kindness—and their *pardon*, like their *love*, should "not unsought be won."[1]

Capt. ABSOLUTE.

I have not patience to listen to you:—thou'rt incorrigible!—so say no more on the subject.—I must go to settle a few matters—let me see you before six—remember—at my lodgings.——A poor industrious devil like me, who have toil'd, and drudg'd, and plotted to gain my ends, and am at last disappointed by other people's folly—may in pity be allowed to swear and grumble a little;—but a captious sceptic in love,—a slave to fretfulness and whim—who has no difficulties but of *his own* creating—is a subject more fit for ridicule than compassion! [*Exit Captain* Absolute.

FAULKLAND.

I feel his reproaches!—yet I would not change this too exquisite nicety, for the gross content with which *he* tramples on the thorns of love.—His engaging me in this duel, has started an idea in my head, which I will instantly pursue.—I'll use it as the touch-stone of Julia's sincerity and disinterestedness—if her love prove pure and sterling ore—my name will rest on it with honour!—and once I've stamp'd it there, I lay aside my doubts for ever:—but if the dross of selfishness, the allay[2] of pride predominate—'twill be best to leave her as a toy for some less cautious Fool to sigh for. [*Exit* Faulkland.

---

1   Cf. Adam's description, in Milton's *Paradise Lost*, of Eve's conduct during their courtship: "though divinely brought, / Yet innocence and virgin modesty, / Her virtue and the conscience of her worth, / That would be wooed, and not unsought be won, / Not obvious, not obtrusive, but retired, / The more desirable" (VIII.500-5).

2   Faulkland's metaphors are all drawn from coinage. A "touchstone" is used to test or "prove" the purity of precious metals. What guaranteed

ACT V.

SCENE I.

Julia's Dressing-Room.

Julia, *sola.*

JULIA.
How this message has alarmed me! what dreadful accident
can he mean! why such charge to be alone?——O Faulkland!—
how many unhappy moments!—how many tears have you cost
me!

Enter Faulkland, *muffled up in a Riding-coat.*

JULIA.
What means this?——why this caution, Faulkland?

FAULKLAND.
Alas! Julia, I am come to take a long farewell.

JULIA.
Heav'ns! what do you mean?

FAULKLAND.
You see before you a wretch, whose life is forfeited.—Nay, start
not!—the infirmity of my temper has drawn all this misery on
me.—I left you fretful and passionate—an untoward accident
drew me into a quarrel—the event is, that I must fly this
kingdom instantly.—O Julia, had I been so fortunate as to have
call'd you mine intirely, before this mischance had fallen on me,
I should not so deeply dread my banishment!——But no more
of that—your heart and promise were given to one happy in

---

the value of English coins as "sterling" was both their being pure and
their being stamped with the name and likeness of a monarch (just as
Julia, if she passes the test, will be given Faulkland's name when they
marry). "Dross" is what separates out from the precious metals when
they are melted. An "allay" is a mixture of metals, especially a mixture
which diminishes the value of whatever gold, silver, or copper is
present.

friends, character, and station! they are not bound to wait upon a solitary, guilty exile.[1]

JULIA.
My soul is oppress'd with sorrow at the *nature* of your misfortune: had these adverse circumstances arisen from a less fatal cause, I should have felt strong comfort in the thought that I could *now* chase from your bosom every doubt of the warm sincerity of my love.——My heart has long known no other guardian—I now entrust my person to your honour—we will fly together.—When safe from pursuit, my Father's will may be fulfilled—and I receive a legal claim to be the partner of your sorrows, and tenderest comforter. Then on the bosom of your wedded Julia, you may lull your keen regret to slumbering; while virtuous love, with a Cherub's hand, shall smooth the brow of upbraiding thought, and pluck the thorn from compunction.

FAULKLAND.
O Julia! I am bankrupt in gratitude! but the time is so pressing, it calls on you for so hasty a resolution.—Would you not wish some hours to weigh the advantages you forego, and what little compensation poor Faulkland can make you beside his solitary love?

JULIA.
I ask not a moment.—No, Faulkland, I have lov'd you for yourself: and if I now, more than ever, prize the solemn engagement which so long has pledged us to each other, it is because it leaves no room for hard aspersions on my fame, and puts the seal of duty to an act of love.—But let us not linger.—Perhaps this delay——

FAULKLAND.
'Twill be better I should not venture out again till dark.—Yet am

---

1 Duelists who killed their opponents were typically only prosecuted for manslaughter, not murder (and sometimes were not even prosecuted at all, if the duel appeared to have been conducted fairly). Nonetheless, post-duel attempts to flee the jurisdiction of English law (as Faulkland is pretending to be preparing to do) were fairly common, and even manslaughter was officially a capital crime—hence Faulkland's life is "forfeit"—though such a punishment was rarely imposed.

I griev'd to think what numberless distresses will press heavy on your gentle disposition!

JULIA.
Perhaps your fortune may be forfeited by this unhappy act.—I know not whether 'tis so—but sure that alone can never make us unhappy.—The little I have will be sufficient to *support* us; and *exile* never should be splendid.

FAULKLAND.
Aye, but in such an abject state of life, my wounded pride perhaps may increase the natural fretfulness of my temper, till I become a rude, morose companion, beyond your patience to endure. Perhaps the recollection of a deed, my conscience cannot justify, may haunt me in such gloomy and unsocial fits, that I shall hate the tenderness that would relieve me, break from your arms, and quarrel with your fondness!

JULIA.
If your thoughts should assume so unhappy a bent, you will the more want some mild and affectionate spirit to watch over and console you:—One who, by bearing *your* infirmities with gentleness and resignation, may teach you *so* to bear the evils of your fortune.

FAULKLAND.
O Julia, I have proved you to the quick![1] and with this useless device I throw away all my doubts. How shall I plead to be forgiven this last unworthy effect of my restless, unsatisfied disposition?

JULIA.
Has no such disaster happened as you related?

FAULKLAND.
I am ashamed to own that it was all pretended; yet in pity, Julia, do not kill me with resenting a fault which never can be repeated: But sealing, this once, my pardon, let me to-morrow, in the face of Heaven, receive my future guide and monitress, and expiate my past folly, by years of tender adoration.

---

1 "Proved you to the quick" means "tested you on the most sensitive (or vital) point of all."

JULIA.
Hold, Faulkland!—that you are free from a crime, which I
before fear'd to name, Heaven knows how sincerely I rejoice!—
These are tears of thankfulness for that! But that your cruel
doubts should have urged you to an imposition that has wrung
my heart, gives me now a pang, more keen than I can express!

FAULKLAND.
By Heav'ns! Julia——

JULIA.
Yet hear me.——My Father lov'd you, Faulkland! and you preserv'd the life that tender parent gave me; in his presence I
pledged my hand—*joyfully* pledged it—where before I had given
my heart. When, soon after, I lost that parent, it seem'd to me
that Providence had, in Faulkland, shewn me whither to transfer, without a pause, my grateful duty, as well as my affection:
Hence I have been content to bear from you what pride and
delicacy would have forbid me from another.—I will not
upbraid you, by repeating how you have trifled with my sincerity.——

FAULKLAND.
I confess it all! yet hear——

JULIA.
After such a year of trial—I might have flattered myself that I
should not have been insulted with a new probation of my sincerity, as cruel as unnecessary! A trick of such a nature, as to
shew me plainly, that when I thought you lov'd me best, you
even then regarded me as a mean dissembler; an artful,
prudent[1] hypocrite.

FAULKLAND.
Never! never!

JULIA.
I now see it is not in your nature to be content, or confident in
love. With this conviction—I never will be yours. While I had
hopes that my persevering attention, and unreproaching kind-

---

1 A "probation" is a test. "Prudent" here means something like
   "scheming."

ness might in time reform your temper, I should have been happy to have gain'd a dearer influence over you; but I will not furnish you with a licensed power to keep alive an incorrigible fault, at the expence of one who never would contend with you.

FAULKLAND.
Nay, but Julia, by my soul and honour, if after this——

JULIA.
But one word more.—As my faith has once been given to you, I never will barter it with another.—I shall pray for your happiness with the truest sincerity; and the dearest blessing I can ask of Heaven to send you, will be to charm you from that unhappy temper, which alone has prevented the performance of our solemn engagement.—All I request of *you* is, that you will yourself reflect upon this infirmity, and when you number up the many true delights it has deprived you of—let it not be your *least* regret, that it lost you the love of one—who would have follow'd you in beggary through the world! [*Exit.*]

FAULKLAND.
She's gone!—for ever!—There was an awful resolution in her manner, that rivetted me to my place.——O Fool!—Dolt!—Barbarian!—Curst as I am, with more imperfections than my fellow-wretches, kind Fortune sent a heaven-gifted cherub to my aid, and, like a ruffian, I have driven her from my side!—I must now haste to my appointment.—Well my mind is tuned for such a scene.—I shall wish only to become a principal in it, and reverse the tale my cursed folly put me upon forging here.——O Love!—Tormentor!—Fiend!—whose influence, like the Moon's, acting on men of dull souls, makes idiots of them, but meeting subtler spirits, betrays their course, and urges sensibility to madness![1] [*Exit.*]

Enter Maid *and* Lydia.

MAID.
My Mistress, Ma'am, I know, was here just now—perhaps she is only in the next room. [*Exit* Maid.

---

1 Traditionally, intermittent insanity (or "lunacy") was thought to be the result of the changing phases of the moon.

LYDIA.
Heigh ho!—Though he has used me so, this fellow runs strangely in my head. I believe one lecture from my grave Cousin will make me recall him.

Enter Julia.

LYDIA.
O Julia, I am come to you with such an appetite for consolation.—Lud! Child, what's the matter with you?—You have been crying!—I'll be hanged, if that Faulkland has not been tormenting you!

JULIA.
You mistake the cause of my uneasiness.—Something *has* flurried me a little.—Nothing that you can guess at.——I would not accuse Faulkland to a Sister! *(Aside.)*

LYDIA.
Ah! whatever vexations you may have, I can assure you mine surpass them.——You know who Beverley proves to be?

JULIA.
I will now own to you, Lydia, that Mr. Faulkland had before inform'd me of the whole affair. Had young Absolute been the person you took him for, I should not have accepted your confidence on the subject, without a serious endeavour to counteract your caprice.[1]

LYDIA.
So, then, I see I have been deceived by every one!—but I don't care—I'll never have him.

JULIA.
Nay, Lydia——

LYDIA.
Why, is it not provoking; when I thought we were coming to the prettiest distress imaginable, to find myself made a mere Smith-

---

1 Then, as now, being willing to act as someone's confidante regarding a situation was often taken to be a tacit endorsement of the confider's behavior in that situation.

field bargain of at last——There had I projected one of the most sentimental elopements!—so becoming a disguise!—so amiable a ladder of Ropes!—Conscious Moon—four horses—Scotch parson—with such surprise to Mrs. Malaprop—and such paragraphs[1] in the News-papers!——O, I shall die with disappointment.

JULIA.
I don't wonder at it!

LYDIA.
Now—sad reverse!—what have I to expect, but, after a deal of flimsy preparation with a bishop's licence, and my Aunt's blessing, to go simpering up to the Altar; or perhaps be cried three times in a country-church, and have an unmannerly fat clerk ask the consent of every butcher in the parish to join John Absolute and Lydia Languish, *Spinster*! O, that I should live to hear myself called Spinster!

JULIA.
Melancholy, indeed!

---

1   A "Smithfield bargain" is a woman who is being married for worldly advantage, rather than love; Smithfield was the principal meat market in London, and was known for its fierce and wholly unsentimental haggling. A "conscious moon" is a moon imagined to be privy to the lovers' secrets. "Four horses" would be necessary to pull a carriage fast enough to elude pursuers. A "Scotch parson" is part of Lydia's fantasy because Scotland was not bound by the restrictions of English marriage law, with its requirements that a couple obtain parental consent, if either party was under twenty-one, and either get a license from the local bishop or ask the bans—i.e., have their intention to marry announced—in their parish on the three Sundays leading up to the wedding. In Scotland, on the other hand, boys as young as fourteen and girls as young as twelve could get married right away, without any parental consent. Hence it was a popular destination for elopements or otherwise illegal marriages. "Paragraphs" about elopements were a routine feature of eighteenth-century newspapers (see Introduction, pp. 35-38). Appendix C offers a sampling of such paragraphs as they concerned Sheridan and Elizabeth Linley. Item 3 in Appendix D provides another example.

LYDIA.
How mortifying, to remember the dear delicious shifts I used to
be put to, to gain half a minute's conversation with this
fellow!——How often have I stole forth, in the coldest night in
January, and found him in the garden, stuck like a dripping
statue!—There would he kneel to me in the snow, and sneeze
and cough so pathetically! he shivering with cold, and I with
apprehension! and while the freezing blast numb'd our joints,
how warmly would he press me to pity his flame, and glow with
mutual ardour!——Ah, Julia! that was something like being in
love.[1]

JULIA.
If I were in spirits, Lydia, I should chide you only by laughing
heartily at you: but it suits more the situation of my mind, at
present, earnestly to entreat you, not to let a man, who loves
you with sincerity, suffer that unhappiness from your *caprice*,
which I know too well caprice can inflict.

LYDIA.
O Lud! what has brought my Aunt here!

Enter Mrs. Malaprop, Fag, *and* David.

Mrs. MALAPROP.
So! so! here's fine work!—here's fine suicide, paracide, and salivation going on in the fields! and Sir Anthony not to be found
to prevent the antistrophe![2]

JULIA.
For Heaven's sake, Madam, what's the meaning of this?

Mrs. MALAPROP.
That gentleman can tell you—'twas he enveloped the affair to
me.

---

1 This speech was apparently cut after the disastrous first night (and then
   restored for the printed versions of the play).
2 "Salivation" is a side-effect of being treated for syphilis. The mercury
   used (to kill the infection) would turn the patient's saliva black, and
   make its production far more copious. An "antistrophe" is a repetition
   of words with the order reversed.

LYDIA.
Do, Sir, will you inform us. *(To Fag.)*

FAG.
Ma'am, I should hold myself very deficient in every requisite
that forms the man of breeding, if I delay'd a moment to give
all the information in my power to a lady so deeply interested in
the affair as you are.

LYDIA.
But quick! quick, Sir!

FAG.
True, Ma'am, as you say, one should be quick in divulging
matters of this nature; for should we be tedious, perhaps while
we are flourishing on the subject, two or three lives may be
lost![1]

LYDIA.
O patience!—Do, Ma'am, for Heaven's sake! tell us what is the
matter?

Mrs. MALAPROP.
Why, murder's the matter! slaughter's the matter! killing's the
matter!—but he can tell you the perpendiculars.

LYDIA.
Then, prythee, Sir, be brief.

FAG.
Why then, Ma'am—as to murder—I cannot take upon me to
say—and as to slaughter, or man-slaughter, that will be as the
jury finds it.

LYDIA.
But who, Sir—who are engaged in this?

FAG.
Faith, Ma'am, one is a young gentleman whom I should be very

---

1 To "flourish" on a subject is to speak floridly (and at length) about it—
   as Fag is preparing to do.

sorry any thing was to happen to—a very pretty behaved gentleman!—We have lived much together, and always on terms.

LYDIA.
But who is this? who! who! who!

FAG.
My Master, Ma'am—my Master—I speak of my Master.

LYDIA.
Heavens! What, Captain Absolute!

Mrs. MALAPROP.
O, to be sure, you are frightened now!

JULIA.
But who are with him, Sir?

FAG.
As to the rest, Ma'am, his gentleman can inform you better
than I.

JULIA.
Do speak, friend. *(To David.)*

DAVID.
Look'ee, my Lady——by the Mass! there's mischief going on.
——Folks don't use to meet for amusement with fire-arms, fire-
locks, fire-engines, fire-screens, fire-office, and the devil knows
what other crackers besides!——This, my Lady, I say, has an
angry favour.[1]

JULIA.
But who is there beside Captain Absolute, friend?

DAVID.
My poor Master—under favour, for mentioning him first.—You
know me, my Lady—I am David—and my Master of course is,
or *was* Squire Acres.—Then comes Squire Faulkland.

---

1   David is getting a bit carried away: "fire-screens" block excess heat from
    a fireplace, while a "fire-office" is a fire-insurance company. "Crackers"
    are fireworks. An "angry favour" is an angry-looking appearance.

JULIA.
Do, Ma'am, let us instantly endeavour to prevent mischief.

Mrs. MALAPROP.
O fie—it would be very inelegant in us:—we should only participate things.

DAVID.
Ah! do, Mrs. Aunt, save a few lives—they are desperately given,
believe me.—Above all, there is that blood-thirsty Philistine,[1]
Sir Lucius O'Trigger.

Mrs. MALAPROP.
Sir Lucius O'Trigger!—O mercy! have they drawn poor little
dear Sir Lucius into the scrape?—why, how you stand, girl!
you have no more feeling than one of the Derbyshire
Putrefactions![2]

LYDIA.
What are we to do, Madam?

Mrs. MALAPROP.
Why, fly with the utmost felicity to be sure, to prevent mischief:—here, friend—you can shew us the place?

FAG.
If you please, Ma'am, I will conduct you.—David, do you look
for Sir Anthony. [*Exit* David.

Mrs. MALAPROP.
Come, girls!—this gentleman will exhort us.—Come, Sir, you're
our envoy—lead the way, and we'll precede.

FAG.
Not a step before the ladies for the world!

Mrs. MALAPROP.
You're sure you know the spot.

---

1 A "philistine" is here an unmerciful foe.
2 The Peak District in Derbyshire was famous for its stalactites and other
   "petrifications."

FAG.
I think I can find it, Ma'am; and one good thing is, we shall
hear the report of the pistols[1] as we draw near, so we can't well
miss them; never fear, Ma'am, never fear. [*Exeunt, he talking.*]

SCENE II.

South-Parade.[2]

Enter Captain Absolute, *putting his sword under his greatcoat.*

Capt. ABSOLUTE.
A sword seen in the streets of Bath would raise as great an
alarm as a mad-dog.—How provoking this is in Faulkland!—
never punctual! I shall be obliged to go without him at last.—O,
the devil! here's Sir Anthony!——how shall I escape him?
[*Muffles up his face, and takes a circle to go off.*]

Enter Sir Anthony.

Sir ANTHONY.
How one may be deceived at a little distance! only that I see he
don't know me, I could have sworn that was Jack!—Hey!—
'Gad's life; it is.—Why, Jack, you Dog!—what are you afraid
of?—hey! sure I'm right.—Why, Jack—Jack Absolute! [*Goes up
to him.*]

Capt. ABSOLUTE.
Really, Sir, you have the advantage of me:—I don't remember

---

1 The "report" of pistols is the sound they make when they are fired.
2 According to *The Morning Post* of 18 January 1775 (the morning after
   the play's disastrous first performance), the painted backdrop for this
   scene, "a perspective view through the south parade ... to the late Mr.
   Allen's delightful villa, was universally admired." "Mr. Allen" was Ralph
   Allen, a beloved philanthropist and literary patron. However, those
   scenic pleasures must not have been enough, because, on 30 January, a
   reviewer for the same paper was recommending that the scene be cut
   ("it being an evident obstruction to the business, and that to answer no
   purpose whatever"), and within two years, the scene was being referred
   to as "generally left out at Covent-garden theatre" (*The Morning Post*, 17
   January 1777). It was, however, performed at Drury Lane (where Sheridan had become manager in 1776).

ever to have had the honour————my name is Saunderson, at
your service.

Sir ANTHONY.
Sir, I beg your pardon—I took you—hey!—why, z—ds! it
is————Stay———— [*Looks up to his face.*
So, so—your humble servant, Mr. Saunderson!—Why, you
scoundrel, what tricks are you after now?

Capt. ABSOLUTE.
O! a joke, Sir, a joke!—I came here on purpose to look for you, Sir.

Sir ANTHONY.
You did! well, I am glad you were so lucky:—but what are you
muffled up so for?—what's this for?—hey?

Capt. ABSOLUTE.
Tis cool, Sir; isn't it?—rather chilly somehow:—but I shall be
late—I have a particular engagement.

Sir ANTHONY.
Stay.—why, I thought you were looking for me?—Pray, Jack,
where is't you are going?

Capt. ABSOLUTE.
Going, Sir!

Sir ANTHONY.
Aye—where are you going?

Capt. ABSOLUTE.
Where am I going?

Sir ANTHONY.
You unmannerly puppy!

Capt. ABSOLUTE.
I was going, Sir, to—to—to—to Lydia—Sir to Lydia—to make
matters up if I could;—and I was looking for you, Sir, to—
to————

Sir ANTHONY.
To go with you, I suppose—Well, come along.

Capt. ABSOLUTE.
O! z—ds! no, Sir, not for the world!—I wish'd to meet with you,
Sir, to—to—to———You find it cool, I'm sure, Sir—you'd
better not stay out.

Sir ANTHONY.
Cool!—not at all—Well, Jack—and what will you say to Lydia?

Capt. ABSOLUTE.
O, Sir, beg her pardon, humour her—promise and vow:—but I
detain you, Sir—consider the cold air on your gout.

Sir ANTHONY.
O, not at all!—not at all!—I'm in no hurry.—Ah! Jack, you
youngsters when once you are wounded here. [*Putting his hand
to Captain* Absolute*'s breast.*
Hey! what the deuce have you got here?

Capt. ABSOLUTE.
Nothing, Sir—nothing.

Sir ANTHONY.
What's this?—here's something d—d hard!

Capt. ABSOLUTE.
O, trinkets, Sir! trinkets—a bauble for Lydia!

Sir ANTHONY.
Nay, let me see your taste. [*Pulls his coat open, the sword falls.*
Trinkets!---a bauble for Lydia!---z—ds! sirrah, you are not
going to cut her throat, are you?

Capt. ABSOLUTE.
Ha! ha! ha!---I thought it would divert you, Sir, tho' I didn't
mean to tell you till afterwards.

Sir ANTHONY.
You didn't?---Yes, this is a very diverting trinket, truly.

Capt. ABSOLUTE.
Sir, I'll explain to you.---You know, Sir, Lydia is romantic---
dev'lish romantic, and very absurd of course:---now, Sir, I

intend, if she refuses to forgive me---to unsheath this sword--- and swear---I'll fall upon its point, and expire at her feet![1]

Sir ANTHONY.
Fall upon fiddle-sticks end!---why, I suppose it is the very thing that would please her---Get along, you Fool.—

Capt. ABSOLUTE.
Well, Sir, you shall hear of my success---you shall hear.---"O, Lydia!---forgive me, or this pointed steel"---says I.

Sir ANTHONY.
"O, Booby! stab away, and welcome"---says she---Get along!--- and d—n your trinkets! [*Exit Captain* Absolute.

Enter David, *running.*

DAVID.
Stop him! stop him! Murder! Thief! Fire!---Stop fire! Stop fire! ---O! Sir Anthony---call! call! bid 'em stop! Murder! Fire!

Sir ANTHONY.
Fire! Murder! where?

DAVID.
Oons! he's out of sight! and I'm out of breath, for my part! O, Sir Anthony, why didn't you stop him? why didn't you stop him?

Sir ANTHONY.
Z—ds! the fellow's mad!—Stop whom? stop Jack?

DAVID.
Aye, the Captain, Sir!--there's murder and slaughter———

---

1 According to one account, the event that precipitated Elizabeth Linley's elopement with Sheridan was Thomas Mathews's attempt to force himself upon her, with a threat to commit suicide if she refused him (see Bor and Clelland, 43). Cf. the plot of *The Morning Ramble*, as described in Appendix B, item 10.

Sir ANTHONY.
Murder!

DAVID.
Aye, please you, Sir Anthony, there's all kinds of murder, all
sorts of slaughter to be seen in the fields: there's fighting going
on, Sir---bloody sword-and-gun fighting!

Sir ANTHONY.
Who are going to fight, Dunce?

DAVID.
Every body that I know of, Sir Anthony:---every body is going
to fight, my poor Master, Sir Lucius O'Trigger, your son, the
Captain——

Sir ANTHONY.
O, the Dog!---I see his tricks:---do you know the place?

DAVID.
King's-Mead-Fields.

Sir ANTHONY.
You know the way?

DAVID.
Not an inch;---but I'll call the Mayor---Aldermen----Consta-
bles----Church-wardens----and Beadles[1]---we can't be too many
to part them.

Sir ANTHONY.
Come along---give me your shoulder! we'll get assistance as we
go---the lying villain!---Well, I shall be in such a phrenzy---So
---this was the history of his d—d trinkets! I'll bauble him!
[*Exeunt.*

---

1   A "church warden" is the chief lay administrator for a church. "Beadles"
    deliver messages for a church (and often act as its disciplinarians).
    Neither would have any legal authority to intervene in a duel.

SCENE III.

King's-Mead-Fields.

Sir Lucius *and* Acres, *with pistols.*

ACRES.
By my valour! then, Sir Lucius, forty yards is a good distance---
Odds levels and aims!---I say it is a good distance.

Sir LUCIUS.
Is it for muskets or small field-pieces? upon my conscience, Mr.
Acres, you must leave those things to me.---Stay now---I'll shew
you. [*Measures paces*[1] *along the stage.*
there now, that is a very pretty distance---a pretty gentleman's
distance.

ACRES.
Z—ds! we might as well fight in a sentry-box!---I tell you, Sir
Lucius, the farther he is off, the cooler I shall take my aim.

Sir LUCIUS.
Faith! then I suppose you would aim at him best of all if he was
out of sight!

ACRES.
No, Sir Lucius---but I should think forty or eight and thirty
yards————

Sir LUCIUS.
Pho! pho! nonsense! three or four feet between the mouths of
your pistols is as good as a mile.

ACRES.
Odds bullets, no!—by my valour! there is no merit in killing

---

1   A "field piece" is a relatively light piece of artillery (one which could be
    moved about the battlefield). The stage at both of the London patent
    theaters was little more than thirty feet wide, and "paces" in dueling
    were generally two-and-a-half or three feet each. Shoemaker has calcu-
    lated that later eighteenth-century duels with pistols were conducted at
    an average of ten paces apart (534).

him so near:—do, my dear Sir Lucius, let me bring him down
at a long shot:—a long shot, Sir Lucius, if you love me!

Sir LUCIUS.
Well—the gentleman's friend and I must settle that.—But tell
me now, Mr. Acres, in case of an accident, is there any little will
or commission I could execute for you?

ACRES.
I am much obliged to you, Sir Lucius—but I don't understand———

Sir LUCIUS.
Why, you may think there's no being shot at without a little
risk—and if an unlucky bullet should carry a *Quietus*[1] with it—I
say it will be no time then to be bothering you about family
matters.

ACRES.
A *Quietus*!

Sir LUCIUS.
For instance now—if that should be the case—would you chuse
to be pickled and sent home?—or would it be the same to you
to lie here in the Abbey?—I'm told there is very snug lying in
the Abbey.

ACRES.
Pickled!—Snug lying in the Abbey!—Odds tremors! Sir Lucius,
don't talk so!

Sir LUCIUS.
I suppose, Mr. Acres, you never were engaged in an affair of
this kind before?

ACRES.
No, Sir Lucius, never before.

Sir LUCIUS.
Ah! that's a pity!—there's nothing like being used to a thing.—
Pray now, how would you receive the gentleman's shot?

---

1 A "quietus" is a release from something (e.g., life).

ACRES.
Odds files!¹—I've practised that—there, Sir Lucius—there [*Puts himself in an attitude.*
——a side-front, hey?—Odd! I'll make myself small enough:— I'll stand edge-ways.²

Sir LUCIUS.
Now—you're quite out—for if you stand so when I take my aim—— [*Levelling at him.*

ACRES.
Z—ds! Sir Lucius—are you sure it is not cock'd?

Sir LUCIUS.
Never fear.

ACRES.
But—but—you don't know—it may go off of its own head!

Sir LUCIUS.
Pho! be easy—Well, now if I hit you in the body, my bullet has a double chance—for if it misses a vital part on your right side—'twill be very hard if it don't succeed on the left!

ACRES.
A vital part! O, my poor vitals!

Sir LUCIUS.
But, there—fix yourself so— [*Placing him.*
let him see the broad side of your full front—there—now a ball or two may pass clean thro' your body, and never do any harm at all.

ACRES.
Clean thro' me!—a ball or two clean thro' me!

Sir LUCIUS.
Aye—may they—and it is much the genteelest attitude into the bargain.

---

1   In this context, "files" are soldiers lined up in formation (e.g., "single file").
2   Perhaps a theatrical in-joke? John Quick, the original Acres, was a tiny man (see Appendix A).

ACRES.
Look'ee! Sir Lucius—I'd just as lieve[1] be shot in an aukward posture as a genteel one—so, by my valour! I will stand edgeways.

Sir LUCIUS. *(Looking at his watch.)*
Sure they don't mean to disappoint us.—Hah?—no faith—I think I see them coming.

ACRES.
Hey!—what!—coming!——

Sir LUCIUS.
Aye—Who are those yonder getting over the stile?[2]

ACRES.
There are two of them, indeed!—well—let them come—hey, Sir Lucius!—we—we—we—we—won't run.—

Sir LUCIUS.
Run!

ACRES.
No—I say—we *won't* run, by my valour!

Sir LUCIUS.
What the devil's the matter with you?

ACRES.
Nothing—nothing—my dear friend——my dear Sir Lucius— but—I-I-I don't feel quite so bold, somehow—as I did.

Sir LUCIUS.
O fie!—consider your honour.

ACRES.
Aye—true—my honour——Do, Sir Lucius, hedge in a word or two every now and then about my honour.

---

1 "I'd just as well."
2 A "stile" is a set of steps or rungs to allow people to climb over a fence, while keeping the animals in. Presumably, like other open spaces near cities, King's Mead was used to graze sheep or cattle.

Sir LUCIUS.
Well, here they're coming. [*Looking.*

ACRES.
Sir Lucius—if I wa'n't with you, I should almost think I was afraid—if my valour should leave me!—Valour will come and go.

Sir LUCIUS.
Then, pray keep it fast, while you have it.

ACRES.
Sir Lucius—I doubt it is going—yes—my valour is certainly going!—it is sneaking off!—I feel it oozing out as it were at the palms of my hands!

Sir LUCIUS.
Your honour—your honour——Here they are.

ACRES.
O mercy!—now—that I were safe at *Clod-Hall*! or could be shot before I was aware!

Enter Faulkland *and Captain* Absolute.

Sir LUCIUS.
Gentlemen, your most obedient—hah!—what Captain Absolute!—So, I suppose, Sir, you are come here, just like myself—to do a kind office, first for your friend—then to proceed to business on your own account.

ACRES.
What, Jack!—my dear Jack!—my dear friend!

Capt. ABSOLUTE.
Heark'ee, Bob, Beverley's at hand.

Sir LUCIUS.
Well, Mr. Acres—I don't blame your saluting the gentleman civilly.—So, Mr. Beverley, *(to* Faulkland*)* if you'll chuse your weapons, the Captain and I will measure the ground.

FAULKLAND.
My weapons, Sir.

ACRES.
Odds life! Sir Lucius, I'm not going to fight Mr. Faulkland; these are my particular friends.

Sir LUCIUS.
What, Sir, did not you come here to fight Mr. Acres?

FAULKLAND.
Not I, upon my word, Sir.

Sir LUCIUS.
Well, now, that's mighty provoking. But I hope, Mr. Faulkland, as there are three of us come on purpose for the game—you won't be so cantanckerous as to spoil the party by sitting out.

Capt. ABSOLUTE.
O pray, Faulkland, fight to oblige Sir Lucius.

FAULKLAND.
Nay, if Mr. Acres is so bent on the matter.

ACRES.
No, no, Mr. Faulkland—I'll bear my disappointment like a Christian—Look'ee, Sir Lucius, there's no occasion at all for me to fight; and if it is the same to you, I'd as lieve let it alone.

Sir LUCIUS.
Observe me, Mr. Acres—I must not be trifled with. You have certainly challenged somebody—and you came here to fight him—Now, if that gentleman is willing to represent him—I can't see, for my soul, why it isn't just the same thing.

ACRES.
Z—ds, Sir Lucius—I tell you, 'tis one Beverley I've challenged—a fellow, you see, that dare not shew his face! If *he* were here, I'd make him give up his pretensions directly!——

Capt. ABSOLUTE.
Hold, Bob—let me set you right—there is no such man as Beverley in the case.—The person who assumed that name is before you; and as his pretensions are the same in both characters, he is ready to support them in whatever way you please.

Sir LUCIUS.
Well, this is lucky—Now you have an opportunity—

ACRES.
What, quarrel with my dear friend Jack Absolute—not if he
were fifty Beverleys! Z—ds! Sir Lucius, you would not have me
be so unnatural.

Sir LUCIUS.
Upon my conscience, Mr. Acres, your valour has *oozed* away
with a vengeance!

ACRES.
Not in the least! Odds Backs and Abettors! I'll be your second
with all my heart—and if you should get a *Quietus*, you may
command me entirely. I'll get you a *snug lying* in the *Abbey here*;
or *pickle* you, and send you over to Blunderbuss-hall, or any of
the kind with the greatest pleasure.

Sir LUCIUS.
Pho! pho! you are little better than a coward.

ACRES.
Mind, gentlemen, he calls me a *Coward*; Coward was the word,
by my valour!

Sir LUCIUS.
Well, Sir?

ACRES.
Look'ee, Sir Lucius, 'tisn't that I mind the word Coward—
Coward may be said in joke.—But if you had call'd me a
Poltroon, Odds Daggers and Balls!

Sir LUCIUS.
Well, Sir?

ACRES.
————I should have thought you a very ill-bred man.

Sir LUCIUS.
Pho! you are beneath my notice.

Capt. ABSOLUTE.
Nay, Sir Lucius, you can't have a better second than my friend,
Acres—He is a most *determined dog*—call'd in the country,
Fighting Bob.—He generally *kills a man a week*; don't you,
Bob?

ACRES.
Aye—at home!

Sir LUCIUS.
Well then, Captain, 'tis we must begin—so come out, my little
counsellor, [*draws his sword.*
and ask the gentleman, whether he will resign the lady, without
forcing you to proceed against him?

Capt. ABSOLUTE.
Come on then, Sir; *(draws)* since you won't let it be an amica-
ble suit, here's *my reply.*

Enter Sir Anthony, David, *and the* Women.

DAVID.
Knock 'em all down, sweet Sir Anthony, knock down my
Master in particular----and bind his hands over to their good
behaviour!

Sir ANTHONY.
Put up, Jack, put up, or I shall be in a frenzy---how came you in
a duel, Sir?

Capt. ABSOLUTE.
Faith, Sir, that gentleman can tell you better than I; 'twas he
call'd on me, and you know, Sir, I serve his Majesty.[1]

---

1 While officially forbidden to play any part in a duel, an officer could not
"honorably" refuse a challenge, since to do so would impugn his
courage, and so make him lose the respect of (and perhaps be shunned
by) his fellow officers and those under his command. Indeed, some officers who refused to fight were court-martialed for "conduct unbecom-
ing an officer and a gentleman." For details, see Gilbert.

Sir ANTHONY.

Here's a pretty fellow; I catch him going to cut a man's throat, and he tells me, he serves his Majesty!——Zounds! sirrah, then how durst you draw the King's sword against one of his subjects?

Capt. ABSOLUTE.

Sir, I tell you! That gentleman call'd me out, without explaining his reasons.

Sir ANTHONY.

Gad! Sir, how came you to call my son out, without explaining your reasons?

Sir LUCIUS.

Your son, Sir, insulted me in a manner which my honour could not brook.

Sir ANTHONY.

Zounds! Jack, how durst you insult the gentleman in a manner which his honour could not brook?

Mrs. MALAPROP.

Come, come, let's have no Honour before ladies—Captain Absolute, come here—How could you intimidate us so?—Here's Lydia has been terrified to death for you.

Capt. ABSOLUTE.

For fear I should be kill'd, or escape, Ma'am?

Mrs. MALAPROP.

Nay, no delusions to the past—Lydia is convinc'd; speak child.

Sir LUCIUS.

With your leave, Ma'am, I must put in a word here—I believe I could interpret the young lady's silence—Now mark—

LYDIA.

What is it you mean, Sir?

Sir LUCIUS.

Come, come, Delia, we must be serious now—this is no time for trifling.

LYDIA.

'Tis true, Sir; and your reproof bids me offer this gentleman my hand, and solicit the return of his affections.

Capt. ABSOLUTE.

O! my little angel, say you so?—Sir Lucius—I perceive there must be some mistake here—with regard to the affront which you affirm I have given you—I can only say, that it could not have been intentional.—And as you must be convinced, that I should not fear to support a real injury—you shall now see that I am not ashamed to atone for an inadvertency—I ask your pardon.—But for this lady, while honour'd with her approbation, I will support my claim against any man whatever.

Sir ANTHONY.

Well said, Jack, and I'll stand by you, my Boy.

ACRES.

Mind, I give up all my claim—I make no pretensions to any thing in the world—and if I can't get a wife, without fighting for her, by my Valour! I'll live a bachelor.

Sir LUCIUS.

Captain, give me your hand—an affront handsomely acknowledged becomes an obligation—and as for the Lady—if she chuses to deny her own hand writing here— *(Taking out letters.)*

Mrs. MALAPROP.

O, he will desolve my mystery!—Sir Lucius, perhaps there's some mistake—perhaps, I can illuminate—

Sir LUCIUS.

Pray, old gentlewoman, don't interfere, where you have no business.—Miss Languish, are you my Delia, or not?

LYDIA.

Indeed, Sir Lucius, I am not.

(Lydia and Captain Absolute walk aside.)

Mrs. MALAPROP.

Sir Lucius O'Trigger—ungrateful as you are—I own the soft impeachment—pardon my blushes, I am Delia.

Sir LUCIUS.
You Delia—pho! pho! be easy.

Mrs. MALAPROP.
Why, thou barbarous Vandyke[1]——those letters are mine—When
you are more sensible of my benignity—perhaps I may be
brought to encourage your addresses.

Sir LUCIUS.
Mrs. Malaprop, I am extremely sensible of your condescension;
and whether you or Lucy have put this trick upon me, I am
equally beholden to you.—And to shew you I'm not ungrateful,
Captain Absolute! since you have taken that lady from me, I'll
give you my Delia into the bargain.

Capt. ABSOLUTE.
I am much obliged to you, Sir Lucius; but here's our friend,
fighting Bob, unprovided for.

Sir LUCIUS.
Hah! little Valour—here, will you make your fortune?

ACRES.
Odds Wrinkles! No.—But give us your hand, Sir Lucius, forget
and forgive; but if ever I give you a chance of *pickling* me again,
say Bob Acres is a Dunce, that's all.

Sir ANTHONY.
Come, Mrs. Malaprop, don't be cast down—you are in your
bloom yet.

Mrs. MALAPROP.
O Sir Anthony!—men are all barbarians—

(All retire but Julia *and* Faulkland.*)*

JULIA.
He seems dejected and unhappy—not sullen—there was some

---

1   Flemish artist Sir Anthony Van Dyck (1599-1641) was so admired in the
    1760s and 1770s that it became fashionable to be painted wearing seven-
    teenth-century clothes, in order to resemble the figures depicted in his
    portraits.

foundation, however, for the tale he told me—O woman! how true should be your judgment, when your resolution is so weak!

FAULKLAND.
Julia!—how can I sue for what I so little deserve? I dare not presume—yet Hope is the child of Penitence.

JULIA.
Oh! Faulkland, you have not been more faulty in your unkind treatment of me, than I am now in wanting inclination to resent it. As my heart honestly bids me place my weakness to the account of love, I should be ungenerous not to admit the same plea for yours.

FAULKLAND.
Now I shall be blest indeed!

(Sir Anthony *comes forward.)*

Sir ANTHONY.
What's going on here?—So you have been quarrelling too, I warrant.——Come, Julia, I never interfered before; but let me have a hand in the matter at last.—All the faults I have ever seen in my friend Faulkland, seemed to proceed from what he calls the *delicacy* and *warmth* of his affection for you——There, marry him directly, Julia, you'll find he'll mend surprisingly!

(The rest come forward.)

Sir LUCIUS.
Come now, I hope there is no dissatisfied person, but what is content; for as I have been disappointed myself, it will be very hard if I have not the satisfaction of seeing other people succeed better——

ACRES.
You are right, Sir Lucius.—So, Jack, I wish you joy—Mr. Faulkland the same.—Ladies,—come now, to shew you I'm neither vex'd nor angry, Odds Tabors and Pipes! I'll order the fiddles[1]

---

1 To "order the fiddles" is to hire musicians (presumably as part of hosting a ball).

in half an hour, to the New Rooms—and I insist on you all meeting me there.

Sir ANTHONY.
Gad! Sir, I like your spirit; and at night we single lads will drink a health to the young couples, and a husband to Mrs. Malaprop.

FAULKLAND.
Our partners are stolen from us,[1] Jack—I hope to be congratulated by each other—yours for having checked in time, the errors of an ill-directed Imagination, which might have betray'd an innocent heart; and mine, for having, by her gentleness and candour, reformed the unhappy temper of one, who by it made wretched whom he loved most, and tortured the heart he ought to have ador'd.

Capt. ABSOLUTE.
Well, Jack,[2] we have both tasted the Bitters, as well as the Sweets, of Love—with this difference only, that *you* always prepared the bitter cup for yourself, while *I*———

LYDIA.
Was always obliged to *me* for it, hey! Mr. Modesty?———But come, no more of that—our happiness is now as unallay'd as general.

JULIA.
Then let us study to preserve it so: and while Hope pictures to us a flattering scene of future Bliss, let us deny its pencil those colours which are too bright to be lasting.—When Hearts deserving Happiness would unite their fortune, Virtue would crown them with an unfading garland of modest, hurtless flowers; but ill-judging Passion will force the gaudier Rose into

---

1 "Stolen from us" suggests that Julia and Lydia have "come forward" to a different part of the stage (although, as Lydia's interruption in a moment will suggest, they are perhaps more within earshot than Faulkland and Captain Absolute realize).

2 It is unclear whether the "Jack" here is just a mistake on the part of the printer or if Faulkland has the same first name as Captain Absolute (thereby creating yet another set of doubles in the play).

the wreath, whose thorn offends them, when its Leaves are
dropt!

EPILOGUE.[1]

BY THE AUTHOR.

Spoken by Mrs. BULKLEY.

Ladies for *You*—I heard our Poet say—
He'd try to coax some *Moral* from his Play:
"One moral's plain"—cried I—"without more fuss;
Man's social happiness all rests on Us—
Thro' all the Drama—whether d—n'd or not—
Love gilds the *Scene*, and *Women* guide the *plot*.
From ev'ry rank—obedience is our due—"
D'ye doubt?—The world's great stage shall prove it true.
　　　The Cit[2]—well skill'd to shun domestic strife—
Will sup abroad;—but first—he'll ask his *wife*:
John Trot, his friend—for once, will do the same,
But then—he'll just *step home to tell my dame*.—
　　　The *surly 'Squire*—at noon resolves to rule,
And half the day—"zounds! Madam is a fool!"
Convinc'd at night—the vanquish'd Victor says,
"Ah! Kate! *you women have such coaxing ways!*—"
　　　The *jolly Toper* chides each tardy blade,[3]—
Till reeling Bacchus calls on Love for aid:
Then with each Toast, he sees fair bumpers swim,
And kisses Chloe on the sparkling Brim!

1　This epilogue, and Mary Bulkley's performance of it, was much
　　admired, and it was repeatedly revived for the rest of the century (even
　　though prologues and epilogues were usually dropped after the ninth
　　night, and only retained in print).
2　Technically, a "cit" is just a citizen of a town (i.e., someone with the
　　social and economic standing to participate in local government).
　　However, in the eighteenth century, "cit" was generally a disparaging
　　term reserved for tradesmen and merchants (who supposedly had a
　　more blinkered view of the world than gentlemen).
3　A "toper" is a drunk. A "tardy blade" is a drinker who isn't keeping up
　　with his companions.

Nay, I have heard that Statesmen—great and wise—
Will *sometimes* counsel with a Lady's eyes;
The servile suitors—watch her various face,
She smiles preferment—or she frowns disgrace,
Curtsies a pension here—there nods a place.

Nor with less awe, in scenes of humbler life,
Is *view'd* the *mistress*, or is *heard* the *wife*.
The poorest Peasant of the poorest soil,
The child of Poverty, and heir to Toil—
Early from radiant Love's impartial light,
Steals one small spark, to cheer his world of night:
Dear spark!—that oft thro' winter's chilling woes,
Is all the warmth his little cottage knows!

The wand'ring *Tar*—who, not for *years*, has press'd
The widow'd Partner of his *day* of rest—
On the cold deck—far from her arms remov'd—
Still hums the ditty which his Susan lov'd:
And while around the cadence rude is blown,
The Boatswain whistles in a softer tone.[1]

The *Soldier*, fairly proud of wounds and toil,
Pants for the *triumph* of his Nancy's smile;
But ere the battle should he list' her cries,
The Lover trembles—and the Hero dies!
That heart, by war and honour steel'd to fear,
Droops on a sigh, and sickens at a tear!

But Ye more cautious—ye nice judging few,
Who give to Beauty only Beauty's due,
Tho' friends to Love—*Ye* view with deep regret
Our conquests marr'd—our triumphs incomplete,
'Till polish'd Wit more lasting charms disclose,
And Judgment fix the darts which Beauty throws!
—In female breasts did Sense and Merit rule,
The Lover's mind would ask no other school;
Sham'd into sense—the Scholars of our eyes,
Our Beaux from *Gallantry* would soon be wise;
Would gladly light, their homage to improve,
The Lamp of Knowledge at the Torch of Love!

---

1 A "tar" is a sailor. A "boatswain" (pronounced BO-sun) is the stereotyp-
ically gruff non-commissioned officer in charge of the sails and rigging
on a ship. He used a whistle to give his orders.

Appendix A: The Original Casts of the Plays

[As the Introduction suggests (pp. 26-27), the eighteenth-century theater was a repertory theater in which performers were routinely type-cast, in part to help them manage the sheer number of roles which they had to be ready to play on short notice. Once cast, though, actors regarded their parts as a kind of property, and often hung onto them for years. The result was that every new role created was likely to be shadowed not only by the specific parts which that performer had previously played, but also by other instances of the kind of characters for which he or she was generally known (coquettes, fops, grumpy old men). This may have made radical departures more difficult for an audience to accept, but it also gave them additional tools for figuring out what to expect from a new play. For more on all of these actors, see Highfill, Burnim, and Langhans.]

JANE BARSANTI (?-1795) was the original Lydia Languish in *The Rivals*, and dominated the part until the play moved, with Sheridan, to Drury Lane in 1777 (and she moved to Ireland). Barsanti was trained as a singer in the late 1760s by Charles Burney (father of the novelist Frances Burney) and most of her early theatrical roles involved music. According to her contemporaries, she had an attractive figure and an intelligent face, but also a bit of a lisp. She was rather sickly. Perhaps tellingly, given her similarities to Elizabeth Linley, Barsanti once used, in a brief return to the London theater, the stage name "Lisley."

MARY BRADSHAW (?-1780) was the original Nurse in *Polly Honeycombe*, and monopolized the part at Drury Lane until her death. In her early career, in the mid-1740s, she specialized in playing rambunctious young women. By the time *Polly Honeycombe* debuted, she had switched over to playing comic old women, particularly ones who were secretly a bit lascivious.

ASTLEY BRANSBY (?-1789) was the original Ledger in *Polly Honeycombe*, and dominated the part at Drury Lane until his retirement at the close of the 1776-77 season. From the mid-1740s on, he specialized in supporting roles, especially simpletons and somber older men. He was very tall, and his voice rather monotonous.

MARY BULKLEY (1748-92) was the original Julia in *The Rivals*, and dominated the part until the play moved, with Sheridan, to Drury Lane in 1777. She was particularly praised for her "just and elegant" performance of the epilogue (*The Morning Chronicle*, 18 January 1775). The niece of a theater manager, she was trained as a dancer, and was known at least as much for her talent in that realm, as for her acting. However, she was probably even better known for her love life: she had several high-profile affairs, including running off to Ireland with her lover in the summer of 1774 (after they had been reportedly caught together in bed in Bath). She was the original Miss Hardcastle in Oliver Goldsmith's *She Stoops to Conquer*. By all accounts, she was stunningly beautiful.

LAWRENCE CLINCH (?-1812) took over the role of Sir Lucius O'Trigger after the disastrous first night of *The Rivals*, and monopolized it until he left London at the close of the 1775-76 season. Born in Ireland, he made his London debut in 1772, and played mostly tragic roles until *The Rivals*. Sheridan was so grateful to Clinch for saving the play that he wrote an afterpiece, *St. Patrick's Day*, for Clinch's benefit performance that spring.[1]

JOHN DUNSTALL (1717-78) was the original David in *The Rivals*, but gave up the part for reasons unknown the next season. Although never a star, he played many supporting roles over the four decades of his career, most of them rough or rural comic parts. By the time of *The Rivals*'s debut, his health was failing, but he remained extremely busy, acting almost every single night of the season. He was known for breaking character to acknowledge his friends in the audience.

JAMES FEARON (1746-89) was the original Coachman in *The Rivals*, and monopolized the role at Covent Garden through the 1787-88 season. After several years of working in the provinces, Ireland, Scotland, and the London summer theater, he made his debut at Covent Garden just a few months before the premiere of *The Rivals*. His other roles that season were a mixture of comic and tragic parts, with no particular specialty.

---

1 In addition to their salaries, eighteenth-century actors were generally guaranteed a benefit performance (or, for the more minor members of the company, a share in such a performance), from which they got to keep the net profits. Since these benefits could often double their annual income, actors tried to pack the house any way they could, including offering new plays that would show off their talents.

JANE GREEN (1719-91) was the original Mrs. Malaprop in *The Rivals*, and monopolized the part at Covent Garden until the play moved, with Sheridan, to Drury Lane in 1777. The daughter of a comic actor, she began performing in her teens, both in London and the provinces. By the time *The Rivals* debuted, she had become a specialist in sly chambermaids and eccentric maiden aunts. Like Jane Pope, she was often compared to Kitty Clive, though not always as favorably. Green was the original Mrs. Hardcastle in Goldsmith's *She Stoops to Conquer*, and the original Margaret, the Duenna, in Sheridan's *The Duenna*. Apparently, she was rather fat by the point at which Sheridan entered her career.

ELIZABETH KENNEDY (c. 1730-74) was the original Mrs. Honeycombe, and monopolized the part at Drury Lane through the 1761-62 season, after which she left London to work in the Dublin and Edinburgh theaters, where her career had begun. However, she returned to the role in the summer of 1765 at the Haymarket. Her first season in London was the one in which *Polly Honeycombe* had its debut. Most of her other parts that year were scheming or otherwise morally dubious women (such as Mrs. Marwood in William Congreve's *The Way of the World*). The prompter at Drury Lane recorded on the third night of the initial run that "Polly Honeycombe goes off very well—much pleas'd with Mrs Kennedy in the last scene" (quoted in Stone, 2:829). According to one of her contemporaries, "she was far from handsome," perhaps because of a skin condition, but had "a good figure" (George Anne Bellamy, *An Apology for the Life of George Anne Bellamy* [London, 1785], 4:3).

THOMAS KING (1730-1805) was the original Scribble in *Polly Honeycombe*, and dominated the part at Drury Lane through the 1765-66 season, after which he handed off the role to a younger actor. As a teenager, King trained to be a lawyer (and so could understand Scribble's closing threats), but gave it up to become an actor. After upwards of a decade working in the provinces and Ireland, he moved to the London stage in 1759, where he quickly established himself as second only to David Garrick as a comic actor at Drury Lane, especially when it came to playing impudent young men, and (later in his career) eccentric, but ultimately good-hearted old men—including Sir Anthony Absolute in *The Rivals*. He was also renowned for his ability to banter with the audience in prologues and epilogues. He was the original Lord Ogleby (a self-satisfied, mildly lecherous aristocrat on the side of young love) in Colman and Garrick's *The Clandestine Marriage*, the original Sir Peter Teazle in Sheridan's *The School for Scandal*, and the original Puff in Sheridan's *The Critic*.

JOHN LEE (1725-81) played Sir Lucius O'Trigger on the disastrous first night of *The Rivals*, and was widely criticized for his performance (though the problems partially lay in how the role was initially written: see "A Note on the Texts"). Thereafter, the part was transferred to Lawrence Clinch. Quarrelsome, passionate, and rather unlucky, Lee spent his career moving from theater to theater, both in London and in the provinces, Ireland, and Scotland—a situation that his supporters thought kept him from ever getting the recognition he deserved. Apparently he was prone to making long pauses and to giving odd emphases to his lines. One of his daughters was Sophia Lee, author of one of the earliest historical novels in English: *The Recess* (1783-85).

JANE LESSINGHAM (c. 1739-83) was the original Lucy, and dominated the part at Covent Garden until the play moved, with Sheridan, to Drury Lane in 1777. She was a competent comic actress, but, like Mary Bulkley, she was perhaps best known for her life off-stage. In 1765 she was divorced by her husband (a rare and expensive proceeding in the eighteenth century) for bearing an illegitimate child while he was away at sea. A few years later, she became the mistress of Thomas Harris, the manager of Covent Garden whom Sheridan thanks in his Preface. She also supposedly enjoyed dressing up in men's clothing and hanging around the coffee houses. Among her other attractions, a 1768 poem claims that her breasts would have "tempted *Antony* away" from Cleopatra (*The Ring. An Epistle Addressed to Miss L------------m*, 5).

CHARLES LEE LEWES (1740-1804) was the original Fag in *The Rivals*, and monopolized the part at Covent Garden until the play moved, with Sheridan, to Drury Lane in 1777. After some time in the provincial theaters, he made his London debut in 1767, where his talents lay in pantomime and smart repartee, including a stint as Scribble in *Polly Honeycombe*. One of his daughters played Julia in *The Rivals* in the 1790s, and his grandson was George Henry Lewes, George Eliot's longtime companion. He was the original Young Marlowe in Goldsmith's *She Stoops to Conquer*.

WILLIAM THOMAS LEWIS (c. 1746-1811) was the original Faulkland in *The Rivals*, and monopolized the role at Covent Garden through the 1788-89 season. The son of an actor, he grew up performing on the Irish stage. He made his London debut in 1773, and soon established himself as a dashing and elegant comic actor. In the season in which *The Rivals* debuted, Lewis played another suspicious lover as well: Claudio in Shakespeare's *Much Ado About Nothing*.

JANE POPE (1744-1818) was the original Polly Honeycombe, and monopolized the role at Drury Lane through the 1778-79 season. She grew up around the theater (her father was the wig-maker and barber for Drury Lane), and performed several times as a child. Her adult debut came in the 1759-60 season, during which she was taken under the wing of Kitty Clive (1711-85; the best comic actress of her generation), and was soon hailed as Clive's natural successor. In the years of *Polly Honeycombe*'s greatest success, Pope played a range of parts, including Beatrice in Shakespeare's *Much Ado About Nothing*, which involved being appealingly pert. In her later years, she grew fat, and turned to specialize in maiden aunts and other sorts of comic old women, including Mrs. Malaprop in *The Rivals* (and one night, for her benefit performance in 1795, Lucy). She was the original Miss Sterling (a jealous, petty, social-climbing heiress) in Colman and Garrick's *The Clandestine Marriage*, the original Mrs. Candour in Sheridan's *The School for Scandal*, and the original Tilberina in Sheridan's *The Critic*.

JOHN QUICK (1748-1831) was the original Bob Acres in *The Rivals*, and monopolized the part at Covent Garden through the 1792-93 season. After a slow start, his career took off in 1773, when he played the original Tony Lumpkin in Goldsmith's *She Stoops to Conquer* (even though, in terms of his body, he was anything but the hulking bruiser which that character usually conjures up). Thereafter, he was a specialist in low comedy, including Mr. Honeycombe, and Isaac Mendoza in Sheridan's *The Duenna*. He was said to be George III's favorite actor.

EDWARD SHUTER (c. 1728-76) was the original Sir Anthony Absolute in *The Rivals*, but went into semi-retirement at the close of the play's first season. An extremely popular comic actor, especially among those who sat in the galleries, Shuter was known for his ability to farcically (and blasphemously) ad-lib and play the buffoon. He was also familiar to audiences well beyond London, since he regularly appeared in the provincial, Irish, and Scots theaters in the summer. However, in the years leading up to *The Rivals*, he grew fat enough to play Falstaff, his drinking grew more and more disruptive, and he frequently neglected to properly learn his lines—which helped contribute to the play's disastrous first night. By all accounts, he had an extraordinarily expressive face. He was the original Hardcastle in Goldsmith's *She Stoops to Conquer*.

HENRY WOODWARD (1714-77) was the original Captain Absolute in *The Rivals*, and monopolized the role at Covent Garden until his death. From the time he was a teenager, Woodward was a popular and versatile performer, renowned for his abilities in dance, mimicry, and pantomime, as well as comedy. While handsome and genteel in appearance, he was generally best loved in less than genteel roles, such as awkward servants, braggart soldiers, and busybodies. However, his performance of Mercutio in Shakespeare's *Romeo and Juliet* set the standard for many years. Among his many other roles, he was the original Sir Christopher Cripple, the aging rake on the verge of reformation who helps foil Solomon Flint (Walter Long)'s plan to marry Miss Linnet (Elizabeth Linley) in Samuel Foote's *The Maid of Bath*. By the time *The Rivals* debuted, Woodward was in ill health (and about fourteen years older than the actor playing his character's father), but was still vivacious, at least on stage, though a reviewer for *The Morning Chronicle* (27 January 1775) complained that he didn't look "the young, gay, handsome Officer, likely to captivate a romantic girl."

RICHARD YATES (c. 1706-96) was the original Mr. Honeycombe, and monopolized the role at Drury Lane through the 1766-67 season, after which he left the company. From the mid-1730s on, he was a versatile comic actor, especially in "low" parts, such as sailors, resourceful valets (including Fag in *The Rivals*), and cranky old men. In the summers surrounding the first few seasons of *Polly Honeycombe*, he also regularly performed variety shows at (the often raucous) Bartholomew Fair. When he forgot his lines, he would often repeat what he had just said (such as the variations on "Hark ye" which come up so frequently in *Polly Honeycombe*). In his later years, he was described as "dwarf-like" ("a wag," quoted in W.T. Parke, *Musical Memoirs* [London, 1830], 1:126). He was the original Sterling (a pretentious City merchant eager for his daughters to marry into the aristocracy) in Colman and Garrick's *The Clandestine Marriage*, and the original Sir Oliver Surface in Sheridan's *The School for Scandal*.

Appendix B: Novel-Reading and Its Discontents

[As the Introduction suggests (pp. 31-35), novel-reading, and the circulating libraries which supported it, were often the objects of a hysteria every bit as over-the-top as the ravings of Mr. Honeycombe or Sir Anthony Absolute. However, as the selections in this appendix reveal, this panic was hardly monolithic: there were probably as many devotees of the novel, as detractors. The latter, though, tended to be far louder, and so collectively convinced many eighteenth-century parents and other authorities that novel-reading was a disreputable, defiant, or at least potentially embarrassing activity.]

1. From [Samuel Johnson], *The Rambler* 4 (31 March 1750)[1]

Simul et jucunda et idonea dicere Vitæ   HOR.[2]

The Works of Fiction, with which the present Generation seems more particularly delighted, are such as exhibit Life in its true State, diversified only by the Accidents that daily happen in the World, and influenced by those Passions and Qualities which are really to be found in conversing with Mankind.

This Kind of Writing may be termed not improperly the Comedy of Romance, and is to be conducted nearly by the Rules of Comic Poetry. Its Province is to bring about natural Events by easy Means, and to keep up Curiosity without the Help of Wonder; it is therefore precluded from the Machines and Expedients of the Heroic Romance, and can neither employ Giants to snatch away a Lady from the nuptial Rites, nor Knights to bring her back from Captivity; it can neither

---

1   *The Rambler* (1750-52), a twice-a-week essay periodical, helped forge the reputation of Johnson (1709-84) as the preeminent moralist and man of letters of his age. While the initial sales of the paper were relatively small, it became more and more influential (and reprinted) as Johnson's authority grew.

2   The epigraph is from Horace's *Ars Poetica* and refers to how poets want "to speak words which are at once enjoyable and useful to our lives." Many essay periodicals, including *The Rambler*, began each issue with a relevant epigraph in Greek or Latin.

Figure 11: The spine and front of a "half-bound volume, with marbled covers" (the typical binding for books from a circulating library). Courtesy of The Ohio State University Rare Books and Manuscripts Library.

bewilder its Personages in Desarts, nor lodge them in imaginary Castles [...][1]

The Task of our present Writers is very different; it requires, together with that Learning which is to be gained from Books, that Experience which can never be attained by solitary Diligence, but must arise from general Converse, and accurate Observation of the living World. Their Performances have, as *Horace* expresses it, *plus oneris quantum veniæ minus*, little Indulgence, and therefore more Difficulty. They are engaged in Portraits of which every one knows the Original, and can therefore detect any Deviation from Exactness of Resemblance. Other Writings are safe, except from the Malice of Learning; but these are in danger from every common Reader [...]

These Books are written chiefly to the Young, the Ignorant, and the Idle, to whom they serve as Lectures of Conduct, and Introductions into Life.[2] They are the Entertainment of Minds unfurnished with Ideas, and therefore easily susceptible of Impressions; not fixed by Principles, and therefore easily following the Current of Fancy; not informed by Experience, and consequently open to every false Suggestion and partial Account.

That the highest Degree of Reverence should be paid to Youth, and that nothing indecent or unseemly should be suffered to approach their Eyes or Ears, are Precepts extorted by Sense and Virtue from an ancient Writer[3] by no Means eminent for Chastity of Thought. The same Kind, tho' not the same Degree of Caution, is required in every thing which is laid before them, to secure them from unjust Prejudices, perverse Opinions, and improper Combinations of Images.

In the Romances formerly written every Transaction and Sentiment was so remote from all that passes among Men, that the Reader was in very little danger of making any Applications to himself; the Virtues and Crimes were equally beyond his Sphere of Activity; and he

---

1 Cf. the similar opposition of "NOVEL" to "ROMANCE" in the Prologue to *Polly Honeycombe* (pp. 67-69). "Machines" are here fantastic or supernatural interventions (such as chivalric romances were often full of, and more modern kinds of fiction—except for the gothic—generally avoided).

2 Johnson inverted this formula in a 9 March 1751 letter to Samuel Richardson praising *Clarissa* as "not a performance to be read with eagerness and laid aside for ever; but [one that] will be occasionally consulted by the busy, the aged, and the studious" (*The Letters of Samuel Johnson*, ed. Bruce Redford [Princeton: Princeton UP, 1992], 1:48). "Occasionally" here means "on appropriate occasions."

3 Presumably Juvenal, whose *Satire* 14 warns parents against setting bad examples for their children.

amused himself with Heroes and with Traitors, Deliverers and Perse-
cutors, as with Beings of another Species, whose Actions were regulated upon Motives of their own, and who had neither Faults nor
Excellencies in common with himself.

But when an Adventurer is levelled with the rest of the World, and
acts in such Scenes of the universal Drama, as may be the Lot of any
other Man, young Spectators fix their Eyes upon him with closer
Attention, and hope by observing his Behaviour and Success to regu-
late their own Practices, when they shall be engaged in the like Part.

For this Reason these familiar Histories may perhaps be made of
greater Use than the Solemnities of professed Morality, and convey
the Knowledge of Vice and Virtue with more Accuracy[1] than Axioms
and Definitions. But if the Power of Example is so great, as to take
Possession of the Memory by a kind of Violence, and produce Effects
almost without the Intervention of the Will, Care ought to be taken
that, when the Choice is unrestrained, the best Examples only should
be exhibited; and that which is likely to operate so strongly, should not
be mischievous or uncertain in its Effects [...]

The Purpose of these Writings is surely not only to show Mankind,
but to provide that they may be seen hereafter with less Hazard; to
teach the Means of avoiding the Snares which are laid by TREACH-
ERY for INNOCENCE, without infusing any Wish for that Superior-
ity with which the Betrayer flatters his Vanity; to give the Power of
counteracting Fraud without the Temptation to practise it; to initiate
Youth by mock Encounters in the Art of necessary Defence, and to
increase Prudence without impairing Virtue [...]

2. From [Francis Coventry], Dedication "To Henry Fielding, Esq.," *The History of Pompey the Little: or, The Life and Adventures of a Lap-Dog*, 3rd ed. (London, 1752)[2]

SIR,

My design being to speak a word or two in behalf of novel-writing,
I know not to whom I can address myself with so much propriety as

---

1 Perhaps tellingly, Johnson revised "Accuracy" to "efficacy" almost immediately (while the initial run of *The Rambler* was still underway).

2 *The History of Pompey the Little* (originally published in 1751 without the dedication to Fielding [1707-54]) is a successful novel that relates, in mock-heroic
   and vaguely Fielding-esque fashion, the story of a lapdog as he moves from
   one owner to another. Coventry (1725-54) was a somewhat worldly priest in
   the Church of England, who had literary ambitions.

to yourself, who unquestionably stand foremost in this species of composition.

To convey instruction in a pleasant manner, and mix entertainment with it, is certainly a commendable undertaking, perhaps more likely to be attended with success than graver precepts; and even where amusement is the chief thing consulted, there is some little merit in making people laugh, when it is done without giving offence to religion, or virtue, or good manners. If the laugh be not raised at the expense of innocence or decency, good humour bids us indulge it, and we cannot well laugh too often.

Can one help wondering therefore at the contempt, with which many people affect to talk of this sort of composition? they seem to think it degrades the dignity of their understandings, to be found with a novel in their hands, and take great pains to let you know that they never read them. They are people of too great importance, it seems, to misspend their time in so idle a manner, and much too wise to be amused.

Now, tho' many reasons may be given for this ridiculous and affected disdain, I believe a very principal one, is the pride and pedantry of learned men, who are willing to monopolize reading to themselves, and therefore fastidiously decry all books that are on a level with common understandings, as empty, trifling and impertinent.

Thus the grave metaphysician for example, who after working night and day perhaps for several years, sends forth at last a profound treatise, where *A.* and *B.* seem to contain some very deep mysterious meaning; grows indignant to think that every little paltry scribbler, who paints only the characters of the age, the manners of the times, and the working of the passions, should presume to equal him in glory.

The politician too, who shakes his head in coffee-houses, and produces now and then, from his fund of observations, a grave, sober, political pamphlet on the good of the nation; looks down with contempt on all such idle compositions, as lives and romances, which contain no strokes of satire at the ministry, no unmannerly reflections upon *Hannover*,[1] nor any thing concerning the balance of power on the continent. These gentlemen and their readers join all to a man in depreciating works of humour: or if they ever vouchsafe to speak in

---

1   A "politician" is here a seeker after (and participant in) political debate, especially as it was conducted in pamphlets and newspapers. Coffee houses were notorious for being full of such men. "Hanover" is a state in Germany that was also ruled by George II. Many Britons resented how much of "their" money and manpower was devoted to the defense of their monarch's other realm.

their praise, the commendation never rises higher than, "yes, 'tis well enough for 'such a sort of a thing;'" after which the grave observator retires to his news-paper, and there, according to the general estimation, employs his time *to the best advantage*.

But besides these, there is another set, who never read any modern books at all. They, wise men, are so deep in the learned languages, that they can pay no regard to what has been published within these last thousand years. The world is grown old; men's geniuses are degenerated; the writers of this age are too contemptible for their notice, and they have no hopes of any better to succeed them. Yet these gentlemen of profound erudition will contentedly read any trash, that is disguised in a learned language, and the worst ribaldry of *Aristophanes*, shall be critiqued and commented on by men, who turn up their noses at *Gulliver* or *Joseph Andrews*.

But if this contempt for books of amusement be carried a little too far, as I suspect it is, even among men of science and learning, what shall be said to some of the greatest triflers of the times, who affect to talk the same language? these surely have no right to express any disdain of what is at least equal to their understandings. Scholars and men of learning have a reason to give; their application to severe studies may have destroyed their relish for works of a lighter cast, and consequently it cannot be expected that they should approve what they do not understand. But as for beaux, rakes, petit-maitres[1] and fine ladies, whose lives are spent in doing the things which novels record, I do not see why they should be indulged in affecting a contempt of them. People, whose most earnest business is to dress and play at cards, are not so importantly employed, but that they may find leisure now and then to read a novel. Yet these are as forward as any to despise them; and I once heard a very fine lady, condemning some highly finished conversations in one of your works, sir, for this curious reason—"because," said she, "'tis such sort of stuff as passes every day between me and my own maid" [...]

> *Your constant reader,*
> *and sincere admirer,*

---

1   Like beaux, *petit maîtres* (literally, "little masters" in French) were men thought to be foppish or otherwise overly concerned with their manners and appearance.

3. [William Whitehead], *The World* 19 (10 May 1753)[1]

To Mr. FITZ-ADAM.

Sir,

The present age is over-run with romances, and yet so strong does the appetite for them continue, that as Otway says on a less delicate occasion, ———*every rank fool goes down.*[2]

I am not surprised that any sketch of human nature, howsoever imperfect, should attract the attention of the generality of readers. We are easily delighted with pictures of ourselves, and are sometimes apt to fancy a strong likeness where there is not even the least resemblance. Those great masters of every movement of the human mind, Homer and Shakespear, knew well this propensity of our dispositions. The latter, from the nature of his writings, had more frequent opportunities of opening the most minute avenues to the heart. The former, though his province was more confined, has let no occasion pass of exerting this affecting talent. He has not only contrasted a vast variety of characters, and given all the passions their full play, but even in the stiller parts of his work, the similes and descriptions, every thing is full of human life. It is the Carian woman who stains the ivory; if a torrent descends from the mountains, some cottager trembles at the sound of it; and the fine broken landskip of rocks and woods by moon-light, has a shepherd to gaze at and admire it.[3]

---

1 *The World* (1753-56) was a highly successful weekly essay periodical to which at least thirty different writers contributed. Like many similar papers, it had a fictional editor to whom contributions would be addressed: in this case, "Adam Fitz-Adam," a genial commentator on contemporary life, especially among the urban elite. Whitehead (1715-85) was a well-connected poet and playwright. In 1757, he became poet laureate, after Thomas Gray refused the position.

2 In Thomas Otway's *The Orphan* (1680), the rakish Polydore denounces the heroine, his foster-sister Monimia, after she has refused his advances, for the ways in which "Vertue you affect, Inconstancy's your practice; / And when your loose desires once get dominion, / No hungry Churle feeds coarser at a Feast; / Every rank Fool goes down———."

3 In order to drive home the image of "dark blood [...] spurting from the wound" in a warrior's groin, Homer instructs his audience to "picture a woman dyeing ivory blood red ... a Carian or Maeonian staining a horse's cheekpiece" (*The Iliad*, trans. Robert Fagles [New York: Viking, 1990], IV.159-61). Later in that book, the "cries and crash of war" are compared to "two winter torrents raging down from the mountains, / flash floods from the well-springs plunging down in a gorge / and miles away in the hills *(continued)*

But it is not with such painters as these that I am at present concerned. They drew really from nature; and ages have felt, and applauded the truth of their designs. Whereas our modern artists (if we may guess from the motley representations they give us of our species) are so far from having studied the natures of other people, that they seldom seem to have the least acquaintance with themselves.

The writers of heroic romance, or the loves of Philodoxus and Urania, professedly soar *above nature*.[1] They introduce into their descriptions trees, water, air, &c. like common mortals; but then all their rivers are clearer than chrystal, and every breeze is impregnated with the spices of Arabia. The manners of their personages seem full as extraordinary to our gross ideas. We are apt to suspect the virtue of two young people who are rapturously in love with each other, and who travel whole years in one another's company; though we are expressly told, that at the close of every evening, when they retire to rest, the hero leans his head against a knotted oak, whilst the heroine seeks the friendly shelter of a distant myrtle. This, I say, seems to us a little unnatural; however, it is not of dangerous example. There can no harm follow if unexperienced persons should endeavour to imitate what may be thought inimitable. Should our virgins arrive but half way towards the chastity of a Parthenia,[2] it will be something gained; and we, who have had learned educations, know the power of early prejudices; some of us having emulated the public spirit, and other obsolete virtues of the old Grecians and Romans to the age of fifteen or sixteen, some of us later, even to twenty or one and twenty.

But peace be to the manes[3] of such authors. They have long enjoyed that elysium which they so frequently described on earth. The present race of romance-writers run universally into a different extreme. They spend the little art they are masters of in weaving into intricacies the

---

a shepherd hears the thunder" (IV.524-27). In Book Eight, the exulting Trojans around their campfires are likened to how "stars in the night sky glittering / round the moon's brilliance blaze in all their glory / when the air falls to a sudden, windless calm ... / all the lookout peaks stand out and the jutting cliffs / and the steep ravines and down from the high heaven bursts / the boundless bright air and all the stars shine clear / and the shepherd's heart exults" (641-47).

1   There are several different Philodoxuses and Uranias, none of whom appear in a romance together. Presumably this is either a made-up title or simply an indication of the typical content of any number of romances.

2   "Parthenia" is Greek for "maiden," and so was a name given to several different chaste young heroines of romance.

3   Ancestral spirits, especially those worthy of homage.

more familiar and more comical adventures of a Jack Slap, or a Betty Sallet; these, though they endeavour to copy after a very great original, I chuse to call our writers *below nature*; because very few of them have as yet found out their master's peculiar art of writing upon low subjects without writing in a low manner. Romances, judiciously conducted, are a very pleasing way of conveying instruction to all parts of life. But to dwell eternally upon orphan-beggars, and *serving-men of low degree*,[1] is certainly what I have called it, writing *below nature*; and is so far from conveying instruction, that it does not even afford amusement.

The writers *below nature* have one advantage in common with the writers above it, that the originals they would seem to draw from are no where to be found. The heroes and heroines of the former are undoubtedly children of the imagination; and those of the latter, if they are not all of them incapable of *reading* their own adventures, are at least unable to inform us by *writing* whether the representations of them are just, and whether people in their station did ever think or act in the manner they are described to have done. Yet the authors, even in this particular, are not quite so secure as they may imagine; for when, toward the end of the third or fourth volume, the He or She of the piece (as is usually the custom) emerges into what they call genteel life, the whole cheat is frequently discovered. From seeing their total ignorance of what they are then describing, we on good grounds conclude that they were equally unacquainted with the inferior parts of life, though we are not able to detect the falshood. Bath, one should imagine, the easiest place in the world to get a thorough knowledge of; and yet I have observed, in books of this kind, several representations of it so excessively erroneous, that they not only shewed the authors to be intirely ignorant of the manners of living there, but of the geography of the town.

But it is not the ignorance of these writers which I would principally complain of; though of that, as a Censor,[2] you ought to take notice, and should assure our young men and young women that they

---

1   "Jack Slap" and "Betty Sallet" seem to be made-up characters. The "very great original" being copied is presumably Fielding, who was often accused of being "low" because of his focus upon servants, foundlings, and other less than genteel social types. Tom Potts, the hero of a popular ballad, is described as "a serving-man of low degree," but (like a novelistic hero?) he wins the love of an heiress, despite her father's attempts to marry her to another.

2   A "Censor" is here a supervisor of public morals. This was an actual position in ancient Rome; a number of eighteenth-century periodicals claimed that they were serving a similar function.

may read fifty volumes of this sort of trash, and yet, according to the phrase which is perpetually in their mouths, *know nothing of life*. The thing I chiefly find fault with is their extreme indecency. There are certain vices which the vulgar call Fun, and the people of fashion Gallantry; but the middle rank, and those of the gentry who continue to go to church, still stigmatize them by the opprobrious names of fornication and adultery. These are confessed to be in some measure detrimental to society, even by those who practice them most; at least, they are allowed to be so in all but themselves. This being the case, why should our novel-writers take so much pains to spread these enormities? It is not enough to say in excuse that they write nonsense upon these subjects as well as others; for nonsense itself is dangerous here. The most absurd ballads in the streets, without the least glimmering of meaning, recommend themselves every day both to the great and small vulgar only by obscene expressions. Here therefore, Mr. Fitz-Adam, you should interpose your authority, and forbid your readers (whom I will suppose to be all persons who can read) even to attempt to open any novel, or romance, unlicensed by you; unless it should happen to be stamped FIELDING, &c.

Your power should extend likewise to that inundation of obscenity which is daily pouring in from France; and which has too frequently the wit and humour of a Crebillon to support it. The gentlemen, who never read any thing else, will I know be at a loss for amusement, and feel their half-hour of morning hang rather too heavy on their hands. But surely, Mr. Fitz-Adam, when they consider the good of their country (and all of them have that at heart) they will consent to meet a little sooner at the hazard[1] table, or while away the tedious interval in studying new chances upon the cards.

If it be said that the heroic romances which I have recommended for their virtue, are themselves too full of passionate breathings upon some occasions, I allow the charge; but am of opinion that these can do little more harm to the minds of young ladies than certain books of devotion, which are put into their hands by aunts and grandmothers; the writers of which, from having suffered the softer passions to mix

---

1   Claude Prosper Jolyot de Crébillon (1707-77) was a French novelist known for his elegant, but unabashed depictions of erotic behavior. The gentlemen have a "half-hour of morning" because they don't rise until 11:30—as Ledger reminds us in *Polly Honeycombe*, the fashionable world was on a completely different schedule than the world of business. "Hazard" is a dice game similar to craps.

too strongly with their zeal for religion, are now generally known by the name of the *amorous divines*.[1]

I am, SIR,

Your most humble servant,

I. T.

4. From [William Dodd], *The Sisters; or, The History of Lucy and Caroline Sanson, Entrusted to a false Friend* (London, 1754)[2]

[...] Mrs. *Stevens* was proceeding, when her narration was interrupted by a letter, which having first run over, she burst into tears, and gave it to Mr. *Jaison* to read—the contents were these.

Honoured Madam,

For so I still think myself obliged to call you, tho' as the poet says, *Cruelty destroys all duty*; and indeed your cruelty to me, as you must know yourself, is very great and dreadful. I am sure there has never been a more dutiful child, and why shou'd you be averse to my making my fortune, and myself happy, is utterly unaccountable, except on the same motives that the charming *Clarissa*'s inhuman and brutish parents prevented her happiness with that most delightful creature sweet Mr. *Lovelace*.[3] As I have read, and I hope to advantage, I have well consider'd the reasons wherefore these persons as Miss *Clarissa*

---

1   Devotional writers and evangelical preachers were often denounced for drawing upon erotic language (and energy) for spiritual purposes.

2   *The Sisters* is a moderately successful novel that tells the story of two sisters who come to London and meet markedly different fates (one marries and lives happily ever after; the other dies squalidly after a prolonged downward trajectory). Dodd (1729-77) was a fashionable priest in the Church of England who routinely lived beyond his means, and so turned to various sorts of writing (including, at the end of his life, forgery—for which he was hanged).

3   Robert Lovelace is the villain of Samuel Richardson's immensely influential *Clarissa* (1747-48). In order to escape a loathsome arranged marriage, Clarissa Harlowe runs away with the aristocratic Lovelace, only to discover that she is as much a prisoner with him as she was with her own family (he wants to marry her in order to revenge himself upon the Harlowes for their ill treatment of him). Eventually he drugs and rapes her, after which she escapes and dies an exemplary Christian death.

Harlowe, Miss *Sophia Western, Arabella, Amelia,*[1] and the rest, have met with so much uneasiness and disappointment in life, and I have perceived it to proceed from a foolish notion imbibed early in youth, (and prejudices you know Madam, *Fielding* inimitably observes are not easily got the better of,)—what was I saying?—Oh their misfortunes all arose from an absurd regard to scrupulous virtue, a false phantom, which they frighted themselves with; for if they had each given way a little, it is plain they had avoided infinite mischiefs and misery. Now, Madam, as I am assur'd you have a much better opinion of me than to think I have so ill-distinguishing a head as to read without making proper reflections and improvement, and as I conceive this moral way of writing, in which we of this age so much excel, and which to be sure is the finest, best and most instructive way of writing that ever was invented, is to teach us life, and to direct us in the knowledge of things, so I have read with this view, and greatly improv'd my way of thinking, avoiding the errors there recorded, and following my better judgment, have without any of their troubles made myself happy. For never did a man, no, not all the *Lovelaces*, or *Jones*'s, or *Booths*, or *Pickles*, or *Randoms*,[2] or all the men in the world, never did they love a woman as dear charming Mr. *Fortebrand* loves me—he sits by me and kisses me, and bids me say so—nay, now he insists upon it, that I let him put in a word—(here was written in Mr. *Fortebrand's hand*) "Madam, what she says is true, d—me, *Fortebrand*."

Well, never was any woman more happy, and can I distrust his love? no, he declares he will marry me, if I desire it, tho' to be sure as he observes, there is no great matter in it, only just to satisfy one's friends and the world, tho' indeed I think, it rather more fashionable not to marry: as to marriage, Madam, it is only a ceremony, and ceremonies cannot tie hearts.

> *Hearts united are the thing,*
>   *Love alone can hearts unite:*
> *Priests may join with words and ring,*
>   *Nought but love can hold us tight.*

---

1 "Miss Sophia Western, Arabella, [and] Amelia" are, respectively, the heroines of Fielding's *Tom Jones* (1749), Charlotte Lennox's *The Female Quixote* (1752), and Fielding's *Amelia* (1751). Like Clarissa, they are all mistreated by those who are supposed to care for them.

2 Booth is the hero of Fielding's *Amelia*, and Peregrine Pickle and Roderick Random are the eponymous heroes of two novels (1751 and 1748, respectively) by Tobias Smollett (1721-71). None of the men mentioned are renowned for their chastity or strict fidelity.

So true are the words of that delightful poet—what—who? I forget his name but no matter for that.[1] However I tend Madam to the business and conclusion of my letter: I wou'd not have you uneasy: for I am not so: if you can be tolerably civil, I shall be glad to see you at my lodgings with my dear sweet *Forte:* if not, I beg you wou'd not interrupt my happiness, but believe me always to be and ever to continue,

Your most happy,
Most fortunate,
and delighted daughter,
JANE FORTEBRAND.

Mr. *Jaison* on concluding the letter promis'd Mrs. *Stevens* all the assistance in his power, and advis'd, as the least evil of the two, that Mrs. *Stevens* should dissemble any dislike, visit her daughter, and if possible procure a marriage between them: the poor unfortunate woman was in such violent grief that advice was then unavailing [...][2]

5. From [Owen Ruffhead], *The Monthly Review* 24 (1761)[3]

ALMORAN *and* HAMET: *An Oriental Tale.* 2 vols. 12mo. 5s. bound. Payne.[4]

The Genius of Romance seems to have been long since drooping among us; and has, of late, been generally displayed only for the basest purposes; either to raise the grin of Ideotism by its buffoonry, or stimulate the prurience of Sensuality by its obscenity. Novels, therefore, have circulated chiefly among the giddy and licentious of both sexes, who read, not for the sake of thinking, but for want of thought.

---

1   These verses, like her earlier quotation from "the poet," appear to be made up.

2   Fortebrand later abandons Jane and their unborn child, forcing her to return home, where she remained as "undutiful and ungrateful as she before had been" (2:239).

3   *The Monthly Review* (1749-1844) was the first periodical in English devoted entirely to reviewing new books of interest to the general public. For more on its power (and that of its rival, *The Critical Review*), see Introduction, pp. 34-35. Ruffhead (1723-69) was a lawyer, a political pamphleteer, and a regular reviewer for the *Monthly*.

4   The information given after the title was a standard part of eighteenth-century book reviews. In this case, it means that *Almoran and Hamet* was available as a two-volume set, in a duodecimo (12mo) format, at a price of 5 shillings. It came already bound, and was being published by Henry Payne. Duodecimos were small books (about the size of a modern paperback).

So shameful a prostitution has brought this species of writing into such disrepute, that if the more serious and solid Reader is at any time tempted to cast an eye over the pages of Romance, he almost blushes to confess his curiosity.

Compositions of this kind, nevertheless, when conducted by a Writer of fine talents and elegant taste, may be rendered as beneficial as delectable. They have this peculiar advantage, that, by making a forcible impression on the imagination, they answer the purposes of conviction and persuasion, with the generality of mankind, much better than a direct appeal to the judgment.

Very few are disposed to relish the dry precepts of morality, or to connect a lengthened chain of reasoning; the majority must be entertained with novelty, humoured with fiction, and, as it were, cheated into instruction [...]

These principles may be of use to us, in judging of the little volumes before us, which are not, we are afraid, among the number of those of which Mr. Lownds need provide a vast many sets for the accomodation of his fair customers. Here they will find no winding up of Clocks,—no wanton double entendres,—no asterisms pregnant with gross ideas,—no lambent pupilability.—In short, every thing here is chaste, elegant and moral [...][1]

6. From *The Critical Review* 20 (1765)[2]

The History of Miss Clarinda Cathcart, *and Miss* Fanny Renton. *Two Vols.* 12mo. Pr. 6s. Noble.

The principal subject of this novel, which appears to be the production of a female pen, is, like that of most others, Love. From the usual strain of these compositions, one would be apt to conclude, that love is not only the principal, but almost the sole passion that actuates the human heart. This we consider as one of the most dangerous conse-

---

1 Thomas Lownds ran one of the largest circulating libraries in London (see the map in Figure 9, p. 58). Laurence Sterne's *Tristram Shandy* (1759-67) opens with the narrator's mother mentally associating the winding up of a clock with sex (both were monthly events in her household). *Tristram Shandy* is full of double-entendres, many of which involve typography, including "asterisms" (asterisks). Slawkenbergius, the supposed author of a tale inset within *Tristram Shandy,* describes "the lambent pupilability of slow, low, dry chat" (4:76) between lovers, which sentimentally affects the heart in a way that completely by-passes the brain.

2 *The Critical Review* (1756-1817), founded by Smollett and run by him until 1763, was the principal competitor of *The Monthly Review.*

quences resulting from the too general prevalence of these kind of writings. The youth of both sexes, having their minds early tinctured with this unhappy prejudice, are thereby rendered liable to the grossest delusions. They fondly imagine, agreeably to what they have read in romances, that every thing must yield to the irresistible influence of all conquering love: but, upon mixing with the world, and studying mankind, not as they are represented in Novels, but as they exist in reality, they find, to their cost, that they have been miserably deceived; that they have viewed human nature through a false medium; and that though love has a strong influence on the actions of men, yet is it frequently over-powered by avarice, ambition, vanity, and a thousand other passions. With this defect, however, which this piece has in common with many others of the same nature, it must likewise be confessed to have some share of merit [...]

Thus the present Novel, like most others, concludes not with one only, but with two marriages. Two other matches are made in the course of the work, and several, though unfinished, are left in great forwardness; for, as we have observed, love, gallantry, courtship, and marriage, form the very soul of modern romance [...]

7. From [James Fordyce], *Sermons to Young Women* (London, 1766)[1]

[...] But I proceed [...] to caution you against that fatal poison to virtue, which is conveyed by Profligate and by Improper Books.

When entertainment is made the vehicle of instruction, nothing surely can be more harmless, agreeable, or useful. To prohibit young minds the perusal of any writings, where Wisdom addresses the affections in the language of the imagination, may be sometimes well meant, but must be always injudicious. Some such writings undoubtedly there are; the offspring of real genius enlightened by knowledge of the world, and prompted, it is to be hoped, by zeal for the improvement of youth [...]

Amongst the few works of this kind which I have seen, I cannot but look on those of Mr. Richardson as well entitled to the first rank [...] an author, to whom your sex are under singular obligations for his uncommon attention to their best interests; but particularly for presenting, in a character sustained throughout with inexpressible pathos

---

1 Fordyce (1720-96) was a fashionable Presbyterian minister. His *Sermons to Young Women* was probably the single most influential conduct book of the later eighteenth century, and was often given to young women. Lydia Languish exploits the display value of her copy in Act One, Scene Two of *The Rivals*.

and delicacy, the most exalted standard of female excellence that was ever held up to their imitation [...]

Besides the beautiful productions of that incomparable pen, there seem to me to be very few, in the style of Novel, that you can read with safety, and yet fewer that you can read with advantage.—What shall we say of certain books, which we are assured (for we have not read them) are in their nature so shameful, in their tendency so pestiferous, and which contain such rank treason against the royalty of Virtue, such horrible violation of all decorum, that she who can bear to peruse them must in her soul be a prostitute, let her reputation in life be what it will. But can it be true—say, ye chaste stars, that with innumerable eyes inspect the midnight behaviour of mortals—can it be true, that any young woman, pretending to decency, should endure for a moment to look on this infernal brood of futility and lewdness?

Nor do we condemn those writings only, that, with an effrontery which defies the laws of God and men, carry on their very forehead the mark of the beast. We consider the general run of Novels as utterly unfit for you. Instruction they convey none. They paint scenes of pleasure and passion altogether improper for you to behold, even with the mind's eye. Their descriptions are often loose and luscious in a high degree; their representations of love between the sexes are almost universally overstrained. All is dotage, or despair; or else ranting swelled into burlesque. In short, the majority of their lovers are either mere lunatics, or mock-heroes. A sweet sensibility, a charming tenderness, a delightful anguish, exalted generosity, heroic worth, and refinement of thought; how seldom are these best ingredients of virtuous love mixed with any judgment or care in the composition of their principal characters! [...]

To come back to the species of writing which so many young women are apt to doat upon, the offspring of our present Novelists, I mean the greater part; with whom we may join the common herd of Play-writers. Beside the remarks already made on the former, is it not manifest with respect to both, that such books lead to a false taste of life and happiness; that they represent vices as frailties, and frailties as virtues; that they engender notions of love unspeakably perverting and inflammatory; that they overlook in a great measure the finest part of the passion, which one would suspect the authors had never experienced; that they turn it most commonly into an affair of wicked or of frivolous gallantry; that on many occasions they take off from the worst crimes committed in the prosecution of it, the horror which ought ever to follow them; on some occasions actually reward those very crimes, and almost on all leave the female reader with this persuasion at best, that it is their business to get husbands at any rate, and by whatever means? Add to the account, that repentance for the

foulest injuries which can be done the sex, is generally represented as the pang, or rather the start, of a moment; and holy wedlock converted into a sponge, to wipe out at a single stroke every stain of guilt and dishonour, which it was possible for the hero of the piece to contract.
———Is this a kind of reading calculated to improve the principles, or preserve the Sobriety, of female minds? How much are those young women to be pitied, that have no wise parents or faithful tutors to direct them in relation to the books which are, or which are not, fit for them to read! How much are those parents and tutors to be commended, who with particular solicitude watch over them in so important a concern! [...]

8. From [Hester Chapone], *Letters on the Improvement of the Mind, Addressed to a Young Lady* (London, 1773)[1]

[...] I would by no means exclude the kind of reading, which young people are naturally most fond of—though I think the greatest care should be taken in the choice of those *fictitious stories*, that so enchant the mind—most of which tend to inflame the passions of youth, whilst the chief purpose of education should be to moderate and restrain them.—Add to this, that both the writing and sentiments of most novels and romances are such as are only proper to vitiate your stile, and to mislead your heart and understanding.—The expectation of extraordinary adventures—which seldom ever happen to the sober and prudent part of mankind—and the admiration of extravagant passions and absurd conduct, are some of the usual fruits of this kind of reading—which, when a young woman makes it her chief amusement, generally renders her ridiculous in conversation, and miserably wrongheaded in her pursuits and behaviour.—There are however works of this class, in which excellent morality is joined with the most lively pictures of the human mind, and with all that can entertain the imagination and interest the heart.—But, I must repeatedly exhort you, never to read any thing of the sentimental kind, without taking the judgment of your best friends in the choice—for, I am persuaded, that the indiscriminate reading of such kind of books corrupts more female hearts than any other cause whatsoever [...]

---

1 Chapone (1727-1801) was a genteel, but not wealthy writer and moralist, who was encouraged by the "bluestocking" Elizabeth Montagu to publish the letters that she had sent her teenage niece in the later 1760s. Like Fordyce's *Sermons*, Chapone's *Letters* were highly successful, and a popular present for young women. Lydia Languish exploits their display value in Act One, Scene Two of *The Rivals*.

9. From *The Monthly Review* 49 (1773)

The Fatal Connexion. By Mrs. Fogerty, Author of Col. Digby and
Miss Stanby. 12mo. 2 Vols. 5s. Bladon. 1773.[1]

Surely Mrs. Fogerty was begotten, born, nursed, and educated in a
circulating library, and sucked in the spirit of romance with her
mother's milk! Novel-writing seems quite natural to her; and while she
lives there is no fear that the reading Misses and reading Masters who
cultivate this profitable study at the easy rate of ten shillings and six-
pence per ann. will ever want a due supply of adventures, memoirs,
and genuine histories of Lady this, and Lord that, and Colonel t'other
thing. In the manufacturing of all which, the greatest difficulty seems
to be—the hitting off a new title page: for as to the stories told, and
the characters drawn, they are all echoes of echoes, and shadows of
shades.

10. From [William Enfield], *The Monthly Review* 52 (1775)[2]

The Morning Ramble; or History of Miss Evelyn. 12mo. 2 Vols. 6s.
bound. Noble. 1775.

A young lady in love with her supposed uncle.—An old dotard in love
with this same young lady, his supposed grand-daughter.—These
amours made honest by the help of a gypsy, whose child the loved
and loving fair one is said to be.—Her virgin chastity attempted by the
ancient lover, and rescued by the younger.—Her virgin chastity again
attempted by the friend of her beloved *Adonis*, and again rescued by a
mad adventurer.—The rescued fair conducted by her new inamorato
to the mouth of a dismal cave, (in which he threatens instantly to end
his life before her eyes, unless she consents to repay his services with
those charms which he had preserved) and there terrified into a
promise of marriage.[3]—A *third ravishment*, and a murder, introduced
for the sake of *variety* and *entertainment*, into the husband's story of
himself.—The wife, unmindful of her holy vow, on a sudden suffering

---

1   This is one of the titles that Lucy has been unsuccessfully seeking in Act One,
    Scene Two of *The Rivals*.
2   Enfield (1741-97) was a Unitarian minister, a tutor at Warrington Academy (a
    school for dissenting Protestants), and a regular reviewer for the *Monthly*.
3   Thomas Mathews supposedly attempted a similar move (not involving a cave)
    with Elizabeth Linley, which prompted her elopement with Sheridan (see Bor
    and Clelland, 43). Cf. Captain Absolute's version of this scenario in Act Five,
    Scene Two, of *The Rivals*.

her first passion to rekindle.—Her husband in a fit of jealousy, encountering his innocent rival.—The hapless fair rushing between their swords. Wounded.—Expiring.—Lamented.

This is a true bill of fare of the Morning's Ramble. A very pretty, *romantic*, *sentimental* morning's entertainment for *Miss in her Teens*.[1]

11. From *The Critical Review* 39 (1775)

The Correspondents, an Original Novel; in a Series of Letters. 12*mo*. 2*s*. 6*d. sewed*. Becket.

The title of Novel prefixed to this little piece may excite in persons of different tastes, prejudices which it little merits. The graver sort of readers will take for granted that it is perfectly a-kin to those seducing publications which constitute the chief furniture of circulating libraries; while miss at boarding-school, whose imagination is fired with the perusal of the tender scenes which those publications exhibit, is impatient till she has an opportunity to procure *The Correspondents*. The judgment formed of this piece from its title will be, however, in these cases, very erroneous. In this novel, no female laments that the tyranny of her parents prevents her from eloping with the dear, dear, man she loves; no cooing turtle pours forth her soul in tender epistles, which the faithful chambermaid conveys to the favourite swain; no rake triumphs over, and forsakes, the fair one he has deceived; in short, no intrigue is carried on; and, for that reason alone, a true novel reading girl would not give six-pence for the book.[2] Thus far for its negative merit; and negative merit is all we can allow it. Without plot, without connexion, and with very little sentiment, it is one of the most uninteresting, insipid, futile productions, which has ever come under our notice.

---

1 Perhaps an allusion to David Garrick's extremely popular afterpiece, *Miss in Her Teens* (1747), which features a heroine much like Polly Honeycombe and Lydia Languish, and a reluctant duel not unlike the one which almost occurs in the final scene of *The Rivals*.

2 A "turtle" is here a turtle-dove, and so a nickname for a lover (since turtle-doves were known for their affection and fidelity). A "swain" is a poetic name for a rural laborer, especially a shepherd. In pastoral and romance, shepherds hardly ever have to work, and so can pass their days as lovers.

Appendix C: "Such Paragraphs in the News-Papers!"

[As the Introduction suggests (pp. 33-38), Sheridan was famous for his love life several years before he gained any sort of celebrity for his writing. Audiences at the early performances of *The Rivals* would almost certainly have recognized—or thought they recognized—glimpses of Sheridan's own elopement with Elizabeth Linley in the story of Captain Absolute and Lydia Languish, and the duels and deceit that surround them. This is not to say that the play is simply or straightforwardly autobiographical—any attempt to pin down one-to-one correspondences immediately ties itself in knots—but it certainly draws upon and tries to exploit the thrill of momentary connection and felt intimacy that lies at the heart of our relation to celebrities. It should be noted that eighteenth-century newspapers routinely copied from one another, so one need not have encountered these particular issues in order to have read these "paragraphs." Almost all of them appeared in several other newspapers and magazines as well.]

1. Report of Sheridan's Elopement with Elizabeth Linley, *The Daily Advertiser*, 26 March 1772

Bath, March 23. Wednesday Evening [i.e., 18 March] the eldest Miss Linley, of this City, justly celebrated and admired for her Musical Abilities, set off with Mr. Sheridan, jun. on a Matrimonial Expedition to Scotland.[1]

2. Thomas Mathews's Denunciation of Sheridan, *The Bath Chronicle*, 9 April 1772

BATH, Wednesday, April 8, 1772.
MR. RICHARD S******* having attempted, in a Letter left behind him for that Purpose, to account for his scandalous Method of running away from this Place, by Insinuations, derogating from *my* Character, and that of a young Lady, *innocent* as far as relates to *me* or *my Knowledge*; since which he neither has taken any Notice of Letters, or even informed his own Family of the Place where he has hid himself.---I can no longer think he deserves the Treatment of a Gentleman, and

---

1 Scotland was not bound by the restrictions of English marriage law, and so was a popular destination for elopements and otherwise illegal weddings.

Figure 12: Thomas Gainsborough's portrait of *Elizabeth and Thomas Linley* (c. 1768), which was exhibited in his studio in Bath. Oil on canvas, 27.48 x 24.53 in. Sterling and Francine Clark Art Institute, Williamstown, Massachusetts. 1955.955. © Sterling and Francine Clark Art Institute.

therefore shall trouble myself no further about him, than in this public Method to post him as a *L**** and a *treacherous S*********.[1]

And as I am convinced there have been many malevolent Incendiaries concerned in the Propagation of this infamous Lie, if any of them, unprotected by *Age, Infirmities,* or *Profession,* will dare to acknowledge the Part they have acted, and affirm *to,* what they have *of* me, they may depend on receiving the proper Reward of their Villainy, in the most public Manner. The World will be candid enough to judge properly (I make no Doubt) of any *private* Abuse on this Subject for the future; as nobody can defend himself from an Accusation he is ignorant of.   THOMAS MATHEWS.

3. Report of the First Duel, *The London Evening-Post*, 2-5 May 1772

Saturday morning Th—s M—th—s, Esq; and Mr. Sh—r—d—n, met in Crutched-friars, and came to an immediate decision of their well-known quarrel; when the latter was run through the body, and carried to Mr. E——'s, Thames-street; where, it appears, the wound is not mortal.[2] Mr. M——— is gone to France with Capt. K—t, his second.

4. Contradiction of *The London Evening-Post* Report, *The Bath Chronicle*, 7 May 1772

We can with authority contradict the account in the London Even. Post of last night, of a duel between Mr. M--t--ws and Mr. S--r---n, as to the time and event of their meeting, Mr. S. having been at this place on Saturday, and both those gentlemen being here at present.[3]

---

1 The words concealed by asterisks are, presumably, "Liar" and "Scoundrel." The easiest way to provoke a duel was to publicly accuse a gentleman of lying (since to do so suggested that he lacked the courage to speak truthfully, and so didn't deserve the honor which his status had granted him). Challenges to duels were increasingly made in writing in the later eighteenth century, but it was rare to do so in print (although duels resulting from other sorts of items in the papers were not uncommon, and duelists often tried to use the press to publicize their side of a quarrel).

2 "Crutched Friars" was an old, somewhat run-down street near the Tower of London. It is also mentioned in the final scene of *Polly Honeycombe*. See the map in Figure 9, p. 58. Thames Street is nearby. Note the totally erroneous information regarding the location of the duel, Sheridan's injury, and Mathews's whereabouts.

3 The correction here is a bit misleading: Sheridan was in Bath that Saturday, and both he and Mathews were back in Bath before this issue came out. But their actual duel was in London (though not in Crutched Friars, as *The London Evening-Post* had it).

Figure 13: Thomas Gainsborough's portrait of *The Linley Sisters* [Elizabeth and Mary], which was exhibited at the Royal Academy in London in the late spring of 1772. Oil on canvas, 78 3/8 x 60 1/4 in. Dulwich Picture Gallery, London. 320. By Permission of the Trustees of Dulwich Picture Gallery.

5. **Mathews's Apology to Sheridan,** *The Bath Chronicle*, **7 May 1772**

Being convinced that the Expressions I made Use of to Mr. SHERI-DAN's Disadvantage, were the Effects of Passion and Misrepresentation, I retract what I have said to that Gentleman's Disadvantage, and particularly beg his Pardon for my Advertisement in the Bath Chronicle.

THOMAS MATHEWS.

6. **Draft of an unsent (?) letter from Sheridan, "written in the Parade coffee-house 9 o'clock Tuesday night" [presumably the eve of the second duel] and apparently intended for** *The Bath Chronicle*[1] **[c. late June 1772]**

It has ever been esteem'd impertinent to appeal to the *publick* in concerns merely private but there now & then occurs a *private* incident which by being explain'd may be productive of *publick* advantage. this consideration, and the precedent of a *publick* appeal in this same affair, are my only apologies for the new following lines.

Mr. *T. Mathews* thought himself essentially injured by Mr. *R. Sheridan*'s having co-operated in the virtuous efforts of a young Lady to escape the snares of vice & dissimulation. He wrote several most abusive threats to Mr. S.—then in France. He labour'd with a cruel industry to vilify his character in England. He publickly posted him as a scoundrel & a Liar.——Mr. S. answered him from France (hurried & surprised) that he would never sleep in England 'till *he* had thank'd him as he deserved.

Mr. S. arrived at London at 9 o'clock at night. At 10 he is informed by Mr. S. Ewart that Mr. M. is in town. Mr. S. had sat up at Canterbury to keep his idle promise to Mr. M. He resolved to call on *Mr. M.* that night, as, (in case he had not found him in town he had call'd on Mr. Ewart to accompany him to *Bath*, being bound by Mr. Linley not to let any thing pass between him & Mr. M. till he had arrived thither.) Mr. S. came to Mr. Cochlins in crutched Friars (where Mr. M. was lodged) about half after twelve.—The key of Mr. C's door was lost. Mr. S. was denied admittance. by 2 o clock He got in. Mr. M. had been previously down to the door & told Mr. S. he should be admitted, & had retired to bed again. He dressed—complained of the cold,

---

1 This account is bound into an extra-illustrated copy of Thomas Moore, *Memoirs of the Life of the Right Honourable Richard Brinsley Sheridan* (Frampton, 1877) held by the Beinecke Rare Book and Manuscript Library, Yale University [call number Im Sh53 +W825a, Vol. 1]. I am grateful to the staff of the Beinecke for their help in locating this document and making it available for transcription.

endeavour'd to get heat into him, call'd Mr. S. his *dear Friend*, & *forced* him to—*sit down.*

Mr. S. had been informed that Mr. M. had *sworn* his death, that Mr. M. had in numberless companies produced *bills*[1] on France, whither he meant to retire on the completion of his revenge. Mr. M. had warn'd Mr. Ewart to advise his Friend not even to come in his way without a sword, as he could not answer for the consequence.

Mr. M. had left two Letters for Mr. S. in which he declares he is to be met with at *any* hour, & begs Mr. S. will not *"deprive himself of so much sleep,* or stand upon *any ceremony."* Mr. S. called on him at the hour mentioned. Mr. S. was admitted with the *difficulty* mentioned. Mr. S. declares that on Mr. M.'s perceiving that he came with Pistols to answer *then* to his challenge he does not remember ever to have seen a *Man* behave so perfectly dastardly. Mr. M. detained Mr. S. 'till 7 o clock the next morning. *He* (Mr. M.) said he never meant to quarrel with Mr. *S.* He convinced Mr. S. that his enmity ought to be directed solely against his brother, & another Gentleman at Bath. Mr. S. went to Bath. in an hour he found every one of Mr. M.['s] assertions totally & positively disavow'd. Mr. S. staid but 3 hours in Bath. he returned to London, he sent to Mr. M. from *Hyde-parck.*[2] Mr. M. came with Capt. *Knight* his second. He objected *frequently* to the ground. They adjourned to the Hercules' Pillers.[3] They returned to Hyde-parck. Mr. M. *objected* to the observation of an officer. they returned to the Hercules' Pillers. they adjourned (by agreement) to the Bedford Coffee-house. Mr. M. was gone to the Castel Tavern.[4] Mr. S. follow'd with Mr. E. Mr. M. made many declarations in favour of Mr. S. They engaged. Mr. M. was disarm'd. Capt. K. run in, Mr. M. begg'd his life, & afterwards denied the advantage. Mr. S. was provoked by (the really well-ment) interposition of Capt. K. & the elusion of Mr. M. He insisted since Mr. M. denied the advantage, that he should give up his sword, Mr. M. denied but sooner than return to his ground he gave it up—it was broke. & Mr. M. offer'd another. He was then called on to retract his abuse, & beg Mr. S.'s pardon. with much altercation & much ill grace *He* complied.—The affair was settled. The sword's being broke was not to be mentioned, if Mr. M. never misrepresented the affair. Mr. S. came to Bath. he gave Mr. M. credit. Mr. *M.*

---

1 "Bills" here are bills of exchange (Mathews was apparently transferring money to France, in anticipation of fleeing the jurisdiction of English law, if he killed Sheridan).

2 Hyde Park is a large park in western London, and was a popular site for duels. See the map in Figure 9, p. 58.

3 An inn at the southeast corner of Hyde Park.

4 The Bedford Coffeehouse and the Castle Tavern were both in Covent Garden, a mile-and-a-half east of Hyde Park. See the map in Figure 9, p. 58.

came to Bath—he misrepresented the whole transaction: He wrote to all his acquaintance. He told *his own story*. Mr. S. wrote to—nobody. he contradicted whatever was told him as Mr. M.'s misrepresentation. Mr. M. found that *Truth* prevailed. He feared the aspersion of want of resolution. He grew desperate & seems resolved to *force* Mr. S. to hazard *life* (which He confessed he had once received from him) to establish his reputation. Mr. S. flatters his own charity, that he has in this representation treated Mr. M. *most tenderly*. as to the truth of it, let their Seconds (Mr. Ewart & Capt. Knight) decide.

R B Sheridan.

7. Report of Sheridan's Second Duel with Mathews, *The Bath Chronicle*, 2 July 1772

This morning [i.e., 1 July] about three o'clock, a second duel was fought with swords between Capt. Mathews and Mr. R. Sheridan, on Kingsdown,[1] near this city, in consequence of their former dispute respecting an amiable young lady, which Mr. M. considered as improperly adjusted, Mr. S. having, since their first rencountre, declared his sentiments respecting Mr. M. in a manner that the former thought required satisfaction. Mr. Sheridan received three or four wounds in his breast and sides, and now lies very ill, Mr. M. was only slightly wounded, and left this city soon after the affair was over.

8. Report of Sheridan's Wounding in the Second Duel, *The London Chronicle*, 2-4 July 1772

Extract of a Letter from Bath, dated July 1. Young Sheridan and Capt. Mathews of this town, who lately had a rencounter in a Tavern in London upon account of the Maid of Bath, Miss Linley, have had another this morning upon Kingsdown, about four miles hence. Sheridan is much wounded, but whether mortally or not is yet unknown. Both their swords breaking upon the first lunge, they threw each other down, and with the broken pieces hacked at each other rolling upon the ground, the seconds standing by quiet spectators. Mathews is but little, if at all, wounded, and is since gone off.

9. Another Report of the Second Duel, *The London Evening-Post*, 2-4 July 1772

Extract of a letter from Bath, July 2. Yesterday morning a duel was fought near this place between Mr. Mathew and a Mr. Sheridan; the

---

1 "Kingsdown" is a hill east of Bath.

latter declining pistols, they engaged with swords. Sheridan, after receiving several wounds, closed with Mr. Matthew; their swords breaking in the fall, the engagement was continued on the ground with the pointed ends. Sheridan was brought to the White Hart, and it's said here Matthew is gone to Calais.[1]

10. Report on Sheridan's Wounds, *The Public Advertiser*, 8 July 1772

By a private Letter from Bath we are informed, the general Opinion of the Faculty[2] is, that Mr. Sheridan will not recover from the Wounds he received in the Duel with Mr. Mathews last week. In the Rencounter both their Swords broke, and the Combatants fell to the Ground, where Mr. Sheridan received a Wound in his Throat from his Antagonist's broken Sword.

11. Another Report on Sheridan's Wounds, *The Bath Chronicle*, 9 July 1772

The last affair between Mr. Matthews and Mr. Sheridan, we are now assured, was occasioned by Mr. S's refusal to sign a paper, testifying the *spirit* and *propriety* of Mr. M's behaviour in their former rencounter. This refusal induced Mr. M to send him a challenge, which was accepted, and Kingsdown was the place appointed for the decision of their quarrel: After a few passes, both their swords were broken, Mr. S's almost to the hilt, who thereupon closed with Mr. Matthews, and they both fell:—Mr. M. having then considerably the advantage, called on S. to beg his life, which he refused, (having in their former duel given M. his life;) upon which M. picked up a broken piece of his sword, gave him the wounds of which he last Wednesday [the day of the duel] lay dangerously ill, and immediately left this city as before mentioned.—The seconds stood by quiet spectators.

---

1   The "White Hart" was an inn on the edge of Bath. Travellers crossing the English Channel to France (e.g., in order to flee the jurisdiction of English law) would first arrive in Calais.

2   The "Faculty" here are surgeons. According to his niece, when Sheridan "was recovering of his wounds, it was one of his amusements to read the daily accounts of himself in the papers and say, 'Let me see what they report of me to-day; I wish to know whether I am dead or alive'" (Alicia LeFanu, *Memoirs of the Life and Writings of Mrs. Frances Sheridan* [London, 1824], 406).

'Tis with great pleasure we inform our readers, that Mr. Sheridan is declared by his surgeon to be out of danger.[1]

12. From "Anecdotes *of the* Maid of Bath (*With an* Elegant Engraving)," *The London Magazine: or, Gentleman's Monthly Intelligencer* 41 (September 1772)[2]

While the biographers of beauty and intrigue are continually ransacking the gay[3] world for heroines and histories, and racking their invention for lying anecdotes to supply the place of real ones, it is astonishing that the fair *Maid of Bath* should have escaped them. We do not insinuate, by this observation, that this lady ought to be ranked with those detested demi-reps, whether real or fictitious, who are exhibited to the world in a certain scandalous magazine;[4] by no means: but that her life has already been marked with events sufficiently important to engage the attention of the public. She has been sung by bards, and fought for by heroes. It is hardly necessary to inform our readers, that we are speaking of Miss L. [...]

Our heroine was born about the year 1754; and even from her infancy [...] gave numerous indications of a natural genius for music. Her father very carefully fostered her rising talents; and she received instruction with so great facility, that at 12 years of age she made her public appearance in the rooms[5] at Bath. Even in these first efforts she charmed all who listened: there was in her voice, the extensive power of commanding all sounds, and every sound was harmonized by such softness, that it was impossible to resist her influence; she sung to the

---

1 The type for each issue of an eighteenth-century newspaper was set as the stories and advertisements became available, so this second paragraph most likely represents a "late-breaking development."

2 The elegance of the engraving (see Figure 14, p. 290)—and its claim to be what the table of contents for this issue terms "an exact Likeness"—are perhaps open to challenge, but it's nonetheless significant that Linley was thought to be of sufficient public interest to warrant a full-page portrait: there were only two such illustrations in each roughly fifty-page issue of *The London Magazine*.

3 "Gay" here means glamorous and hedonistic. The word doesn't acquire its associations with homosexuality until the twentieth century.

4 Probably *The Town and Country Magazine* (1769-95), which regularly reported on the love affairs of celebrities, especially those involving male aristocrats and "demi-reps" (fashionable women whose reputations were suspect, but not yet wholly beyond the pale). Perhaps tellingly, these accounts were accompanied by oval portraits of the lovers in question that resemble the "Elegant Engraving" accompanying this item (except that in *The Town and Country Magazine*, the names beneath the portraits would be dashed-out, or converted into pseudonyms).

5 The "rooms" are the Assembly Rooms (see Introduction, pp. 39-40 and Appendix D).

MISS LINLEY.

Figure 14: The "Elegant Engraving" of Elizabeth Linley which accompanied "Anecdotes *of the* Maid of Bath," in *The London Magazine* (September 1772).

heart: from this time therefore she was present at every concert, and held the station of principal singer.

Thus glided away two years, in which she enjoyed all the delirium of panegyric and applause. She was complimented in private, and applauded in public; and her young heart met their praises with rapture, and fluttered at the sounds.—But it was doomed to flutter still more: they had often called her a *siren*, but she was now fourteen, and they called her *angel* too. Her charms expanded, and as they expanded they mellowed: they became daily more dangerous; and, without seeking to conquer, they conquered—A method I would recommend to all young ladies in the kingdom, as the most successful in the world; let them never *begin* the engagement, and they will be sure to conquer.

It is not our intention to record in these anecdotes every man who paid our heroine the common tribute of sighs and kind looks. We shall mention those only whose passion has been productive of some business and adventure, among the earliest of these in his attendance on Miss L. was Mr. M—ws, a circumstance which was far from being favourable to her fame, for this gentleman was at the time married; and, whether he admired her for her personal or professional perfections, he was her constant attendant. The censorious, as usual, took the alarm, and became very anxious for her virtue, without knowing whether it was in danger.

We now pass over two years, and come to the grand æra which made our heroine known to the world, and which appeared to the modern Aristophanes[1] sufficiently important for the business of the Dramatic Muse. Mr. L—ng, though the son of a carpenter now living in Bath, is a man of good fortune and paid his addresses to the Maid of Bath upon honourable terms. However, the humour of a poet has fashioned the story for his own convenience, it is certain that Mr. L—ng was shot to the heart, and nothing could cure him but marriage. He told this to the lady, and to her parents: and the latter received it with rapture, but the former with disgust. The daughter confessed that the offer was good, but then the *age*—the *age* of the lover she could never reconcile to her inclinations: the father confessed all this to be very true, but, then the *money*—the *money* ought to reconcile every thing. This dispute, so usual in families, was terminated in the usual way—the father insisted on the thing, and the daughter *promised* to comply. Now mark the consequence.

When a father, from motives of ambition, avarice, or low prudence, presumes to *oblige* a daughter, who is neither whimsical nor foolish, to marry the man she hates; when a father, I say, thus attempts to overrule nature and justice by his arbitrary will, thus dares sacrifice a daughter to humour his own passions—may he meet, like the father of our heroine, with contradiction and disappointment!—It happened thus—All the necessary preparations for the celebration of the nuptials were making and the expected day almost arrived, when an unexpected accident happened; it was, the absolute refusal of the lady to consent to the match. The thought of being dragged from the kind eye of the public, who had so often caressed and applauded her, and of resigning all her hopes, her pleasures, to be eternally imprisoned in an obscure country-house,—

---

1 Samuel Foote (c. 1721-77), whose *The Maid of Bath* (first staged 1771; first printed c. 1775) told a thinly disguised and highly partisan version of Walter Long's courtship of Linley.

without, nothing but baleful yew-trees and dreary avenues—within, nothing but an old husband—these thoughts were insupportable, and she told her father so; and added, with a truly English spirit, "that if she married at all, she would marry only to be *free*." This stroke fell upon him like thunder; it overturned the gaudy structure which ambition had raised in his imagination, and with it fell all his hopes. She was now too resolute to be compelled, and his prudence therefore advised him to "make the best of a bad bargain."

In the matrimonial treaties between the lover and the father it had been settled, that, as Miss L. was an apprentice to her father, her lover should pay the trifling sum of one thousand pounds, as a compensation for the loss her father should sustain by resigning the remainder of her time. Now, though the match was entirely broke off, the prudent old man still insisted that this part of the treaty should be fulfilled, because his daughter had not been allowed to appear in public since her connections with Mr. L—ng began—a circumstance by which he was considerably a loser. Mr. L—ng refused to acquiesce, and the matter was finally left to the discussion of certain friends, who adjudged that the money should be paid to the young lady, and placed in trust in her father's hands till she arrived at age. Matters being thus settled, Miss L. did not appear in public during some months after; her father's income felt the defection, and he obliged her to resume her profession.

About the time Mr. L—ng paid his addresses to our heroine, Mr. Sheridan and his family came to reside at Bath. An acquaintance soon commenced between Miss L—y and his children (two sons and two daughters;) and it was supposed the eldest of the young gentlemen distinguished her in a very particular manner. However, if he felt any tender emotions for the lady, these were sufficiently damped by the more weighty applications of old L—ng, who was seconded by the powerful influence of gold. He therefore judiciously retreated for some time, till he was informed that connection was broke off. He now rose with new hope and redoubled vigour, but was still unsuccessful, for the lady seemed to eye the younger brother with more tenderness.

We are now to inform our readers, that Miss L. during her connections with Mr. L—, had not relinquished all her former acquaintance, but was still treated with great civility by Mr. M—ws, whose name we have mentioned already. We are also to inform them, that this gentleman and the younger Sheridan were inseparable companions; and Miss L. in her visits at Mr. M—ws's house, found frequent opportunities of seeing and conversing with Mr. Sheridan, who began at length to treat her with great gallantry. As the civility seemed to be mutual, a marriage was expected, but the young gentleman's father was averse to it. Business, however, soon called old Mr. Sheridan to

Ireland; and the lovers, seizing the favourable moment, eloped. They pursued their route to France, and the lady was lodged in a convent for security; but the father soon discovered her place of residence, and returned with the lovers to England.

Soon after the above elopement had taken place, it was buzzed about in Bath that Mr. M—ws had been privy to it, which he constantly persisted in denying, and at the same time unluckily took some indecent liberties with Mr. Sheridan's name, though he was absent. Officious persons are never wanting; and on young Sheridan's arrival he was informed that Mr. M—ws had used his name disrespectfully. By the laws of honour he called him to account for this, and a duel was the consequence. Our readers already know, that this duel was fought in a tavern in the neighbourhood of Covent-Garden in London, and that Mr. M—ws, being disarmed, was obliged to beg his life. But this circumstance being, it seems, by the laws of honour deemed *ungentleman-like*, Mr. M—ws was actually obliged to leave Bath, and fly to the mountains of Wales to forget his infamy among strangers. But scandal travels with surprising speed, and the news of the duel reached Wales almost as soon as he did himself. The tale of infamy was again revived; he was universally talked of and shunned like the pestilence. In short, he found that there was but one method of regaining his reputation and his peace, and that was, by challenging Sheridan to a second combat: with this resolution he left Wales, and soon appeared in Bath. His first visit was to Sheridan, who promised to meet him. Each of them was to have a second, but not to interfere, whatever might be the consequence. They met the next morning about four: the first onset was fierce. Sheridan attempted to disarm his antagonist, as before, but was baffled, and obliged to close. In the struggle they fell, by which both the swords were broken. M—ws, having now greatly the advantage by pressing on him, asked the other if he would beg his life; he was answered, that he scorned it; and the contest was renewed in this aukward situation. They mangled each other for some time with their broken swords; and S—n having received some dangerous wounds was left on the field with few signs of life. He was conveyed to Bath, while M—ws and his second drove off to London.

Thus ended an unmanly combat, which did not prove fatal to Mr. S—n, for he was confined only a few weeks. During the time of his indisposition Miss L—y was uncommonly affected by it, but she was denied the favour of visiting him, even tho' she begged it by the tender appellation of *husband*. Whether they are married or not, their respective parents have since that time been very industrious in keeping them separate.

13. Yet Another Report on Sheridan's Wounds, *The St. James's Chronicle; or, British Evening-Post*, 10-12 November 1772

Mr. Sheridan, jun. who last Summer fought a Duel with Capt. Mathews, about the Maid of Bath, is entirely recovered of his Wounds, but has lost the Use of his Right Arm, from receiving a Shot between the Bones at the Joint.[1]

14. "Miss Linley, the syren of Bath," *The Westminster Magazine; or, The Pantheon of Taste* 1 (March 1773)

One of those whims by which the Public are continually influenced, has made it the *ton* to resort to this theatre [Drury Lane] to hear and see Miss Linley, the syren of Bath. This young lady, who is greatly indebted to Nature for the *eclât*[2] with which she is followed, and not a little to the fortuitous concurrence of remarkable incidents in her life, has drawn crowded houses incessantly; and this success has been insured by the constant attendance of his majesty and the royal family at this theatre.

15. Report of a Sheridan-Linley Marriage, *The Bath Chronicle*, 1 April 1773

It is now publicly said, that Mr. Richard Sheridan is actually married to Miss Linley,[3] and has been for some time.—Thus this charming Syren has put it out of her power to listen to the addresses of any man.

16. Letter probably written by Sheridan, *The Bath Chronicle*, 15 April 1773

The following letters are confidently said to have passed between Lord G——r, and the celebrated English Syren, Miss L——y. I send them to you for publication, not with any view to encrease the volume of literary scandal, which, I am sorry to say, at present needs no assistance, but with the more laudable intent of setting an example for our modern belles, by holding out the character of a young woman, who, notwithstanding the solicitations of her profession, and the flattering

---

1 Note the supposed source of the injury (both duels were fought with swords).
2 *Ton* is French for "tone"; in this context, it simply means "the fashion." *Éclat* is French for "brightness" or "splendor"; in this context, it means something like "avid public attention."
3 Sheridan and Linley weren't actually married until 13 April 1773.

example of higher ranks, has added *incorruptible virtue* to a number of the most elegant qualifications.

Yours, &c.

HORATIO[1]

Grosvenor-square.

   Lord G—— to Miss L——y.

   Adorable Creature!

Permit me to assure you, in the most tender and affectionate manner, that the united force of your charms and qualifications have made so complete a prisoner of my art,[2] that I despair of its being set at liberty but through your means.

Under this situation, I have it ever to lament, that the laws will not permit me to offer you my hand. Here I cannot resist my fate; but what I can dispose of, my *heart* and my *fortune*, are entirely at your devotion, thinking myself the happiest of mankind should either be acceptable.

Lady A. who will deliver you this, and who obligingly vouchsafes to be my mediator, will, I flatter myself, urge the sincerity of my heart on this occasion, so as to obtain a permission for me to throw myself at your feet to-morrow evening. In momentary expectation of which,

I am, your devoted admirer,

G-------R.

Wednesday Evening, 4 o'clock.

   Miss L—— to Lord G——.

My Lord,—Lest my silence should bear the most distant interpretation of listening to your proposals, I condescend to answer your infamous letter.

You lament the laws will not permit you to offer me your hand. I lament it too, my Lord, but on a different principle—to convince your

---

1 Sheridan used the pseudonym "Horatio" in some of the poems and love-letters he secretly sent to Linley in the time between his first duel and their wedding, when their parents were trying to keep them apart. It would seem that these letters, the first of which purports to be the work of Richard, Lord Grosvenor (1731-1802), a famous libertine, who was involved in an extremely high-profile adultery case in 1770, were an attempt to force Thomas Linley's hand to allow Sheridan to marry Elizabeth before she was involved in any more scandal. *The Bath Chronicle* only came out weekly, so this issue actually appeared two days after their wedding. It is unclear whether Mr. Linley saw copies of these letters in advance, was simply warned that they were coming out, or if he finally relented and allowed the marriage for other reasons.

2 "Art" here presumably means something like "skill and self-control in the ways of love" (though it may simply be a misprint for "heart").

dissipated heart, that I have a soul capable of *refusing* a coronet,[1] when the owner is not the object of my affections—*despising* it when the offer of an unworthy possessor.

The reception your *honourable* messenger met with in the execution of her embassy, saves me the trouble of replying to the other parts of your letter, and (if you have any feeling left) will explain to you the *baseness*, as well as the *inefficacy* of your design.

—— L——y.[2]

17. Report on *The Rivals*, *The Gazetteer and New Daily Advertiser*, 17 January 1775

It having been reported, that the story of the new comedy of The Rivals was not a fictitious one, we have authority to assert, that such a report is entirely void of foundation, and that there is not the slightest local or personal allusion whatever throughout the piece.[3]

18. Another Report on *The Rivals*, *The Town and Country Magazine; or, Universal Repository of Knowledge, Instruction and Entertainment* 7 (January 1775)

It was believed by the friends of the author that it would meet with opposition from a certain quarter, as it was thought by many to have a close connexion with a certain affair at Bath, in which the celebrated Miss Linley (now Mrs. Sheridan) was the subject of rivalship; but in this respect they seem to have been mistaken, as no comedy that we recollect has met with fairer play. After a pretty warm contest towards the end of the last act, it was suffered to be given out for the ensuing night.[4]

---

1 A crown worn by a noble on ceremonial occasions.

2 In signing just her last name (as male aristocrats traditionally did), "Linley" is implicitly asserting her equality to (the then Baron) Grosvenor.

3 Rumors of this sort were also swirling around Bath: Mary Linley wrote to her sister around this time that "I was told last night that it was his [i.e., Sheridan's] own story, and therefore called 'The Rivals'; but I do not give any credit to this intelligence" (quoted in Thomas Moore, *Memoirs of the Life of the Right Honourable Richard Brinsley Sheridan* [London, 1825], 100).

4 However, at some point after *The Rivals* was "given out for the ensuing night" (and advertisements were sent to the papers to announce such a performance), Sheridan withdrew the play for revision. See "A Note on the Texts."

Appendix D: The Narrative Possibilities of Bath

[As the Introduction suggests (pp. 38-40), *The Rivals* wouldn't work nearly as well set anywhere other than Bath. The play relies upon that city's preexisting reputation as a place for courtship and fortune hunting and temporary reinvention, a reputation that it owed as much to literature as anything else. Not all of Sheridan's early audiences would have actually been to Bath, but almost all of them would have thought that they knew what sorts of things happened there—much as we might imagine that we know what goes on in the gang territories of Los Angeles or the posher parts of Manhattan, whether or not we have ever visited those places.]

1. **From [Christopher Anstey],** *The New Bath Guide: or, Memoirs of the B—r—d Family. In a Series of Poetical Epistles.* **3rd ed. (London, 1766)**[1]

Miss Jenny W—d—r to Lady Eliz. M—d—ss, at —— Castle, North.[2]

[...] Take then, my Friend, the sprightly Rhyme,
While you inglorious waste your Prime,
At Home in cruel Durance pent,
On dull domestic Cares intent,
Forbid, by Parent's harsh Decree,
To share the Joys of *Bath* with me.
Ill-judging Parent! blind to Merit,
Thus to confine a Nymph of Spirit!
With all thy Talents doom'd to fade
And wither in th'unconscious Shade!

---

1 *The New Bath Guide* is an extremely successful narrative poem that jauntily tells the story of the "B—r—d" [i.e., "Blunderhead"] family's visit to Bath, where they immerse themselves in the pleasures of the town, in most cases to their ultimate chagrin. With the exception of the Epilogue added to the third edition, the whole tale is told through letters written to their friends back home. Anstey (1724-1805) was a country gentleman, and regular visitor to Bath.

2 This excerpt is from a letter described in the prefatory address "To the Reader" as being "from a Romantic young Lady ... to her Friend in the Country." The dashed-out names apparently stand in for "Wildair" (or "Wonder") and "Modeless," respectively.

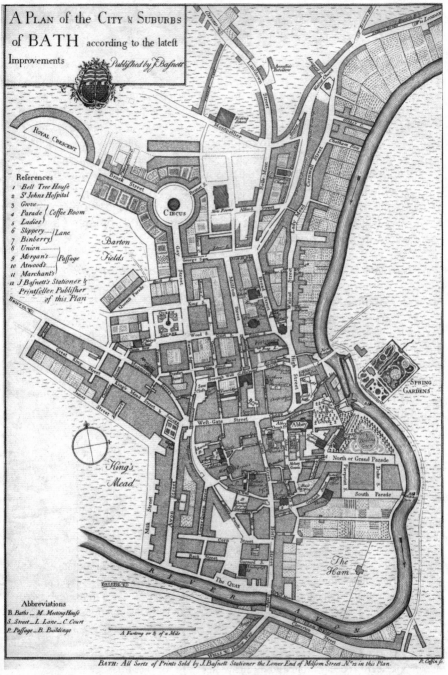

Figure 15: A map of Bath in 1775. Bath Record Office. 0596/1/9. Courtesy of Bath Record Office.

I vow, my Dear, it moves my Spleen,
Such frequent Instances I've seen
Of Fathers, cruel and unkind,
To all paternal Duty blind.
What Wretches do we meet with often,
Whose Hearts no Tenderness can soften!
Sure all good Authors should expose
Such Parents, both in Verse and Prose,
And Nymphs inspire with Resolution
Ne'er to submit to Persecution.
This wholesome Satire much enhances
The Merit of our best Romances,
And modern Plays, that I could mention, ⎫
With Judgment fraught, and rare Invention, ⎬
Are written with the same Intention [...] ⎭

A JOURNAL.[1]

[...] But come, CALLIOPE,[2] and say
How Pleasure wastes the various Day:
Whether thou art wont to rove
By Parade, or Orange Grove,
Or to breathe a purer Air
In the Circus or the Square;[3]
Wheresoever be thy Path,
Tell, O tell the Joys of *Bath*.
        Ev'ry Morning, ev'ry Night,
Gayest Scenes of fresh Delight:
When AURORA sheds her Beams,
Wak'd from soft Elysian Dreams,
Music calls me to the Spring
Which can Health and Spirits bring;
There HYGEIA, Goddess, pours
Blessings from her various Stores;

---

1   As the title suggests, this excerpt is from a journal supposedly kept by Miss
    Jenny, though it's improbably full of mock-heroic allusions (and a few echoes
    of Milton's *L'Allegro*).
2   Calliope is the Muse who oversees epic poetry. Of the deities mentioned later,
    Aurora is the Goddess of the Dawn, Hygeia the Goddess of Health, Cupid
    the God of Erotic Love, and Hymen the God of Weddings.
3   For these and the other locations mentioned (all fashionable parts of Bath in
    which to stroll, see, and be seen), see Introduction (pp. 39-40) and the map in
    Figure 15 (p. 298). The North Parade is depicted in Figure 16 (p. 319).

Let me to her Altars haste,
Tho' I ne'er the Waters taste,
Near the Pump to take my Stand,
With a Nosegay[1] in my Hand,
And to hear the Captain say,
"How d'ye do, dear Miss, to-day?"
The Captain!—Now you'll say my Dear,
"Methinks I long his Name to hear,"—
Why then—but don't you tell my Aunt,
The Captain's Name is—CORMORANT:[2]
But hereafter, you must know,
I shall call him ROMEO,
And your Friend, dear Lady BET,
JENNY no more, but JULIET.

      O ye Guardian Spirits fair,
All who make true Love your Care,
May I oft my ROMEO meet,
Oft enjoy his Converse sweet;
I alone his Thoughts employ
Through each various Scene of Joy!
Lo! where all the jocund Throng
From the Pump-Room hastes along,
To the Breakfast all invited
By Sir TOBY, lately knighted.[3]
See with Joy my ROMEO comes,
He conducts me to the Rooms;[4]
There he whispers, not unseen,
Tender Tales behind the Screen;
While his Eyes are fix'd on mine,
See each Nymph with Envy pine,
And with Looks of forc'd Disdain,
Smile Contempt, but sigh in vain.

---

1 The Pump Room was a fashionable place to gather in the morning, check out one's fellow visitors, and listen to music, whether or not one was drinking the supposedly healing (and quite foul-tasting) waters. A "nosegay" is a small, fragrant bouquet of flowers.

2 A bird of prey that swallows fish whole (often used as a figure for insatiable greed). It may be telling that when Satan first scouts out Eden in *Paradise Lost* he "sat like a cormorant" "on the Tree of Life" (IV.196, 194).

3 Newly arrived (and sometimes newly wealthy) visitors would often give public breakfasts, complete with music, as a way of calling attention to themselves.

4 The "Rooms" here are the Assembly Rooms, where balls (and public breakfasts) would be held.

O the charming Parties made!
Some to walk the South Parade,
Some to LINCOMB's shady Groves,
Or to SIMPSON's proud Alcoves;[1]
Some for Chapel trip away,
Then take Places for the Play:
Or we walk about in Pattins,
Buying Gauzes, cheap'ning[2] Sattins,
Or to PAINTER's we repair,
Meet Sir PEREGRINE HATCHET there,
Pleas'd the Artist's Skill to trace
In his dear Miss GORGON's Face:
Happy Pair, who fix'd as Fate ⎫
For the sweet connubial State, ⎬
Smile in Canvas *Tête à Tête*.[3] ⎭
If the Weather, cold and chill,
Calls us all to Mr. GILL,
ROMEO hands to me the Jelly,
Or the Soup of Vermicelli;[4]
If at TOYSHOP I step in,
He presents a Diamond Pin;[5]
Sweetest Token I can wear,
Which at once may grace my Hair,
And, in Witness of my Flame,
Teach the Glass to bear his Name:[6]

---

1 "Lincomb" (or Lyncombe) is a village south across the river from Bath. There
   was a pleasure garden located there. "Simpson's proud Alcoves" are the
   private walks surrounding the Assembly Rooms run by Charles Simpson.
2 "Pattens" are thick wooden shoes strapped onto the bottoms of one's regular
   shoes in order to keep the latter out of the mud. To "cheapen" something is to
   haggle for it.
3 *Tête à tête* is French for "head to head." The studios of portrait painters were
   generally open to visitors, and often contained canvases beyond those being
   currently worked upon (e.g., for about six years, one could walk into Thomas
   Gainsborough's studio and see his portrait of the young Elizabeth Linley and
   her brother [Figure 12, p. 282]).
4 Charles Gill is elsewhere described in the poem as "*an eminent Cook at
   BATH*." "Jelly" was often eaten as dessert in the eighteenth century. "Vermicelli" is any thin pasta (still a somewhat exotic food in the later eighteenth
   century, especially for visitors from the country).
5 "Toyshops" sold all sorts of small precious items, including jewelry.
6 That is, she can scratch the Captain's name into a mirror or window using the
   diamond in her pin.

See him turn each Trinket over,
If for me he can discover
Aught his Passion to reveal,
Emblematic Ring or Seal;
CUPID whetting pointed Darts,
For a Pair of tender Hearts;
HYMEN lighting sacred Fires,
Types of chaste and fond Desires:
Thus enjoy we ev'ry Blessing,
Till the Toilet[1] calls to Dressing;
Where's my Garnet, Cap, and Sprig?
Send for SINGE to dress my Wig:
Bring my silver'd Mazarine,[2]
Sweetest Gown that e'er was seen:
TABITHA, put on my Ruff:
Where's my dear delightful Muff?
Muff, my faithful ROMEO's Present!
Tippet[3] too from Tail of Pheasant!
Muff from downy Breast of Swan!
O the dear enchanting Man!
Muff that makes me think how JOVE
Flew to LEDA from above.——[4]
Muff that——TABBY, see who rapt then.
"Madam, Madam, 'tis the Captain!"
Sure his Voice I hear below,
'Tis, it is my ROMEO;

---

1   A "toilet" here is a dressing table.
2   A "sprig" is here probably a sprig-shaped piece of jewelry worn on her cap or
    in her hair. "Singe" is a stock-name for a hairdresser (curling irons could
    singe); it's also French for "monkey." A "mazarine" is a deep blue garment.
3   Tabitha is the family's maid. A "ruff" is a pleated linen or lace collar. A
    "muff" is a hollow cylinder of fur or feathers into which one could put one's
    hands to keep warm. A "tippet" is a short cape.
4   In classical mythology, Jove (a.k.a. Jupiter or Zeus) came down to earth in the
    form of a swan in order to have sex with Leda, the Queen of Sparta. In some
    versions of the story, he seduces her; in others, it's a rape. Either way, Jenny
    seems to be hinting—unwittingly?—at the eroticism underlying her courtship,
    an eroticism also brought out by the double entendres surrounding the
    Captain's presentation of the ticket to the private ball (i.e., a ball that, by not
    being open to everyone, reinstated some of the social distinctions that the
    usual rules of Bath suspended).

Shape and Gait, and careless Air,⎫
Diamond Ring, and Solitaire,[1] ⎬
Birth and Fashion all declare. ⎭
How his Eyes, that gently roll,
Speak the Language of his Soul!
See the Dimple on his Cheek,
See him smile and sweetly speak,
"Lovely Nymph, at your Command,
I have something in my Hand,
Which I hope you'll not refuse,
'Twill us both at Night amuse:
What tho' Lady WHISKER crave it,
And Miss BADGER longs to have it,
'Tis, by JUPITER I swear,
'Tis for you alone, my Dear:
See this Ticket, gentle Maid,
At your Feet an Off'ring laid;
Thee the Loves and Graces call
To a little private Ball:
And to Play I bid adieu, ⎫
Hazard, Lansquenet, and Loo,[2] ⎬
Fairest Nymph, to dance with you.—" ⎭
—I with Joy accept his Ticket,
And upon my Bosom stick it:
Well I know how ROMEO dances,
With what Air he first advances,
With what Grace his Gloves he draws on,
Claps, and calls up *Nancy Dawson*;[3]
Me through ev'ry Dance conducting,
And the Music oft instructing;
See him tap the Time to shew,
With his light fantastic Toe;
Skill'd in ev'ry Art to please,
From the Fan to waft the Breeze,
Or his Bottle to produce

---

1 In this context, a "solitaire" is probably a loose piece of black silk worn
   around the neck. It could also mean a single gem set by itself (usually in a
   ring).
2 "Hazard" is a dice game similar to craps. "Lansquenet" and "loo" are both
   card games. All involved extensive gambling ("play").
3 "Nancy Dawson" was a popular dance to a nautical tune (now best known as
   "Here We Go Round the Mulberry Bush"), which was named after a famous
   dancer of hornpipes on the London stage.

Fill'd with pungent *Eau de Luce.*——[1]
Wonder not, my Friend, I go
To the Ball with ROMEO.
      Such Delights if thou canst give,
Bath, at Thee I choose to live [...]

Mr. S—— *B—n—r—d, to Lady B—n—r—d, at* —— *Hall, North.*[2]

[...] For my Means are so small, and my Bills are so large,
I ne'er can come home till you send a Discharge.[3]
Let the Muse speak the Cause, if a Muse yet remain,
To supply me with Rhimes, and express all my Pain.
      Paid Bells, and Musicians,
        Drugs, Nurse, and Physicians,
Balls, Raffles, Subscriptions, and Chairs;
      Wigs, Gowns, Skins, and Trimming,
      Good Books for the Women,
Plays, Concerts, Tea, Negus,[4] and Prayers [...]
A Sum, my dear Mother, far heavier yet,
Captain CORMORANT won when I learn'd Lansquenet;
Two Hundred I paid him, and Five am in Debt.
For the Five I had nothing to do but to *write*,
For the Captain was very well bred, and polite,
And took, as he saw my Expences were great,
My Bond, to be paid on the *Clodpole* Estate;

---

1   "Eau de Luce" is a kind of smelling salts (to revive Jenny if she faints from over-stimulation).

2   This excerpt is from a letter written by Jenny's cousin to his mother, and contains his "Serious REFLECTIONS" at the end of the family's stay in Bath. His first name is apparently "Simkin," an old term for a fool, and so a fitting appellation for someone still so taken in by Captain Cormorant.

3   A "discharge" is a release from debt (Simkin needs his mother to send him a lot of money).

4   The "bells" of the Abbey would be rung when socially prominent visitors arrived in Bath. "Musicians" would then go to their lodgings. In both cases, a substantial tip was expected (somewhere between five and twenty-one shillings). "Subscriptions" are here probably for tickets to a series of balls and concerts (but visitors also typically paid on arrival for the use of the private walks of the Assembly Rooms, for membership in a circulating library, and for supplies to write letters at the coffeehouse). "Chairs" are sedan chairs (the standard mode of transportation for visitors to Bath). "Skins" are presumably animal furs, with which to line clothes for greater warmth. "Trimmings" are decorations for a dress. "Negus" is a mixture of wine, warm water, sugar, and sometimes spices or fruit.

And asks nothing more, while the Money is lent,
Than Interest paid him at Twenty per Cent.[1]
But I'm shocked to relate what Distresses befall
Miss JENNY, my Sister, and TABBY and all:
Miss JENNY, poor Thing, from this *Bath* Expedition,
Was in hopes very soon to have chang'd her Condition;
But Rumour has brought certain Things to her Ear,
Which I ne'er will believe, yet am sorry to hear,
"That the Captain, her Lover, her dear ROMEO,
Was banished the Army, a great while ago:
That his Friends and his Foes he alike can betray,
And picks up a scandalous Living by Play."
But if e'er I could think that the Captain had cheated,
Or my dear Cousin JENNY unworthily treated,
By all that is sacred I swear, for his Pains
I'd cudgel him first, and then blow out his Brains.
For the Man I abhor like the Devil, dear Mother,
Who one Thing conceals, and professes another [...]

The GHOST *of Mr.* QUIN.[2]

[...] 'Tis true, such Insects as thy Tale has shewn
Breathe not the Atmosphere of *Bath* alone,
Tho' there, in Gaiety's meridian Ray
Do Fools, like Flies, their gaudy Wings display;
Awhile they flutter, but, their Sunshine past,
Their Fate, like SIMKIN, they lament at last [...]

---

1   In order to cover his gambling debts, Simkin has taken out a mortgage on one
    of the family properties. If he fails to pay either the principal or the usurious
    interest, the estate (which is presumably worth significantly more than £500)
    will go to Captain Cormorant. Since lansquenet was notorious for how it
    favored the dealer, and the legal limit on interest was five per cent, Simkin has
    clearly been taken advantage of.
2   This excerpt is from the epilogue Anstey added to the third edition in order to
    counter charges that he was engaged in obscenity (there's a scene in which a
    recent convert to Methodism mistakes a wet dream for the experience of
    being born again), or the slander of particular individuals. As part of denying
    the latter, the ghost of a famous actor, James Quin (1693-1766), who retired
    to Bath, appears to the Guide—a personified copy of the poem itself—and
    assures it that its critics are all mistaken.

2. From [Tobias Smollett], *The Expedition of Humphry Clinker. By the Author of Roderick Random* (London, 1771)[1]

To Miss WILLIS, at Gloucester.[2]

Bath, April 26.

MY DEAREST COMPANION,

[...] Bath is to me a new world——All is gayety, good-humour, and diversion. The eye is continually entertained with the splendor of dress and equipage; and the ear with the sound of coaches, chaises, chairs, and other carriages. *The merry bells ring round*, from morn till night. Then we are welcomed by the city-waits[3] in our own lodgings: we have musick in the Pump-room every morning, cotillons every fore-noon in the rooms, balls twice a week, and concerts every other night, besides private assemblies and parties without number—As soon as we were settled in lodgings, we were visited by the Master of the Ceremonies; a pretty little gentleman, so sweet, so fine, so civil, and polite, that in our country he might pass for the prince of Wales; then he talks so charmingly, both in verse and prose, that you would be delighted to hear him discourse; for you must know he is a great writer, and has got

---

1   *Humphry Clinker* is an extremely successful epistolary novel which tells the story of a Welsh family's extended tour of Great Britain. Each member of the family writes to a friend elsewhere and often the same events are narrated several times from different perspectives (thereby shedding light on the writer, and his or her preoccupations). Smollett was a novelist, a historian, and the founder of *The Critical Review* (selections from which appear in Appendix B).

2   Laetitia Willis is the best friend and confidante of the seventeen-year-old Lydia Melford, the writer of this letter. Lydia is, in turn, the niece and ward of Matt Bramble, the gouty, grumpy, but ultimately kind-hearted patriarch of the family. Shortly before this point in the novel, Lydia's plans to elope with an actor going by the name of "Wilson" were discovered, and she was removed from boarding school, and forced to come on this family trip. Matt complains at one point that she "reads romances."

3   "Equipage" is a term for a carriage and all its accompanying horses and servants. "The merry bells ring round" is a line from Milton's *L'Allegro* (written c. 1631, first published 1645), which introduces a scene of rural gaiety. Matt Bramble has already complained about the ringing of bells upon the arrival of important visitors to Bath. "The city waits" are the musicians who would go to the lodgings of such visitors.

five tragedies ready for the stage.[1] He did us the favour to dine with us, by my uncle's invitation; and next day 'squired my aunt and me to every part of Bath; which, to be sure, is an earthly paradise. The Square, the Circus, and the Parades, put you in mind of the sumptuous palaces represented in prints and pictures; and the new buildings, such as Princes-row, Harlequin's-row, Bladud's-row, and twenty other rows, look like so many enchanted castles, raised on hanging terraces.

At eight in the morning, we go in dishabille to the Pump-room; which is crowded like a Welsh fair; and there you see the highest quality, and the lowest trades folks, jostling each other, without ceremony, hail-fellow well-met. The noise of the musick playing in the gallery, the heat and flavour of such a crowd, and the hum and buz of their conversation, gave me the head-ach and vertigo the first day; but, afterwards, all these things became familiar, and even agreeable [...]

Hard by the Pump-room, is a coffee-house for the ladies; but my aunt says, young girls are not admitted, inasmuch as the conversation turns upon politics, scandal, philosophy, and other subjects above our capacity; but we are allowed to accompany them to the booksellers' shops, which are charming places of resort; where we read novels, plays, pamphlets, and news-papers, for so small a subscription as a crown a quarter;[2] and in these offices of intelligence, (as my brother calls them) all the reports of the day, and all the private transactions of the Bath, are first entered and discussed. From the bookseller's shop, we make a tour through the milliners and toy-men; and commonly stop at Mr. Gill's, the pastry-cook, to take a jelly, a tart, or a small bason of vermicelli. There is, moreover, another place of entertainment on the other side of the water, opposite to the Grove; to which the company cross over in a boat—It is called Spring Garden; a sweet retreat, laid out in walks and ponds, and parterres of flowers;[3] and there is a long-room for breakfasting and dancing. As the situation is low and damp, and the season has been remarkably wet, my uncle won't suffer me to go thither, lest I should catch cold: but my aunt says it is all a vulgar prejudice; and, to be sure, a great many gentlemen and ladies of Ireland frequent the place, without seeming to be the worse for it. They say, dancing at Spring Gardens, when the air is

---

1 Although published in 1771, *Humphry Clinker* is apparently set in the mid-1760s, as this description fits Samuel Derrick (1724-69), the Master of Ceremonies from 1763-69. The Prince of Wales (the future George IV) was only born in 1762, so Derrick's ability to "pass" for him may be a rather mixed compliment.

2 A "crown" is five shillings.

3 Flower beds, arranged into a pattern and framed by gravel paths and tightly clipped hedges.

moist, is recommended to them as an excellent cure for the rheumatism. I have been twice at the play; where, notwithstanding the excellence of the performers, the gayety of the company, and the decorations of the theatre, which are very fine, I could not help reflecting, with a sigh, upon our poor homely representations at Gloucester—But this, in confidence to my dear Willis—You know my heart, and will excuse its weakness.——

After all, the great scenes of entertainment at Bath, are the two public rooms; where the company meet alternately every evening— They are spacious, lofty, and, when lighted up, appear very striking. They are generally crowded with well-dressed people, who drink tea in separate parties, play at cards, walk, or sit and chat together, just as they are disposed. Twice a-week there is a ball; the expence of which is defrayed by a voluntary subscription among the gentlemen; and every subscriber has three tickets. I was there Friday last with my aunt, under the care of my brother, who is a subscriber; and Sir Ulic Mackilligut recommended his nephew, captain O Donaghan, to me as a partner; but Jerry excused himself, by saying I had got the head-ach; and, indeed, it was really so, though I can't imagine how he knew it. The place was so hot, and the smell so different from what we are used to in the country, that I was quite feverish when we came away. Aunt says it is the effect of a vulgar constitution, reared among woods and mountains; and, that as I become accustomed to genteel company, it will wear off.—Sir Ulic was very complaisant, made her a great many high-flown compliments; and, when we retired, handed her with great ceremony to her chair.[1] The captain, I believe, would have done me the same favour; but my brother, seeing him advance, took me under his arm, and wished him good-night. The Captain is a pretty man, to be sure; tall and strait, and well made; with light-grey eyes, and a Roman nose; but there is a certain boldness in his look and manner, that puts one out of countenance— But I am afraid I have put you out of all patience with this long unconnected scrawl; which I shall therefore conclude, with assuring you, that neither Bath nor London, nor all the diversions of life, shall ever be able to efface the idea of my dear Letty, from the heart of her ever affectionate

LYDIA MELFORD.

---

1 To "hand" someone to a chair is to take her by the hand and lead her to a sedan chair.

To Dr. LEWIS.[1]

DEAR DICK,

[...] I have other reasons for abridging my stay at Bath—You know sister Tabby's complexion—If Mrs. Tabitha Bramble had been of any other race, I should certainly have looked upon her as the most—But, the truth is, she has found means to interest my affection; or, rather, she is beholden to the force of prejudice, commonly called the ties of blood. Well, this amiable maiden has actually commenced a flirting correspondence with an Irish baronet of sixty-five. His name is Sir Ulic Mackilligut. He is said to be much out at elbows;[2] and, I believe, has received false intelligence with respect to her fortune. Be that as it may, the connexion is exceedingly ridiculous, and begins already to excite whispers. For my part, I have no intention to dispute her free-agency; though I shall fall upon some expedient to undeceive her paramour, as to the point which he has principally in view. But I don't think her conduct is a proper example for Liddy, who has also attracted the notice of some coxcombs in the Rooms; and Jerry tells me, he suspects a strapping fellow, the knight's nephew, of some design upon the girl's heart. I shall, therefore, keep a strict eye over her aunt and her, and even shift the scene, if I find the matter grow more serious—You perceive what an agreeable task it must be, to a man of my kidney, to have the cure of such souls as these—But, hold, you shall not have another peevish word (till the next occasion) from

yours,

Bath, April 28.   MATT. BRAMBLE.

To Sir WATKIN PHILLIPS, of Jesus college, Oxon.[3]

DEAR KNIGHT,

I think those people are unreasonable, who complain that Bath is a contracted circle, in which the same dull scenes perpetually revolve,

---

1 Richard Lewis is not only Matt Bramble's physician, but also his closest friend (and his agent for many acts of surreptitious charity).

2 To be "out at elbows" is to be in need of money.

3 Sir Watkin Phillips is a friend from Oxford ("Oxon.") of the recently graduated Jery Melford, the writer of this letter. Jery is Matt Bramble's nephew, Lydia's brother, and the most genteel and least eccentric member of the family. He was challenged by "Wilson" (Lydia's beloved) to a duel, but it was interrupted by the local authorities before any fighting could take place.

without variation—I am, on the contrary, amazed to find so small a place, so crowded with entertainment and variety. London itself can hardly exhibit one species of diversion, to which we have not something analogous at Bath, over and above those singular advantages that are peculiar to the place. Here, for example, a man has daily opportunities of seeing the most remarkable characters of the community. He sees them in their natural attitudes and true colours; descended from their pedestals, and divested of their formal draperies, undisguised by art and affectation—Here we have ministers of state, judges, generals, bishops, projectors, philosophers, wits, poets, players, *chemists, fiddlers*, and *buffoons*.[1] If he makes any considerable stay in the place, he is sure of meeting with some particular friend, whom he did not expect to see; and to me there is nothing more agreeable, than such casual rencounters—Another entertainment, peculiar to Bath, arises from the general mixture of all degrees assembled in our public rooms, without distinction of rank or fortune. This is what my uncle reprobates, as a monstrous jumble of heterogeneous principles; a vile mob of noise and impertinence, without decency or subordination. But this chaos is to me a source of infinite amusement.

I was extremely diverted, last ball-night, to see the Master of the Ceremonies leading, with great solemnity, to the upper end of the room, an antiquated Abigail, dressed in her lady's cast-clothes;[2] whom he (I suppose) mistook for some countess just arrived at the Bath. The ball was opened by a Scotch lord, with a mulatto heiress from St. Christopher's; and the gay colonel Tinsel danced all the evening with the daughter of an eminent tinman from the borough of Southwark— Yesterday morning, at the Pump-room, I saw a broken-winded Wapping landlady squeeze through a circle of peers, to salute her brandy-merchant, who stood by the window, prop'd upon crutches; and a paralytic attorney of Shoe-lane, in shuffling up to the bar, kicked the shins of the chancellor of England, while his lordship, in a cut bob,[3] drank a glass of water at the pump. I cannot account for my

---

1 "Projectors" are promotors (sometimes naïve or dishonest) of a new business venture. In John Dryden's *Absalom and Achitophel* (1681), "Zimri" (a clear stand-in for the Duke of Buckingham) is mocked for, among other things, his short attention span: "Stiff in Opinions, always in the wrong; / Was every thing by starts, and nothing long: / But, in the course of one revolving Moon, / Was Chymist, Fiddler, States-Man, and Buffoon" (ll. 547-50).

2 An "abigail" is a maid. Servants often received their employers' old clothes as a perquisite of their jobs.

3 "Gay" here means flashily dressed. The word doesn't acquire its associations with homosexuality until the twentieth century. "Southwark," "Wapping," and "Shoe Lane" are all unfashionable parts of London. A "cut bob" is an

being pleased with these incidents, any other way than by saying, they are truly ridiculous in their own nature, and serve to heighten the humour in the farce of life, which I am determined to enjoy as long as I can.— [...][1]

I want to see this phenomenon in his cups; and have almost prevailed upon uncle to give him a small turtle at the Bear.[2] In the mean time, I must entertain you with an incident, that seems to confirm the judgment of those two cynic philosophers. I took the liberty to differ in opinion from Mr. Bramble, when he observed, that the mixture of people in the entertainments of this place was destructive of all order and urbanity; that it rendered the plebeians insufferably arrogant and troublesome, and vulgarized the deportment and sentiments of those who moved in the upper spheres of life. He said, such a preposterous coalition would bring us into contempt with all our neighbours; and was worse, in fact, than debasing the gold coin of the nation. I argued, on the contrary, that those plebeians who discovered such eagerness to imitate the dress and equipage of their superiors, would likewise, in time, adopt their maxims and their manners, be polished by their conversation, and refined by their example; but when I appealed to Mr. Quin, and asked if he did not think that such an unreserved mixture would improve the whole mass?—"Yes," (said he) "as a plate of marmalade would improve a pan of sirreverence."[3]

I owned I was not much conversant in high-life, but I had seen what were called polite assemblies in London and elsewhere; that those of Bath seemed to be as decent as any; and that, upon the whole, the individuals that composed it, would not be found deficient in good manners and decorum. "But let us have recourse to experience," (said

---

informal wig usually worn by men of a rather lower social standing than the Chancellor of England (a very senior government official and the highest ranking judge in the land).

1 In a passage here omitted, Jery writes that Matt Bramble has renewed his old friendship with the actor James Quin, now retired to Bath. Quin was renowned for his performance of Falstaff (and kept up a rather Falstaffian life off-stage).

2 A "turtle" is here a feast of turtle (an eighteenth-century delicacy). "The Bear" was a fashionable inn in Bath. Later in the novel, Jery gets his wish and witnesses Quin "carried home with six good bottles of claret under his belt," where "it being then Friday, he gave orders, that he should not be disturbed till Sunday at noon" ("claret" is red wine, especially Bordeaux. Eighteenth-century wine bottles were typically about two-thirds the capacity of modern 750ml bottles, and the wine was sometimes weaker, so Quin's consumption— though still staggering—was not perhaps quite as life-threatening as it would be today).

3 "Sir-reverence" is human excrement.

I) "—Jack Holder, who was intended for a parson, has succeeded to an estate of two thousand a year, by the death of his elder brother. He is now at the Bath, driving about in a phaeton and four, with French horns. He has treated with turtle and claret at all the taverns in Bath and Bristol, till his guests are gorged with good chear: he has bought a dozen suits of fine clothes, by the advice of the Master of the Ceremonies, under whose tuition he has entered himself: he has lost some hundreds at billiards to sharpers, and taken one of the nymphs of Avon-street into keeping; but, finding all these channels insufficient to drain him of his current cash, his counsellor has engaged him to give a general tea-drinking to-morrow at Wiltshire's room.[1] In order to give it the more eclat, every table is to be furnished with sweet-meats[2] and nosegays; which, however, are not to be touched till notice is given by the ringing of a bell, and then the ladies may help themselves without restriction. This will be no bad way of trying the company's breeding—"

"I will abide by that experiment," (cried my uncle) "and if I could find a place to stand secure, without the vortex of the tumult, which I know will ensue, I would certainly go thither and enjoy the scene." Quin proposed that we should take our station in the musick-gallery; and we took his advice. Holder had got thither before us, with his horns perdue;[3] but we were admitted. The tea-drinking passed as usual; and the company having risen from the tables, were sauntering in groupes, in expectation of the signal for attack, when the bell beginning to ring, they flew with eagerness to the dessert, and the whole place was instantly in commotion. There was nothing but justling, scrambling, pulling, snatching, struggling, scolding, and screaming. The nosegays were torn from one another's hands and bosoms; the glasses and china went to wreck; the tables and floor were strewed with comfits. Some cried; some swore; and the tropes and figures of Billingsgate[4] were used without reserve in all their native zest and

---

1 A "phaeton and four" is a fast open carriage drawn by four horses. The nouveaux-riche would sometimes hire French horn players to accompany them and announce their arrival (earlier in the novel, Matt Bramble is annoyed by two slaves who are playing the French horn in the stairway of his lodgings). "The nymphs of Avon-street" are prostitutes. "Wiltshire's room" is one of the Assembly Rooms. Later in the novel, Matt mentions a man who paid over £68 to host one of these Assembly Room teas. For more on money and the comparative costs of things, see Introduction, pp. 20-22 and 33-34.

2 "Eclat" here means "greater effect." "Sweet-meats" are desserts.

3 "Purdue" means "waiting in ambush."

4 "Billingsgate" was the principal fish market in London. The women who worked there were notorious for their profanity.

flavour; nor were those flowers of rhetoric unattended with significant gesticulation. Some snapped their fingers; some forked them out; some clapped their hands, and some their back-sides; at length, they fairly proceeded to pulling caps, and every thing seemed to presage a general battle; when Holder ordered his horns to sound a charge, with a view to animate the combatants, and inflame the contest; but this manœuvre produced an effect quite contrary to what he expected. It was a note of reproach that roused them to an immediate sense of their disgraceful situation. They were ashamed of their absurd deportment, and suddenly desisted. They gathered up their caps, ruffles, and handkerchiefs; and great part of them retired in silent mortification.

Quin laughed at this adventure; but my uncle's delicacy was hurt. He hung his head in manifest chagrin, and seemed to repine at the triumph of his judgment—Indeed, his victory was more complete than he imagined; for, as we afterwards learned, the two amazons who singularized themselves most in the action, did not come from the purlieus of Puddle-dock, but from the courtly neighbourhood of St. James's palace.[1] One was a baroness, and the other, a wealthy knight's dowager—My uncle spoke not a word, till we had made our retreat good to the coffee-house; where, taking off his hat and wiping his forehead, "I bless God" (said he) "that Mrs. Tabitha Bramble did not take the field to-day!" "I would pit her for a cool hundred" (cried Quin) "against the best shake-bag of the whole main."[2] The truth is, nothing could have kept her at home but the accident of her having taken physick before she knew the nature of the entertainment [...]

Yours,

Bath, April 30.   J. MELFORD.

To Sir WATKIN PHILLIPS, of Jesus college, Oxon.

[...] You desire to have further acquaintance with the person of our aunt, and promise yourself much entertainment from her connexion with Sir Ulic Mackilligut: but in this hope you are baulked already; that connexion is dissolved. The Irish baronet is an old hound, that, finding her carrion, has quitted the scent [...]

---

1 "Puddle Dock" was a wharf in the City of London, which gave its name to the (rather squalid) surrounding neighborhood. In terms of social status, its denizens were about as far from St. James's Palace as one could get.

2 A "shake-bag" is a large cock kept in a bag until the beginning of a cockfight (and so an unknown, but fearsome opponent). "The whole main" is all the cocks who are part of a given fight.

You must know, she yesterday wanted to steal a march of poor Liddy, and went to breakfast in the Room without any other companion than her dog, in expectation of meeting with the Baronet, who had agreed to dance with her in the evening—Chowder no sooner made his appearance in the Room than the Master of the Ceremonies, incensed at his presumption, ran up to drive him away, and threatened him with his foot; but the other seemed to despise his authority, and displaying a formidable case of long, white, sharp teeth, kept the puny monarch[1] at bay—while he stood under some trepidation, fronting his antagonist, and bawling to the waiter, Sir Ulic Mackilligut came to his assistance; and seeming ignorant of the connexion between this intruder and his mistress, gave the former such a kick in the jaws, as sent him howling to the door——Mrs. Tabitha, incensed at this outrage, ran after him, squalling in a tone equally disagreeable; while the Baronet followed her on one side, making apologies for his mistake; and Derrick on the other, making remonstrances upon the rules and regulations of the place.

Far from being satisfied with the Knight's excuses, she said she was sure he was no gentleman; and when the Master of the Ceremonies offered to hand her into the chair, she rapped him over the knuckles with her fan. My uncle's footman being still at the door, she and Chowder got into the same vehicle, and were carried off amidst the jokes of the chairmen and other populace——I had been riding out on Clerkendown, and happened to enter just as the *fracas* was over—The Baronet, coming up to me with an affected air of chagrin, recounted the adventure; at which I laughed heartily, and then his countenance cleared up. "My dear soul," (said he) "when I saw a sort of a wild baist, snarling with open mouth at the Master of the Ceremonies, like the red cow going to devour Tom Thumb,[2] I could do no less than go to the assistance of the little man; but I never dreamt the baist was one of Mrs. Bramble's attendants——O! if I had, he might have made his breakfast upon Derrick and wellcome—But, you know, my dear friend, how natural it is for us Irishmen to blunder, and to take the wrong sow by the ear—However, I will confess judgment, and cry her mercy; and, 'tis to be hoped, a penitent sinner may be forgiven." I told

---

1 The Master of Ceremonies was traditionally called the "King of Bath," and Derrick was a small and apparently unimpressive-looking man. Hence he's "the puny monarch."

2 In the traditional English folk tale of Tom Thumb (a boy who never grows any larger than his father's thumb), Tom's mother tied him to a thistle to keep him safe on a windy day, while she milked a red cow. However, the cow took a bite of thistle, and so inadvertently swallowed Tom.

him, that as the offence was involuntary of his side, it was to be hoped he would not find her implacable.

But, in truth, all this concern was dissembled. In his approaches of gallantry to Mrs. Tabitha, he had been misled by a mistake of at least six thousand pounds, in the calculation of her fortune; and in this particular he was just undeceived.[1] He, therefore, seized the first opportunity of incurring her displeasure decently, in such a manner as would certainly annihilate the correspondence; and he could not have taken a more effectual method, than that of beating her dog. When he presented himself at our door, to pay his respects to the offended fair, he was refused admittance; and given to understand, that he should never find her at home for the future. She was not so inaccessible to Derrick, who came to demand satisfaction for the insult she had offered to him, even in the verge of his own court. She knew it was convenient to be well with the Master of the Ceremonies, while she continued to frequent the Rooms; and, having heard he was a poet, began to be afraid of making her appearance in a ballad or lampoon.— She therefore made excuses for what she had done, imputing it to the flutter of her spirits; and subscribed handsomely for his poems: so that he was perfectly appeased, and overwhelmed her with a profusion of compliment. He even solicited a reconciliation with Chowder; which, however, the latter declined; and he declared, that if he could find a precedent in the annals of the Bath, which he would carefully examine for that purpose, her favourite should be admitted to the next public breakfasting—But, I believe, she will not expose herself or him to the risque of a second disgrace—Who will supply the place of Mackilligut in her affections, I cannot foresee; but nothing in the shape of man can come amiss. Though she is a violent church-woman, of the most intolerant zeal, I believe in my conscience she would have no objection, at present, to treat on the score of matrimony with an Anabaptist, Quaker, or Jew; and even ratify the treaty, at the expence of her own conversion. But, perhaps, I think too hardly of this kinswoman; who, I must own, is very little beholden to the good opinion of

Yours,

Bath, May 6.   J. MELFORD.

---

1   Tabitha's maid had earlier reported to Sir Ulic's servant that "all" her mistress "had to trust to" was a "poor ten thousand pounds." The servant, in turn, had claimed that his master had "an estate of fifteen hundred a year." The latter is presumably as exaggerated a figure as the former.

To Sir WATKIN PHILLIPS, Bar[t].[1] of Jesus college, Oxon.

[...] Now we are upon the subject of parsons, I must tell you a ludicrous adventure, which was atchieved the other day by Tom Eastgate, whom you may remember on the foundation of Queen's. He had been very assiduous to pin himself upon George Prankley, who was a gentleman-commoner of Christ-church, knowing the said Prankley was heir to a considerable estate, and would have the advowson[2] of a good living, the incumbent of which was very old and infirm. He studied his passions, and flattered them so effectually, as to become his companion and counsellor; and, at last, obtained of him a promise of the presentation, when the living should fall. Prankley, on his uncle's death, quitted Oxford, and made his first appearance in the fashionable world at London; from whence he came lately to Bath, where he has been exhibiting himself among the bucks and gamesters of the place. Eastgate followed him hither; but he should not have quitted him for a moment, at his first emerging into life. He ought to have known he was a fantastic, foolish, fickle fellow, who would forget his college-attachments the moment they ceased appealing to his senses. Tom met with a cold reception from his old friend; and was, moreover, informed, that he had promised the living to another man, who had a vote in the county, where he proposed to offer himself a candidate at the next general election.[3] He now remembered nothing of Eastgate, but the freedoms he had used to take with him, while Tom had quietly stood his butt, with an eye to the benefice; and those freedoms he began to repeat in common place sarcasms on his person and his cloth,[4] which he uttered in the public coffee-house, for the entertainment of the company. But he was egregiously mistaken in giving his own wit credit for that tameness of Eastgate, which had been entirely

---

1 An abbreviation for baronet.

2 Being "on the foundation" of an Oxford college (such as Queen's or Christ Church) meant that one was supported by a scholarship; being a "gentleman-commoner" meant that one paid full fees. Gentleman-commoners received all sorts of special treatment in eighteenth-century Oxford. The "advowson" of a "living" is the right to "present"—i.e., appoint—a priest to a given parish (typically this power was held by the local landowner).

3 Running for Parliament in the eighteenth century routinely involved bribing voters, both directly—with food and drink, or, more rarely, cash—and through promises of future patronage or threats of retaliation. In his first election to Parliament, Sheridan spent approximately £1,250 on beer, food, and well-timed charitable contributions, and £750 on direct payments to about three-quarters of the eligible voters.

4 A "benefice" is a living (in the sense used earlier in this letter). A priest's "cloth" is his profession.

owing to prudential considerations. These being now removed, he retorted his repartee with interest, and found no great difficulty in turning the laugh upon the aggressor; who, losing his temper, called him names, and asked, *If he knew whom he talked to?* After much altercation, Prankley, shaking his cane, bid him hold his tongue, otherwise he would dust his cassock for him. "I have no pretensions to such a valet"; (said Tom) "but if you should do me that office, and overheat yourself, I have here a good oaken towel[1] at your service."

Prankley was equally incensed and confounded at this reply. After a moment's pause, he took him aside towards the window; and, pointing to the clump of firs on Clerken-down, asked in a whisper, if he had spirit enough to meet him there, with a case of pistols, at six o'clock to-morrow morning. Eastgate answered in the affirmative; and, with a steady countenance, assured him, he would not fail to give him the rendezvous at the hour he mentioned. So saying, he retired; and the challenger stayed some time in manifest agitation. In the morning, Eastgate, who knew his man, and had taken his resolution, went to Prankley's lodgings, and roused him by five o'clock—

The 'squire, in all probability, cursed his punctuality in his heart, but he affected to talk big; and having prepared his artillery over-night, they crossed the water at the end of the South Parade. In their progress up the hill, Prankley often eyed the parson, in hopes of perceiving some reluctance in his countenance; but as no such marks appeared, he attempted to intimidate him by word of mouth. "If these flints do their office," (said he) "I'll do thy business in a few minutes." "I desire you will do your best"; (replied the other) "for my part, I come not here to trifle. Our lives are in the hands of God; and one of us already totters on the brink of eternity—" This remark seemed to make some impression upon the 'squire, who changed countenance, and with a faultering accent observed, "That it ill became a clergyman to be concerned in quarrels and blood-shed—" "Your insolence to me" (said Eastgate) "I should have bore with patience, had not you cast the most infamous reflections upon my order, the honour of which I think myself in duty bound to maintain, even at the expence of my heart's blood; and surely it can be no crime to put out of the world a profligate wretch, without any sense of principle, morality, or religion——" "Thou may'st take away my life," (cried Prankley, in great perturbation) "but don't go to murder my character.—What! has't got no conscience?" "My conscience is perfectly quiet" (replied the other); "and now, sir, we are upon the spot—Take your ground as near as you please; prime your pistol; and the Lord, of his infinite mercy, have compassion upon your miserable soul!"

---

1 The "oaken towel" is, of course, a club.

This ejaculation he pronounced in a loud solemn tone, with his hat off, and his eyes lifted up; then drawing a large horse pistol, he presented,[1] and put himself in a posture of action. Prankley took his distance, and endeavoured to prime, but his hand shook with such violence, that he found this operation impracticable—His antagonist, seeing how it was with him, offered his assistance, and advanced for that purpose; when the poor 'squire, exceedingly alarmed at what he had heard and seen, desired the action might be deferred till next day, as he had not settled his affairs. "I ha'nt made my will" (said he); "my sisters are not provided for; and I just now recollect an old promise, which my conscience tells me I ought to perform—I'll first convince thee, that I'm not a wretch without principle, and then thou shalt have an opportunity to take my life, which thou seem'st to thirst after so eagerly—"

Eastgate understood the hint; and told him, that one day should break no squares;[2] adding, "God forbid that I should be the means of hindering you from acting the part of an honest man, and a dutiful brother—"By virtue of this cessation, they returned peaceably together. Prankley forthwith made out the presentation of the living, and delivered it to Eastgate, telling him at the same time, he had now settled his affairs, and was ready to attend him to the Fir-grove; but Tom declared he could not think of lifting his hand against the life of so great a benefactor—He did more: when they next met at the coffee house, he asked pardon of Mr. Prankley, if in his passion he had said any thing to give him offence; and the 'squire was so gracious as to forgive him with a cordial shake of the hand, declaring that he did not like to be at variance with an old college-companion—Next day, however, he left Bath abruptly; and then Eastgate told me all these particulars, not a little pleased with the effects of his own sagacity, by which he has secured a living worth 160 *l. per annum* [...]

Yours ever,

Bath, May 17.   J. MELFORD.

3. Report of an Elopement, *The Bath Chronicle*, 9 September 1773

A few days since the Hon. Miss ——, daughter of Lady M——s, set off from her Ladyship's house near this city in a post-chaise and four,

---

1 A "horse pistol" is a large pistol designed for use on horseback. To "present" in a duel is to aim one's gun.

2 "Break no squares" means "do no harm."

with Mr. L——, a young gentleman of good family and fortune in Dorsetshire. It is supposed they are gone on a matrimonial visit to France; their first stage was to Devizes, where they hired fresh horses for Marlborough, but as soon as they left the inn, the driver was directed to take the Salisbury road, and by that means their pursuers were put on a wrong scent, and Cupid thus triumphant will no doubt shortly wear the crown of Hymen.[1]

Figure 16: An etching and stipple engraving of the North Parade in Bath (1785). The fashions are slightly different than those current at the debut of *The Rivals*, but the views, architecture, and kinds of social interaction depicted are all essentially the same. Courtesy of the Lewis Walpole Library, Yale University.

---

1 A "post-chaise" is a small fast carriage. It usually seats only two people and is pulled by "four" horses, who are replaced at regular intervals (or "stages"). Devizes is a town to the east of Bath. Marlborough is still further east. Salisbury is to the south of Devizes, however, and so en route to a port from which one could sail to France.

Select Bibliography

Allan, David. *A Nation of Readers: The Lending Library in Georgian England*. London: British Library, 2008.

Andrew, Donna T. "The Code of Honour and Its Critics: The Opposition to Duelling in England, 1700-1850." *Social History* 5.3 (1980): 409-34.

Anstey, Christopher. *The New Bath Guide*. Edited by Gavin Turner. Bristol: Broadcast Books, 1994.

Auburn, Mark S. *Sheridan's Comedies: Their Contexts and Achievements*. Lincoln: U of Nebraska P, 1977.

Bevis, Richard, ed. *Eighteenth-Century Drama: Afterpieces*. London: Oxford UP, 1970.

———. *The Laughing Tradition: Stage Comedy in Garrick's Day*. Athens: U of Georgia P, 1980.

Bor, Margot, and Lamond Clelland. *Still the Lark: A Biography of Elizabeth Linley*. London: Merlin, 1962.

Borsay, Peter. "Image and Counter-Image in Georgian Bath." *British Journal for Eighteenth-Century Studies* 17.2 (1994): 165-79.

Bourque, Kevin. "Blind Items: Anonymity, Notoriety, and the Making of Eighteenth-Century Celebrity." Ph.D. diss., University of Texas, 2012.

Braudy, Leo. *The Frenzy of Renown: Fame and Its History*. Oxford: Oxford UP, 1986.

Brewer, David A. "Print, Performance, Personhood, Polly Honeycombe." *Studies in Eighteenth-Century Culture* 41 (2012): 185-94.

———, and Angus Whitehead. "The Books of Lydia Languish's Circulating Library Revisited." *Notes and Queries* 255.4 (2010): 551-53.

Briggs, Peter. "The Importance of Beau Nash." *Studies in Eighteenth-Century Culture* 22 (1993): 208-30.

Colman, George, the Elder. *Critical Edition of The Jealous Wife and Polly Honeycombe by George Colman the Elder (1732-1794)*. Edited by Thomas Price. Lewiston: Edwin Mellen, 1997.

Donoghue, Frank. "Avoiding the 'Cooler Tribunal of the Study': Richard Brinsley Sheridan's Writer's Block and Late Eighteenth-Century Print Culture." *ELH* 68.4 (2001): 831-56.

———. *The Fame Machine: Book Reviewing and Eighteenth-Century Literary Careers*. Stanford: Stanford UP, 1996.

Downie, J.A. "The Making of the English Novel." *Eighteenth-Century Fiction* 9.3 (1997): 249-66.

Eglin, John. *The Imaginary Autocrat: Beau Nash and the Invention of Bath*. London: Profile, 2005.

Fawcett, Trevor. *Bath Entertain'd: Amusements, Recreations, and Gambling at the Eighteenth-Century Spa*. Bath: Ruton, 1998.

——, comp. *Voices of Eighteenth-Century Bath: An Anthology of Contemporary Texts Illustrating Events, Daily Life, and Attitudes at Britain's Leading Georgian Spa*. Bath: Ruton, 1995.

Freeman, Lisa A. *Character's Theater: Genre and Identity on the Eighteenth-Century English Stage*. Philadelphia: U of Pennsylvania P, 2002.

Gallagher, Catherine. *Nobody's Story: The Vanishing Acts of Women Writers in the Marketplace, 1670-1820*. Berkeley: U of California P, 1994.

Gilbert, Arthur N. "Law and Honour among Eighteenth-Century British Army Officers." *The Historical Journal* 19.1 (1976): 75-87.

Gray, Charles Harold. *Theatrical Criticism in London to 1795*. New York: Columbia UP, 1931.

Highfill, Philip H., Jr., Kalman A. Burnim, and Edward A. Langhans. *A Biographical Dictionary of Actors, Actresses, Musicians, Dancers, Managers, and Other Stage Personnel in London, 1660-1800*. 16 vols. Carbondale: Southern Illinois UP, 1973-93.

Hogan, Charles Beecher, ed. *The London Stage, 1660-1800: A Calendar of Plays, Entertainments, and Afterpieces Together with Casts, Box-Receipts, and Contemporary Comment Compiled from the Playbills, Newspapers, and Theatrical Diaries of the Period. Part 5: 1776-1800*. 3 vols. Carbondale: Southern Illinois UP, 1968.

Holmes, Richard. *Redcoat: The British Soldier in the Age of Horse and Musket*. London: HarperCollins, 2001.

Hughes, Leo. *The Drama's Patrons: A Study of the Eighteenth-Century London Audience*. Austin: U of Texas P, 1971.

Hume, Robert D. "The Economics of Culture in London, 1660-1740." *Huntington Library Quarterly* 69.4 (2006): 487-532.

——, ed. *The London Theatre World, 1660-1800*. Carbondale: Southern Illinois UP, 1980.

[Hunt, Leigh]. "The Play-Goer. By the Original Theatrical Critic in the Examiner," *The Tatler. A Daily Journal of Literature and the Stage*, 2 December 1830.

Hunter, J. Paul. *Before Novels: The Cultural Contexts of Eighteenth-Century English Fiction*. New York: W.W. Norton, 1990.

——. "Making Books, Generating Genres." In *The Commonwealth of Books: Essays and Studies in Honour of Ian Willison*, edited by Wallace Kirsop, 18-47. Melbourne: Centre for the Book, Monash University, 2007.

Kavanaugh, Rachel, director. *The Rivals*, by Richard Brinsley Sheridan. Recorded 12-13 June 2004 at the Bristol Old Vic, Bristol. West Long Branch: Kultur, 2005. DVD.

Leerssen, Joseph Th. *Mere Irish and Fior-Ghael: Studies in the Idea of Irish Nationality, its Development and Literary Expression Prior to the Nineteenth Century.* Amsterdam: John Benjamins, 1986.

Loftis, John. *Sheridan and the Drama of Georgian England.* Oxford: Basil Blackwell, 1976.

McKeon, Michael. *The Origins of the English Novel, 1600-1740.* Baltimore: Johns Hopkins UP, 1987.

Moody, Jane. "Stolen Identities: Character, Mimicry, and the Invention of Samuel Foote." In *Theatre and Celebrity in Britain, 1660-2000,* edited by Mary Luckhurst and Jane Moody, 65-89. Houndsmills, Basingstroke: Palgrave Macmillan, 2005.

Moretti, Franco. *Atlas of the European Novel, 1800-1900.* London: Verso, 1998.

A Nest of Nightingales: Thomas Gainsborough, The Linley Sisters. London: Dulwich Picture Gallery, 1988. Exhibition catalog.

Nettleton, George Henry. "The Books of Lydia Languish's Circulating Library." *Journal of English and Germanic Philology* 5.4 (1905): 492-500.

Nicoll, Allardyce. *The Garrick Stage: Theatres and Audience in the Eighteenth Century.* Manchester: Manchester UP, 1980.

O'Connell, Sheila. *London 1753.* London: British Museum, 2003.

O'Quinn, Daniel. *Entertaining Crisis in the Atlantic Imperium, 1770-1790.* Baltimore: Johns Hopkins UP, 2011.

O'Toole, Fintan. *A Traitor's Kiss: The Life of Richard Brinsley Sheridan, 1751-1816.* New York: Farrar, Straus and Giroux, 1998.

Page, Eugene R. *George Colman the Elder: Essayist, Dramatist, and Theatrical Manager, 1732-1794.* New York: Columbia UP, 1935.

Picard, Liza. *Dr. Johnson's London: Coffee-Houses and Climbing Boys, Medicine, Toothpaste and Gin, Poverty and Press-Gangs, Freakshows and Female Education.* New York: St. Martin's, 2000.

Price, Cecil. "The First Prologue to *The Rivals.*" *Review of English Studies* n.s. 20 (1969): 192-95.

———. *Theatre in the Age of Garrick.* Oxford: Basil Blackwell, 1973.

Raven, James. "Historical Introduction: The Novel Comes of Age." In *The English Novel, 1770-1829: A Bibliographical Survey of Prose Fiction Published in the British Isles, Vol. 1: 1770-1799,* edited by James Raven and Antonia Forster, 15-121. Oxford: Oxford UP, 2000.

———. Introduction to *British Fiction, 1750-1770: A Chronological Check-List of Prose Fiction Printed in Britain and Ireland.* Newark: U of Delaware P, 1987.

Roach, Joseph. *It.* Ann Arbor: U of Michigan P, 2007.

Scott, William. "George Colman's *Polly Honeycombe* and Circulating

Library Fiction in 1760." *Notes and Queries* n.s. 15.12 (1968): 465-67.

Sheridan, Richard Brinsley. *The Dramatic Works of Richard Brinsley Sheridan.* Edited by Cecil Price. 2 vols. Oxford: Clarendon, 1973.

———. *The Letters of Richard Brinsley Sheridan.* Edited by Cecil Price. 3 vols. Oxford: Clarendon, 1966.

———. *The Rivals, A Comedy. As It Was First Acted at the Theatre-Royal in Covent-Garden.* Edited by Richard Little Purdy. Oxford: Clarendon, 1935.

Sherman, Stuart. "Garrick among Media: The '*Now* Performer' Navigates the News." *PMLA* 126.4 (2011): 966-82.

Shoemaker, Robert B. "The Taming of the Duel: Masculinity, Honor, and Ritual Violence in London, 1660-1800." *The Historical Journal* 45.3 (2002): 525-45.

Smollett, Tobias. *The Expedition of Humphry Clinker.* Edited by O.M. Brack, Jr. Athens: U of Georgia P, 1990.

Stern, Tiffany. *Documents of Performance in Early Modern England.* Cambridge: Cambridge UP, 2009.

———. *Rehearsal from Shakespeare to Sheridan.* Oxford: Clarendon, 2000.

Stone, George Winchester, Jr., ed. *The London Stage, 1660-1800: A Calendar of Plays, Entertainments, and Afterpieces Together with Casts, Box-Receipts, and Contemporary Comment Compiled from the Play-bills, Newspapers, and Theatrical Diaries of the Period. Part 4: 1747-1776.* 3 vols. Carbondale: Southern Illinois UP, 1962.

Taylor, John Tinnon. *Early Opposition to the English Novel: The Popular Reaction from 1760 to 1830.* New York: King's Crown, 1943.

Taylor, Richard C. "'Future Retrospection': Rereading Sheridan's Reviewers." In *Sheridan Studies,* edited by James Morwood and David Crane, 47-57. Cambridge: Cambridge UP, 1995.

Thomas, David, and Arnold Hare, comps. *Restoration and Georgian England, 1660-1788. Theatre in Europe: A Documentary History.* Cambridge: Cambridge UP, 1989.

Warner, William B. *Licensing Entertainment: The Elevation of Novel Reading in Britain, 1684-1750.* Berkeley: U of California P, 1998.

Watt, Ian. *The Rise of the Novel: Studies in Defoe, Richardson, and Fielding.* Berkeley: U of California P, 1957.

Werkmeister, Lucyle. *The London Daily Press, 1772-1792.* Lincoln: U of Nebraska P, 1963.

Williams, Ioan, ed. *Novel and Romance, 1700-1800: A Documentary Record.* London: Routledge & Kegan Paul, 1970.

FSC
www.fsc.org

MIX
Paper from
responsible sources
FSC® C103567

LIST
of products used:

982 lb(s) of Rolland Opaque50
50% post-consumer

RESULTS
Based on the Cascades products you selected compared to products in the industry made with 100% virgin fiber, your savings are:

 4 trees

 3,405 gal. US of water
37 days of water consumption

 862 lbs of waste
8 waste containers

 2,640 lbs CO2
5,006 miles driven

 13 MMBTU
63,313 60W light bulbs for one hour

 8 lbs NOx
emissions of one truck during 11 days